MW00781765

FAULKNER'S CARTOGRAPHIES
OF CONSCIOUSNESS

William Faulkner continues to be an author who is widely read, studied, and admired. This book provides an interdisciplinary account of his legacy, one that speaks to the antiracism discourse of our own time and presents concerns about the development of subjecthood in a technologically saturated culture. Combining literary critique with network and complexity science, this study offers a new reading of William Faulkner as a novelist for the information age.

JOHN MICHAEL CORRIGAN earned his PhD from the University of Toronto and currently teaches at National Chengchi University in Taiwan. His books include *American Metempsychosis* (2012) and *Romantic Legacies* (2019). He serves as a senior editor with the University of Virginia's "Digital Yoknapatawpha" project.

FAULKNER'S CARTOGRAPHIES OF CONSCIOUSNESS

JOHN MICHAEL CORRIGAN

National Chengchi University

Shaftesbury Road, Cambridge CB2 8EA, United Kingdom

One Liberty Plaza, 20th Floor, New York, NY 10006, USA

477 Williamstown Road, Port Melbourne, VIC 3207, Australia

314–321, 3rd Floor, Plot 3, Splendor Forum, Jasola District Centre, New Delhi – 110025, India

103 Penang Road, #05-06/07, Visioncrest Commercial, Singapore 238467

Cambridge University Press is part of Cambridge University Press & Assessment, a department of the University of Cambridge.

We share the University's mission to contribute to society through the pursuit of education, learning and research at the highest international levels of excellence.

www.cambridge.org
Information on this title: www.cambridge.org/9781009377850

DOI: 10.1017/9781009377867

First published 2024

A catalogue record for this publication is available from the British Library.

A Cataloging-in-Publication data record for this book is available from the Library of Congress

ISBN 978-1-009-37785-0 Hardback

To my parents, Kevin Corrigan and Elena Glazov-Corrigan.

Contents

Acknowledgments

I have benefited from the support of numerous people and institutions during the writing of this book. I begin by thanking William Bartley, who guided me over twenty years ago when I first entered graduate studies; Sally Wolff-King, who introduced me to Oxford with her Emory class in 2009; Martine Brownley, Keith Anthony, Amy Erbil, Colette Barlow, and the Fox Center at Emory University for a postdoctoral fellowship during the 2012–13 academic year; the Harrison Institute at the University of Virginia for awarding me a Lillian Gary Taylor Fellowship in 2013, and Erich Nunn, who did not just encourage me but made sure I applied; Shiuhhuah Serena Chou and the Institute of European and American Studies at Academia Sinica; and the Ministry of Science and Technology in Taiwan, which has supported my research for a decade.

My first day at the Harrison Institute both changed the direction of this book and opened my life to a wonderful group of people. As I made my first request from the Faulkner Collection, the librarian introduced me to Stephen Railton, who invited me to join the "Digital Yoknapatawpha" project. I thank Steve as well as Theresa M. Towner, Worthy Martin, James Carothers, Johannes Burgers, Jennie J. Joiner, John Padgett, Erin Penner, Christopher Rieger, Ben Robbins, Lorie Watkins, Jay Watson, and Robbie Bingler. Our project has been a resource to which I continually turned during the writing and editing of this book.

I thank Cambridge University Press, particularly Ray Ryan, who guided this book toward publication, Edgar Mendez, Abigail Rothberg, and Franklin Mathews Jebaraj. The support of other colleagues and friends over the years has been invaluable. I thank Alan Ackerman, Arthur Versluis, Dominick Rolle, Graeme Todd, Li-Hsin Hsu, Shun-liang Chao, Justin Hewitson, Justin Prystash, and my colleagues at National Chengchi University.

Portions of this work have appeared previously in other publications, and I am grateful for the permission to reprint this material. Chapter 1 was reworked from "Murder in the House of Memory: Faulkner's Plantation Prototype and the Elite Planter in *Flags in the Dust*," Copyright © 2019 The Johns Hopkins University Press, which first appeared in *modernism/modernity*, Volume 4, Cycle 2, 2019. Sections 3.3 and 3.4 of Chapter 3 originally appeared in "Sourceless Sunlight: Faulkner's *Sanctuary* and the Sacrificial Crisis," *Mosaic: An Interdisciplinary Critical Journal*, Volume 50, Issue 4, 2017, pp. 139–55. Sections 6.1 and 6.2 of Chapter 6 originally appeared in "Faulkner's Human Hive: Complex Systems in *The Hamlet*," *Digitizing Faulkner: Yoknapatawpha in the Twenty-First Century*, edited by Theresa M. Towner, University of Virginia Press, 2022, pp. 125–50. © 2022 by the Rector and Visitors of the University of Virginia. Reprinted by permission of the University of Virginia Press.

In closing, I thank my family: Peggy Lee, my wife, who shared the weight of this journey with me; Sarah Corrigan; Maria Corrigan; Jesse Archibald Barber; Marina Glazov; Tali Glazov; and Yuri Corrigan, who served as an editor and a spiritual anchor when I needed him most. I dedicate this work to my mother and father, Elena Glazov-Corrigan and Kevin Corrigan, both of whom are living testaments to the boundlessness of the interior life.

Introduction
Faulkner in the Information Age

Faulkner's novels express an acute anxiety about the vulnerability of the human subject nestled within the complex systems of modernity. Fascinated by how constructed space culturally co-evolves with the human being, Faulkner crafted a speculative fiction that questions the role of the individual within ever-scaling systems of information. His works painstakingly visualize the architectural intricacies of scale – from houses to plantations, from towns to cities – and imagine how information flows through, and connects, these lived spaces by virtue of an ever-expanding infrastructure of road, rail, energy, and finance. Faulkner was predisposed to his critique of modernity by his own rural upbringing and, like the Romantics, he upheld human consciousness as a mysterious, even sacred faculty that can never be fully enfolded into our social relations. Yet his fiction is poised at a place in history where the rural itself is predicated upon system centralization and the nascent realization that sophisticated flows of information shape the human being's movement, behavior, and thinking across time.

Faulkner, therefore, speaks to us directly in the information age. Never has his vision of the coupling of the exponential growth that began in the eighteenth century and the fragile inner space of the human subject been timelier. And yet for us to benefit from Faulkner's insight, his vision requires elucidation. Faulkner was by no means a systems theorist. Though he spent decades pondering the relationship between external system and internal architecture, nowhere does he outline his conclusions for us. Instead, he self-consciously employed artistic representation itself – from the singular image to the expansive grammatical structure of his long sentences – as the ideal vehicle for investigating human consciousness and its relationship to the sophisticated information networks that underlay the changing plantation system of the South and, beyond it, the industrial networks of global modernity. The work of the scholar, therefore – and the purpose of this book – is to derive a working theory from the practice that is presented throughout Faulkner's Yoknapatawpha novels.

Space and Subject in Faulkner Studies

In seeking to understand Faulkner's meditation on modern information systems and their effects on human consciousness, we begin with the basic premise that his fictional world of Yoknapatawpha County is a place at once based upon, and artistically independent of, Northeast Mississippi. It was not until 1961, one year before Faulkner's death, that the distinction between his native region and the landscape of his imagination emerged in any meaningful way among literary scholars. G. T. Buckley was the first to wonder about the validity of the straightforward correspondence between the two. Previously, it had "been taken for granted that [Faulkner's] Yoknapatawpha County is really Lafayette County, Mississippi, and that his Jefferson, the county seat, is really Oxford" (Brown 1976: 223). With an emerging awareness of the vexed relationship between the two cartographies, the job of the literary scholar appeared relatively simple: to determine the ways in which Faulkner had intermixed his own Southern landscape with his invented county. Yet this task was by no means easy, for the "question of the localization of Faulkner's setting," as Calvin Brown put it in 1976, depended upon "evidence" that was "already beyond the reach of the literary researcher" and a landscape that was itself "fast disappearing" (224).[1]

Scholars have on the whole attended more to Faulkner's fictional country as its own self-enclosed realm than to its similarities with Lafayette, though there can be no strict dividing line between the two, as Faulkner's Yoknapatawpha invariably reflects the place in which he lived and wrote. In recent years, there have been notable efforts to preserve some record of the South's earlier material history as it pertains to Faulkner's artistic vision. George Stewart's photographic reportage (2009) records and recreates that vanishing landscape; and Charles Aiken's *William Faulkner and the Southern Landscape* (2009) concentrates on the ways that Faulkner converted his local geography into his fictional world. Another cartographic approach places its primary emphasis on the fictional county. This method has been adopted over the last decade by the University of Virginia's *Digital Yoknapatawpha*, of which I have been a senior editor. Our team of Faulkner scholars and digital technologists has created a database of interactive maps for the key locations, characters, and events of the Yoknapatawpha fiction. As the project has grown, our work invariably involves preserving and interpreting the material culture of Faulkner's region.

In thinking about Yoknapatawpha as an imagined landscape, two critical tendencies can be roughly discerned. On the one hand, a neo-Romantic or idealist mode emphasizes Faulkner's attention to the imma-nent, or inwardly inviolable, value of human consciousness. On the other hand, a poststructuralist reading opposes the project of human inwardness and advocates a view of the human subject as determined by the material and ideological contexts of its time. The camp that we have roughly designated as "neo-Romantic" or "idealist" is not so much in favor of a Faulknerian self that lies above or beyond its social context; rather, this view holds that the material relationships of Faulkner's novels – whether social or textual – are infused and permeated by the primacy of the human mind. John Pikoulis, in 1982, was one of the first to propose that Yoknapatawpha be understood as a "mental landscape" (2) with an aes-thetic quality that offers a spiritual subtext. In this sense, Faulkner's "characters are facets of their author's mind brooding on itself and extended on to the page with all the complexity of art, fictions masking an inner identity" (1). Pikoulis, therefore, articulates a Romantic notion of the "inner identity" of the artist mirrored in an invented world that simultaneously forms an extended mind construct: "Faulkner treats people less as parts of an observed world than as players in a private drama whose origins may have lain outside himself but who have become, like figures in a family history, part of his expanded consciousness of self, as intimate as memory" (2). Here, consciousness is paramount; inwardness exerts power over a network of material relationships. Pikoulis also suggests the devel-opmental character of an idealist reading. Faulkner's characters "have become" part of an "expanded consciousness," indicating that the artistic process is ongoing, prospectively connecting the author and the latent memory of the text to the dynamic consciousness of the present reader.

Joseph Urgo (2001) has likewise questioned the supposition that Yoknapatawpha signifies place and place alone. Similarly predisposed toward an idealist reading, Urgo argues that Faulkner's Yoknapatawpha manifests "a way of thinking" that "signals less a series of representations and more a mode of cognition" (106). "Faulkner went to the trouble," Urgo (2004) observes, "to implicate [Yoknapatawpha] as a place concep-tually or intellectually distinct from the place on which it is so closely modeled." It "may be less a place than a perspective, less significant for mapping a landscape than for mapping a mode of consciousness" (639). As a consequence, "Yoknapatawpha comes into being to articulate the interior lives of those who people its cartography." And we, the readers, may read Faulkner's map so as to contact "the deeper, spiritual existence shared within the boundaries of its time and place" (647).

This idealist notion of cognitive mapping, however, has been largely overshadowed by other theoretical paradigms. Contemporaneous scholars to Pikoulis and Urgo proposed Yoknapatawpha as a mental landscape outside the terms of an inner life. In 1991, Marc Baldwin emphasized the cultural and economic processes involved in Faulkner's "cognitive mapping." Here the concept of interiority is elided in favor of a transactional paradigm that is historically contingent, since the assignment of value rests not upon any intrinsic qualities, but upon power and capital. Baldwin unpacks Faulkner's "curious metaphor" of Yoknapatawpha as a "postage stamp of native soil" and argues that it enforces "a union between cultural and natural, civilized and primitive, industrial and agrarian" (196). "Like the postage stamp," Baldwin contends, "the land has been squared and measured, zoned, demarcated, assigned a value and bartered." From this perspective, a cartographic reading of Yoknapatawpha entails a transactional paradigm in which "humankind is nearly split up the middle by the joint spaces of real estate and capital, for ownership of land depends upon the spacious resources of a financial institution."

J. Hillis Miller (1995) also provided a brief, farsighted reading in which Faulkner's topography is staged not upon individualistic preconditions, but upon the interlocking mechanisms of capital and ideology. "Faulkner has a strongly topographical imagination," Miller begins. "The events of his novels take place within an elaborately mapped mental or textual landscape in which characters are associated with places" (211). Miller goes on to develop a poststructuralist reading of space to consider the role of ideology in the shaping of Faulkner's topographic vision. "Subjectivity, including its ideological presumptions, is . . . diffused into the landscape," Miller writes. "It is not just projected there but incarnated there." From this point of view, "ideology is not something abstract and dreamlike, the confusion of linguistic with material reality. That confusion is, literally, embodied. It is marked on bodies of the human beings who are mystified by the ideology" (212). For Miller then, ideology shapes subjectivity. Human beings perceive the marks of a culture's ideology in the landscape and are mystified by it. This ideology appears too ubiquitous and material to be mere concept; indeed, it is interwoven into the invented world about us and, as a result, into our very being, since we do more than apprehend it; we internalize and individuate it.

Miller's line of reasoning echoes a larger interpretative and influential framework that Philip Weinstein applied earlier that decade in his seminal *Faulkner's Subject* (1992), which presents Faulkner's subjectivity in the context of critical theory. Weinstein articulates a Faulknerian paradox in a manner closely related to Miller's reading. "The subject," Weinstein writes, "is simultaneously the free human being and the human being subjected to an exterior system of beliefs and practices. Ideology is the missing term that enables this paradox, for ideological practice and the free human subject mutually constitute each other" (89–90). Like Miller who sees ideology incarnated both in the landscape and in ourselves, Weinstein views the construction of selfhood in terms of our "hegemonic consent" to "social scripts" that lie initially outside the self (89–91). For Weinstein, therefore, our very sense of cognitive depth – our subjective perception of an inner life – depends entirely on the process by which we internalize society's scripts.

In these readings, Yoknapatawpha has become its own spatial practice, related less to either Faulkner or Oxford than to the cultural, ontological, and epistemological concerns of the late-twentieth century. In this practice or, at least, in these theoretical versions of this practice, the inner life of the Romantics has been eclipsed in favor of a self wholly submerged in ideology and absolutely reliant upon its environment. Weinstein's ultimate claim is telling and for some may not appear at all questionable. Where he begins with the supposition that our very sense of interiority emerges out of our willful acceptance of social inscription (a model of "noncoercion" [90]), he concludes with the poststructuralist axiom that there is nothing outside this process – in short, there is only an ideological self and, as a consequence, "appearing to be beyond ideology is ideology's defining move" (161). Weinstein's seminal work is now thirty years old, but his conclusions about Faulknerian subjecthood stand more or less uncontested. And this reality puts us at risk, I submit, of losing sight of a vital ethics of interiority in Faulkner's Yoknapatawpha fiction. Indeed, if we assume that there is only the flow of ideology through social and cognitive space, that there is, in short, no "domain deeper than ideology" in our social relations and in our individual person, then we take Faulkner's *warnings* to us as the whole of his humanist project and lose sight of the constructive dimensions of his thought and poetics.

The view of the socially and ideologically constructed subject that Weinstein and Miller attribute to Faulkner is of course symptomatic of a more widespread orthodoxy in the humanities. And yet, despite the continuing critical prevalence of this model, there are some Faulkner scholars who have held to the possibility of a more constructive ethics; who attend, that is, to Faulkner's attempts to preserve notions of interiority and agency even within an ideologically saturated fictional landscape. Already in 1979, Gary Lee Stonum posited a middle path. He recognized that the individuals in Faulkner's fiction are "from the outset part of a world constituted by their relationship[s], constituted, that is, by already established forms which in turn help to determine their subjectivity" (155). Yet this does not preclude the possibility of an emergent individual ethics. According to Stonum, Faulkner abandons the modernist privileging of aesthetics over morality and assumes responsibility for his art, for his own role in transmitting values to his audience (157–9).

Theresa Towner (2000) also sees a Faulkner who is continually "sensitive to the history of the South's peculiar institution and to the precarious means by which any individual's identity forms and develops" (14). She thereby gives voice to a fiction that "repeatedly probes the terrifying moments wherein culture and identity collide" and affirms the possibilities of individual agency therein. Karl Zender (2003) directly questions what he sees as an "irreversible (and largely salutary) change in Faulkner criticism" where "avoidances and silences ... mark the limits of [Faulkner's] artistic vision." While the twenty-first-century critic is predisposed to "read beyond, rather than within, the manifest content of Faulkner's fiction," Zender proposes an "alternative to the present consensus" that can still perceive a "valuable and livable, even a desirable politics ... inside" of Faulkner's fiction (120–1). Hortense Spillers (2004) skillfully maneuvers the idealist and the poststructural interpretations of Faulknerian space, maintaining that the spatial relationship between the self and the environment "remains the problematic encounter that both exceeds the map and remains representable by it" (535). Faulkner's "affirmation of the artist" is thus "one of the most compelling," even while offering an unexpected site of "derangement" (565). Jay Watson (2019) has likewise achieved a fine balance of reading both beyond and within the fictional world of Yoknapatawpha. The Faulkner that he engages is an author self-consciously working to uncover a "legacy" that "disturbs" and defiantly resounds within "a sensibility handed down from the European Enlightenment to the New World Plantation" (277).

These are, of course, just a handful of scholars who implicitly aim to preserve a Faulkner who self-consciously and earnestly attempted to work through the moral dilemmas of his Southern heritage and of global modernity itself. This book makes the case that Faulkner's spatial practice requires extensive reconsideration. In a time where visual mediation has risen to new heights, Faulkner's repeated representation of a self over-whelmed by visual surfaces takes on new urgency. The constructive solutions that he considered in his mature fiction are both nuanced and applicable to our cultural and individual crises today. From his first Yoknapatawpha fiction onward, Faulkner imagines the dilemma of a self that is bombarded with an ever-expanding field of visual surfaces and, in a manner that speaks directly to the antiracism protests of the coronavirus pandemic, he visualizes the monumental statue as a coercive object, erected in the principal vertices of social space to transmit its ideology directly into its perceiver. Faulkner's anticipation of both our increasing reliance on information technology and the rebellion against monumental architecture is no mere happenstance. Indeed, his invention of Yoknapatawpha entailed that he develop a symbolic cartography of social and cognitive space, one capable of representing the manner in which human beings transition from smaller distributed networks to hierarchies of power, privilege, and belief. Instead of an "exterior system of beliefs and practices" that we willingly assume, as Weinstein insisted, the landscape in Faulkner's Yoknapatawpha fiction is a nexus of trajectories in which outer and inner overlap to constitute an intersubjective, dynamic, and adaptive networked system. As they scale, these networks can become tyrannical and coercive – not at all willingly internalized. In Faulkner's Yoknapatawpha, the coercive character of such centralized human net-works is a persistent theme and, from *Flags in the Dust* onward, the individual self – with its fragile architecture of interior space – is under threat of being subsumed by the larger flows of ideology through our networked systems.

The case for individualism in Faulkner's fiction involves first taking these coercive processes seriously and, second, recognizing that Faulkner was an expressly anti-ideological writer. Although these centralized net-works seem both omnipotent and ubiquitous, they are not primary for Faulkner, but emergent properties that can be reconstituted and trans-formed according to the underlying movement, behavior, and thinking of the individuals that constitute them. The postmodern rejection of an older "paradigm of identity as an essentialized sacred space" (86), as Weinstein (1992) called it, misrepresents the character of Faulkner's individualism, conflating the inner life with "enclosed essences" that I argue, here and elsewhere, are caricatures of an idealist way of thinking about cognitive interiority. This book offers a different interpretation of the relationship between self and social body by moving chronologically through the Yoknapatawpha novels to outline an intersubjective way of understanding

Faulkner's spatial practice that hinges upon a deeper architectonics within the self, one that is grounded in our biological and social makeup. Where Faulkner engages in stream-of-consciousness experimentation in many of his earlier Yoknapatawpha narratives, this perspective is always located within an intersubjective vision of dynamic and adaptive networks in which the immanent value of individual life potentially operates as a vital source of novelty and change.

Above all, Faulkner was not responding to nebulous or generic aspects of modern life. His fiction continually focuses on the emergence of the lien-centered plantation system of the New South, placing it within the contexts of industrialization and the way that Jim Crow legally and culturally reinstated the racial and class hierarchy that had existed during slavery. What makes Faulkner's critique of his own heritage all the more striking is that the ethical dimension in his fiction is rarely abstract; rather, it is generated within a clear-sighted systems view of human relations. Faulkner of course lived in a different time, but this book makes the case that he was involved in developing a narrative form that could describe – with a prescience that has aged remarkably – the manner in which this social system scaled from rudimentary interaction networks to complex and coercive hierarchies. It is easy to minimize how immense was the transformation of Mississippi within just a few lifetimes – the shock of which lies at the heart of Faulkner's artistic project. Don Harrison Doyle (2001) reminds us to defamiliarize "our understanding of the Old South" for it "rests on images of older, more settled and finished eastern states like Virginia and South Carolina. In Mississippi, we witness the freshest expression of a dynamic southern society as it regenerated itself in the West" (3). Granted statehood in 1817, Mississippi had been home to indigenous peoples who had practiced nomadic ways of life for thousands of years and whose systemic removal from their homeland began in the 1830s, giving way to slave plantations controlled by a small number of white families. This transition occurred within the lifetime of Faulkner's great-grandfather and, within a few more generations, Mississippi had been completely transformed again. While the antebellum plantation system had occupied at most a mere ten percent of the land (with most of Mississippi remaining wilderness), the state was intensively settled after Reconstruction, with a new lien-centered plantation system and burgeoning industrialization.

Faulkner's narrative form involves a stylistic and metaphoric miniaturization of this historical arc into individual experience. The novels, in other words, treat historical macrocosm in the form of personal microcosm. To aid in the task of elucidating Faulkner's spatial practice, I introduce the term cognitive cartography to denote a narrative form that attempts to condense elements or even the entire arc of this civilizational transition from nomadic life to settled social organization into present experience – to mirror macrocosmic geographies in microcosmic space. I thereby define a cognitive cartography as a history of movement, behavior, and thinking compressed into social space. I show that Faulkner's earliest Yoknapatawpha fiction required much more narrative exposition to produce these cognitive cartographies than in his mature fiction. During the course of his career, the author became increasingly adept at compressing these cartographies into the structure of his prose style, attempting to make the grammatical unit of the sentence capable of enveloping the recurrent behavior of the social body as it builds the complex institutions of the New South. From wilderness to highly systemized infrastructure largely bent on the production of monocultures, Faulkner's Yoknapatawpha serves as a cartography not just for a small rural community that gradually grew in scale, but for the larger human transition to ever more intricate bureaucracies of social interaction and control, bureaucracies in which ideology appears to possess an independence and quasi-agency.

In analyzing these cognitive cartographies, I necessarily employ some of the basic terminology of network theory to assist in close readings of a number of Faulkner's Yoknapatawpha novels: *Flags in the Dust* (1927), *The Sound and the Fury* (1929), *As I Lay Dying* (1930), *Sanctuary* (1931), *Light in August* (1932), *Absalom, Absalom!* (1936), *The Unvanquished* (1938), *Go Down, Moses* (1942), *The Hamlet* (1940), *The Town* (1957), and *The Mansion* (1959), most prominent among them. I show that the modernist author was already discovering the epistemology of networked systems in the creation of his own imagined landscape. Before providing readers with a chapter overview, I first need to describe briefly the language of networks and complexity, a body of theory that does not determine my approach to Faulkner, but offers a frame of reference. Simply to say that Yoknapatawpha is composed of many overlapping interaction networks that together compose a complex system does not, in itself, convey very much about Faulkner's art or the fictional world he populated. Interaction networks can take many different forms – and they also express themselves at different scales ranging from microbiology all the way up to ecosystems and beyond, from the neurons in brains to the individual relationships that constitute a larger community of beings.

Network Theory, a Brief Synopsis

The formal study of networks dates back to 1735 when Swiss-born mathematician Leonhard Euler invented the geometry of position, using basic units of graph theory, namely, nodes or vertices and edges or links (Ferguson 2018: 24–5). Once it was established, nineteenth-century scientists applied Euler's "framework to everything from cartography to electrical circuits to isomers of organic components. That there might also be *social* networks certainly occurred to some of the great political thinkers of that age," but no investigator attempted "to formalize this insight" until the turn of the twentieth century (25–6) when Euler's geometry of position came to underlie the study of networks and the distinct, but overlapping field of complex systems. Put simply, we can visualize a network as a graph where each dot (each vertex or node) represents an object, and the lines between them (the edges or links) represent the connections or relationships between objects.[2] In real life, networks are "weighted," meaning that there are certain nodes that are more important than others for the system; these objects are referred to more often, visited continually, and therefore become central to the information that flows through that system. These nodes are therefore more weighty than other nodes.[3] The layperson can imagine the direction in which information flows through a network. These information flows constitute a self-organizing pattern of behavior – and the more weighted a system, the more such flows favor certain nodes, thereby indicating the centrality of certain nodes in the network.

Nineteenth-century mathematical attempts to calculate and visualize the dynamic nature of networks entailed, moreover, the transition from the flat space of Euclidean geometry to a projective or speculative geometry (Delanda 2016: 115). Toward the end of the century, Henri Poincaré (1854–1912), sometimes called the forefather of relativity theory, made major innovations in the calculation of dynamical systems by capturing "all the possible states" of a two-dimensional space. Exploring the behavior of trajectories in a body of water, Poincaré "noticed that curves tended to converge at *special points* in the space, as if they were attracted to them: it did not matter where the trajectory had its origin, or how it wound its way around the space, its long-term tendency was to end up at a particular point" (120). These "special, remarkable, or singular points were eventually named attractors. When a state space has several attractors, these singularities are surrounded by an area within which they affect trajectories, an area called a 'basin of attraction'" (120). Poincaré's work was revolutionary and had manifold applications, particularly in data analysis of everything from cells to cities, from solar systems to galaxies. For our purposes, Poincaré maps can be described as a projective geometry that allows complex data to be visualized in terms of both space and time.[4] By giving spatial representation to spans of time, these maps can visualize the ways in which a network self-organizes and produces a basin of attraction or a "zone of stability" (120). With this, we achieve more than a snapshot of a moving system; rather, we may visualize a range of behaviors – from the chaotic to the predictable – that form "stable tendencies" characterizing such a system.

The shift from analyzing the essential properties of things to investigating the self-organizing pattern that objects make in the world may appear subtle, but it marks a key distinction that informs the study of networks and systems theory. In the humanities, Gilles Deleuze and Félix Guattari were among the first to understand the importance of dynamical systems theory in their *A Thousand Plateaus* (1980), giving mathematical shape to a philosophy of immanence and the concept of the *agencement* or assemblage. A year before, in the bestselling *Gödel, Escher, Bach* (1979), Douglas R. Hofstadter popularized systems theory as the key to understanding human cognition itself. The "key is not the *stuff* out of which brains are made," he writes in the opening of the book, "but the *patterns* that can come to exist inside the stuff of a brain" (4). "This is a liberating shift," he continues, "because it allows one to move to a different level of considering what brains are: as media that support complex patterns that mirror, albeit far from perfectly, the world, of which, needless to say, those brains are themselves denizens – that is in the inevitable self-mirroring that arises, however partial or imperfect it may be, that the strange loops of consciousness start to swirl" (4). Hofstadter insists, moreover, that one attends to the pattern of individual interactions in order to comprehend the larger aggregate behavior of a system while these interactions, no matter how small, must be imagined as a form of language and communication. Indeed, these interactions exist everywhere, in minds as well as in every other biological network.

Hofstadter draws a parallel between the movement of individual ants within a colony and "the composition of a human brain out of neurons. Certainly no one would insist that individual brain cells have to be intelligent beings on their own in order to explain the fact that a person can have an intelligent conversation" (320). Hofstadter's analogy of brains and ant hills – where higher-order behavior emerges out of, but cannot be reduced to, lower-level interactions – has become a standard way of visualizing the world in the twenty-first century. Consider, for example, Deborah Gordon's critically acclaimed book on ant colonies as interaction networks. Thirty-one-years after Hofstadter, Gordon (2010) similarly dissuades readers from imagining a "hidden program" within the colony and urges us to accept the seemingly counterintuitive supposition that individual ant interactions with their noise, randomness and variability produce larger "patterns of regularities" (47). Here, Gordon describes what has become an elementary tenet of system structure. Though disordered movement may characterize many of the interactions within the ant colony, the aggregate self-organizes, which means that it produces spontaneous pattern formations; or, to use another description, it creates "dynamic patterns synchronized in time and extending over large distances of space many orders of magnitude bigger than a [single] interaction" (Kelso 1995: 8).

Gordon's description of the ant colony arises out of the application of network theory to biological systems – systems so large and robust that one may speak of system complexity, that is, a system that resists simple characterization and requires an examination of the myriad connections that compose it. Scott Page (2011) provides a general definition, stating that "systems that produce complexity consist of *diverse* rule-following entities whose behaviors are *interdependent*. Those entities interact over a contact structure or network," and these "entities often *adapt*" (17). It is important to add that the study of complexity still does not possess a uniform methodology, for there is much disagreement among scholars concerning the application of basic terminology. Renate Sitte (2009), for instance, writes that there is still "no unanimous consensus as to what complexity is" (22), while describing qualities that are generally accepted across disciplines. "Systems are complex," Sitte affirms, "when they undergo changes in structure, changes in functioning, when they have adaptive feedback, are evolving, or simply when they have a large number of components or relations" (25). Scholars thus agree upon a number of the "strongest characteristics of a complex system." Sitte outlines these characteristics as follows:

> (1) intricate interdependencies among many parts; (2) many variables operating simultaneously; (3) generally nonlinear; (4) cause and effect are not close in time and space; (5) intuitive interventions do not produce the expected outcome; (6) reductionist analysis fails or is misleading; (7) emergence; and (8) self-organization. (26; adapted)

Perhaps the most influential term that describes such complexity in systems theory is the notion of the *edge of chaos*, and it is one that I apply to

Faulkner's view of social interaction in his later fiction. First coined by
Norman Packard in 1988, this notion of "adaptation to the edge of chaos"
proposes a dynamic state in which systems – whether biological or com-
putational – when driven towards a state of chaos, adapt from within,
achieving new equilibriums and staving off disorder by self-adjusting,
integrating, and processing information. Scientists have applied this idea
to a range of fields to understand how systems at different scales survive,
achieving stability by adapting to changes in their environment.[5] The *edge
of chaos* has been described in different ways, but the emphasis undoubtedly
falls upon individual interactions self-organizing, generating order from the
bottom up, and maintaining stability through adaptation. If we place
Yoknapatawpha in the context of this history, Faulkner emerges as an
unacknowledged – and as yet untapped – literary pioneer for visualizing
complex social systems and meditating upon the role and value of the
human individual therein.[6] While the centuries-long context above for
the study of networked systems illuminates our subject, the *modus operandi*
of the book is to value Faulkner's own symbolic formulation of
Yoknapatawpha as a self-organizing and dynamical system. This means
that I do not simply apply network or systems theory onto the
Yoknapatawpha fiction; rather, my principal aim is to examine Faulkner's
artistic discovery of the dynamics of social space and interpret how his
formulation changed, matured, and developed over a four-decade span.

Faulkner's Complex Systems

In the chapters to come, I present two major stages in which Faulkner's
discovery took place: (1) an earlier vision portraying how networks scale,
circulate information, centralize, and produce potentially tyrannical paradigms of top-down vertical power; and (2) another view of dynamical
networks that are constantly adapting to produce novel forms of movement and behavior. The first two chapters concentrate on the ways that a
weighed network forms. I begin with Faulkner's first representation of the
plantation system of the New South as a network of agencies – both
human and nonhuman actors – that circulate information and ideology.
Central to this first stage of Faulkner's artistic discovery is a meditation
upon the image or the process of image-making itself as the basis for
higher-order social complexity and the circulation of information through
networked space. The problem that Faulkner immediately intuited was
one of scale. An image or story that is capable of nourishing the creative
energies of a community can also – as a system scales – become a node of

power that regulates, often coercively, the individual lives that constitute that system. Faulkner shows us how certain kinds of images become power-wielding nodes; to use Poincaré's terminology, these images are attractors, special points in space at which flows of information, ideology, and resources tend to converge.

What comes to occupy Faulkner in this first stage of discovery is the question of human interiority within such rapidly scaling social systems – producing a tension so pronounced in his prolific period of writing between 1927 and 1936 that he repeatedly narrativizes the process by which the interior architecture of the self is invaded by certain images and modes of behavior that achieve prominence. The Faulkner that this study evokes is at once the modernist developing a spatial narrative practice describing the emergence of complex social networks and the Romantic for whom the immanent life was paramount and even sacrosanct. That these two trajectories of inquiry and spiritual belief are not easily reconcilable gives philosophical and moral weight to the landscape and characters that Faulkner invented. They also provide a striking meditation on what it means for human beings to find themselves in systems so vast and ubiquitous that they can no longer remember what it was like to live outside them and, thus, to think outside of their ideological dicta.

The second stage of Faulkner's discovery begins, I argue, with *Absalom, Absalom!*. Certainly, there is precedent in the fiction beforehand, but the 1936 novel represents a significant shift in focus, from visualizing the hegemonic centralization that occurs in the circulation of ideology to a more dynamical view of networked space. One can imagine systems dialectically oscillating between information stability and entropy, yet, for Faulkner, it matters what ideology circulates through the nodes of a particular network. The novel, therefore, identifies the racial hierarchy of the South as an escalating incoherence that destabilizes the slave culture and undermines the textual paradigms of power that it has instituted to circulate its ideology. We see the institution of slavery falling in upon itself, as its racist ideology jeopardizes the interpersonal and intersubjective bonds of family and community. The novels to come develop this dynamical view, no longer focusing solely on paradigms of ideological power that eventually jeopardize the life of the whole, but also affirming alternative attractors of novelty and alterity that allow human subjects to protect themselves against the stealthy and often invisible forms of tyranny that Faulkner identified in the earlier fiction. The Snopes trilogy is perhaps the most sustained articulation of this second view. Monopolies of power certainly emerge – as with the iconic villainous depiction of Flem Snopes who first appears as a "spider" lurking "among the ultimate shadows" (H 64) and eventually as a "nothing" that violently etches itself onto the apex of social space in *The Mansion* (177). Yet, despite the everpresent danger of a Flem, the trilogy offers a view of networked systems as dynamically open and unpredictable and of individuals within them as potential generators of social change. In this respect, Faulkner presciently anticipates the concept of *adaptation to the edge of chaos* and provides a model for the preservation and strengthening of human agency and intersubjectivity within a coercive information system.

This book consists of six chapters, each of which is divided into four subsections. In the first chapter, "Murder in the House of Memory," I show how Faulkner's first Yoknapatawpha novel visualizes the expanding plantation network of the New South with the primary nodes of this network being the Sartoris family bank and the plantation complex. In the plantation manor especially, Faulkner articulates a physical and a cognitive architecture that becomes archetypal in his larger body of writing. Indeed, in *Flags in the Dust*, the manor house offers a microcosm for the larger plantation system with Faulkner visualizing two levels of network structure within its architectural design. On one level, the manor house is comprised of a series of discontinuous agencies – both people and things – through which information continuously circulates. At the same time, information does not circulate uniformly through this networked structure, and Faulkner imagines how a coercive and threatening ideology centralizes in various hubs of social space, particularly in artifacts and texts. The monumental statue of the plantation patriarch emerges as a particularly threatening site that assumes a quasi-agency, at once preserving the ideology of the planter system and disseminating its ideology through the nodes of the network and out into the wider world.

Chapter 2, "A Clock in Place of the Sun," interprets *The Sound and the Fury* as a new stage in the design of these cognitive cartographies. As Yoknapatawpha County and its population expand, Faulkner visualizes how human beings invent information systems that grow and multiply into large-scale social orders reaching across generations, so that individuals lose the ability to differentiate their inner lives from these interlocking fields of relationships. The cognitive cartographies of *Flags in the Dust* acquire a far more sinister potency in *The Sound and the Fury*. Faulkner once again imagines the way in which centralized networks rely upon mimetic information objects to circulate ideology through the social body – and, in the clock and the statue of the Confederate soldier particularly, he identifies both planter legacy and Jim Crow segregation as mechanisms of social control.

Chapter 3, "Invasions of Interiority," examines how Faulkner, in *As I Lay Dying* and *Sanctuary*, develops the cognitive cartographies of his earlier novels and the mimetic mechanisms that allow information to be replicated in selves and social groups. I begin by returning to *The Sound and the Fury* to analyze Faulkner's positive depiction of characters like Dilsey and Miss Quentin who offer the first paradigms of alterity and resistance to the flow of ideology within plantation culture. I then apply this view to Faulkner's symbolic characterization of Darl Bundren in *As I Lay Dying* as a hybrid character who evokes a decisive clash between immanent subjectivity and the self as merely a node in the circulation of cultural information. In other words, Darl presents a Faulknerian ontology in which a model for selfhood is mimetically constituted and can thereby be mimetically jeopardized. In the last two sections, I show how *Sanctuary* articulates this dilemma in terms of scale, depicting the hyper-mimetic circulation of information through surfaces and selves. In this light, *Sanctuary* serves as an experimental novel that explores the stages by which a hyper-mimetic information pattern flows through the social body – in individual and group self-expression and from the deliberate conscious actions of an agent to the self-organizing and spontaneous movement of a mob or collective.

Chapter 4, "When Ideology Wavers," explores the artistic culmination of Faulkner's representation of coercive ideologies in two of his most mature novels, *Light in August* and *Absalom, Absalom!*. I show how Faulkner increasingly represents the cognitive cartographies of Yoknapatawpha in terms of coercion, violence, and racial injustice. Here again, the fragile architecture of the self is the stage upon which an information pattern proliferates. Faulkner, I argue, is particularly interested in the process of how a small, individual act can grow in weight and resonance until it becomes a coercive node in a system, acquiring institutional power across generations. Yet there is a significant and meaningful change in Faulkner's strategy, since he begins to show not just the incoherence of the racial ideology of the South, but how such incoherence destabilizes the planter culture from within. Chapter 5, "Beyond the Tyranny of Textual Space," and Chapter 6, "Architecture of Interiority," concentrate on five novels published between 1938 and 1958: *The Unvanquished, Go Down, Moses, The Hamlet, The Town*, and *The Mansion*. These final chapters consider the growth of complex systems not simply in terms of their topographical and technological expansion – as hamlets become towns and towns become cities – but also in terms of the inner architecture of the human self. I make the case that Faulkner emphatically affirms the individual agent and presents an underlying moral anchorage in his later fiction that upholds immanence and the interpersonal bonds between individuals as the principal manner by which the individual may resist coercive systems of social control.

For all his unflinching investigations of the power of faceless and inhuman systems, Faulkner held out hope for the human subject. A generation of critics saw this hope in the erasure of this subject's metaphysical foundations, but this study makes the case that Faulkner held fast to the viability of the inwardly-directed human being not as a vestige of a now-extinct spiritual past, but as a source of novelty that produces and participates in, while never fully subsumed by, the flows of information that form the systems in which we are nestled. In Faulkner's later work particularly, the individual does not merely aid in or resist the production of social order, although this can be the case; he or she is perpetually producing novelty within the life of the whole, a role vital to the long-term wellbeing of our very personhood and our communities, especially in addressing the racial and economic inequalities that threaten to undermine the social fabric. This cognitive interiority is not imagined abstractly either; rather, Faulkner repeatedly returns to an associative web of images that characterize such internal space as a real and substantial underlayer of our networked life.

CHAPTER I

Murder in the House of Memory

Scholars have long emphasized the centrality of the plantation house as both symbol and institution in Faulkner's fictional cosmos. Scott Romine (2015) notes the plantation's foundational importance for "Faulkner's mapping, orienting both the 1936 and 1945 maps." The plantation appears, he writes, "as a historical phenomenon – a space subject to the temporal grammars of past, present, and future tense – there is no space on Faulkner's map marked as historically prior to it" (18–19). It should be no surprise then that Faulkner's first Yoknapatawpha fiction provides a spatial representation of the Sartoris plantation manor more detailed than any other plantation complex in his later works. This level of detail may be the result of an ambitious eagerness on his part, a recognition that he had finally discovered the site for his future artistic endeavors and desired to map systematically a symbolic edifice at the outset. In the original holograph manuscript of *Flags in the Dust*, one can observe the labor-intensive effort that Faulkner put into formulating the spatial symbolism of the plantation manor. Faulkner, in fact, discarded the original beginning that recounted young John Sartoris' death in France, opening the manuscript instead with old Bayard climbing the stairway of the mansion to enter the attic and confront a decisive memory of fatality on the flyleaf of the family bible.[1] In later versions, including the heavily edited *Sartoris*, Faulkner carefully rearranged the chronology of the sequence, developing the details of Bayard's ascent through the manor and using his movements as a way of structuring the narrative remembrances that constitute a significant portion of the first hundred pages of the novel.

This chapter provides a close reading of Faulkner's first depiction of the plantation manor and argues that it provides the prototype for a spatial pattern that will be repeated so often and in so many variable forms as to constitute the foundational archetype of networked space and information flow throughout the whole of the Yoknapatawpha fiction. I begin by providing relevant scholarly findings from plantation studies in order to distinguish Faulkner's representation of the twentieth-century tenant plantation system from the gothic interpretations traditionally ascribed to it. In Section 1.2, I show how *Flags in the Dust* imagines the Sartoris plantation as both a physical and a cognitive architecture that simultaneously preserves, recreates, and disseminates a violent paradigm of power. In developing this idea, Sections 1.3 and 1.4 lay the basis for my broader view of how certain patterns of information circulate both in social space and within the cognitive interiority of the self. Indeed, the Sartoris planter network does more than circulate information through its myriad nodes – in the family bank and manor house, across the freshly tilled fields of cotton, and along the rail lines out to the wider world; Faulkner visualizes a vertically oriented spatial symbolism in which a violent ideology is embedded in the artifacts and aesthetic objects of that network so that it is capable of replicating its content in individuals who inhabit that space. This predicament is most fully realized in Colonel Sartoris's statue, for while the man himself is dead, the ideological information of his mimetic print circulates through the financial and technological infrastructure of bank and rail, using the innovations of modernity to disseminate itself even while reinforcing the racial and class suppositions of the slave system that preceded it. This is the danger that pervades the Yoknapatawpha fiction to come, the fear that an information pattern can acquire a life of its own, overpowering and imprinting itself upon the agents who come into contact with it.

1.1   The Planter Class of the New South

The earliest critical investigations often approached Faulkner's Yoknapatawpha County through a gothic literary lens, equating the plantation culture with the decline of the elite white families of the Old South, a line of inquiry developed in equal measure by a number of contemporary cultural critics.[2] This conflation of the plantation with gothic ruin downplays an important aspect of Faulkner's vision – the institutional success of the plantation system in the first half of the twentieth century and the historical violence at the foundation of this ever-adapting edifice. In his complex representation of the economic and cultural power exercised by elite planters, Faulkner portrays a vision of the New South that resonates with contemporary scholarship in plantation studies and gestures to "a global socioeconomic and cultural matrix" that Amy Clukey terms "plantation modernity."[3] It is necessary to provide briefly the changing view of historians and cultural critics before moving onto Faulkner's first inventory of the New South plantation manor, since it helps to elucidate the initial character of, and context for, Faulkner's portrayal of his twentieth-century fictional county and the place of the plantation therein. Far from being a gothic-tinged world of haunting and ghosts, Yoknapatawpha is, I show, a site upon which Faulkner narrativizes the reconsolidation of economic and cultural power in the hands of the elite planter class and uses the plantation house as his first site to map both social space and the cognitive interiority of his characters.

A mid-twentieth-century consensus argued for the decline of the aristocratic class within a larger history of emergent capitalism and systemic racial inequality. This conventional understanding of a fundamental breach between the antebellum and postbellum social and economic orders of the South was not challenged until 1978 when Jonathan Wiener argued that the plantation system did not vanish and that the "leading prewar planters persisted" (Reidy 2002: 305). Numerous studies of federal policy in the South during Reconstruction emphasized the cooperation between wealthy landowners and politicians and "portrayed the army and the Freedmen's Bureau as working hand in glove with former slaveholders to thwart the freedmen's aspirations and force them to return to plantation labor" (Foner 1990: xiv). Consequently, a new consensus emerged in the 1980s that the disintegration of the older plantation economy during Reconstruction was a popular misconception of a more complex phenomenon.

Postrevisionist scholars, as they came to be called, documented the "continued hold of racism and federalism despite the extension of citizenship rights to blacks and the enhanced scope of national authority" (Foner 1990: xiv). Instead of emphasizing the decline of the old plantation system, scholars described a reorganization that differed from region to region. Gavin Wright (1986) provided an influential analysis that stressed regional and economic specificity. The agricultural producers, Wright wrote, "were not landlords but 'laborlords'" (18) – and this relationship between the elite class and the laborers often involved various crops and lien arrangements. There was one "basic background condition," Wright asserted, "for virtually the whole epoch between the Civil War and World War II," and this entailed the "isolation of the southern unskilled labor market" (70). The lien system reinforced this deepening isolation, for it "locked the farmer into cotton production and forced him to pay outrageously high interest on the funds borrowed, thereby keeping him in perpetual debt to the merchant or the landowner, who were often the same person" (Woodman 2003: 252). The old elite planter families were among this new class of laborlords, and their success involved centralized management (Aiken 1998: 63–84).

A distinctive locus of Faulkner's Mississippi is the so-called Black Belt region, a term originally applied with geographical precision, but eventually used to describe large areas of intensive cotton production in the Deep South. While other parts of the South facilitated the advancement of a postbellum merchant class, composed substantially of foreigners, Black Belt planters "retained supremacy through legislative means, specifically by crafting lien laws that gave them primacy over the merchants" (Reidy 2002: 306). During Reconstruction, these planters initially attempted to recreate the slave system, but could not counteract the ability of freedmen to move from one employer to the next (Wright 1986: 85). The emergence of a lien-centered plantation system solved this problem of decentralization for the elite planters. As a result, the large landownership units persisted, having to become "the most modern, well-organized, [and] closely supervised agricultural operations in the cotton South" if they were to survive in this new period of industrial growth (Woodman 2003: 251).[4] After Reconstruction, when a massive expansion of cotton manufacturing occurred in the South, leading in turn to new forms of social conflict among "rural cultivators, merchants, imperial statesmen, landowners, and industrialists," the old elite planter class solidified control over vast swaths of the Black Belt, within which Mississippi had the largest number of extensive tenant plantations, with Alabama and Georgia following closely behind.[5]

Faulkner's depiction of Yoknapatawpha, Mississippi, in *Flags in the Dust* supports this account of the consolidation of power by the old planter class during and after Reconstruction. The plantation complex arises not simply as a decayed site that exerts a spectral power over the present; the Sartoris plantation is a cartography actively internalized by the social body of a *modern* Yoknapatawpha. Thus, I offer a different way of understanding Faulkner's craft – one that explores how networked systems centralize or become hierarchal over time and, indeed, how intergenerational movement and behavior spatially converge in vertical paradigms of power and belief. Faulkner originally imagines this network centralization by portraying how the interacting nodes of the plantation economy erect a coercive information object that instantiates the ideology of the culture by physically situating it in a central hub of social space, above the men and women who sustain it with their activity. What interests Faulkner, I argue, are the structural features of networks as they become more complex, centralized, and capable of spontaneously supervening upon the individuals who sustain them. From this perspective, Faulkner offers us an interpretative lens through which we can better view the modernization of the plantation network of the South, a reinvention at scale entailing an accompanying infrastructure of finance, bureaucracy, transportation, and ideology.

1.2   Into the House of Memory

Flags in the Dust begins with a portrayal of the economic viability of the twentieth-century Sartoris plantation, charting an expanded network of relations no longer centralized on agriculture alone. In the novel's opening paragraphs, old Bayard Sartoris appears at a major artery of his family's commercial enterprise – in his family's bank with the ghost of his father, Colonel John Sartoris, hovering above him: "John Sartoris seemed to loom still in the room, above and about his son, with his bearded, hawklike face, so that old Bayard sat with his crossed feet propped against the corner of the cold hearth, holding the pipe in his hand, it seemed to him that he could hear his father's breathing even" (FD 3). A traditional critical view places this relationship between father and son within a gothic purview of plantation deterioration. For André Bleikasten (2017b), the scene presets the overarching theme of "decline" (133) where the present self is a stage upon which the ghosts of the past assert their control: "The past breaks through the cracks of the present. The edges of time open up, and a multitude of ghosts readies itself to take over the stage" (132).[6]

Problems arise if one accepts this equation of the scene's gothic elements with plantation decline. Bayard is in this case hardly perturbed or troubled. Sitting in his office, he is inextricably connected to his past through an experience of leisure. He holds his father's pipe, his own teeth tracing the prints his father left, which are, in turn, situated within a historical continuum of artistic and natural ingenuity:

> The bowl of the pipe was ornately carved and it was charred with much usage, and on the bit were the prints of his father's teeth, where he had left the very print of his ineradicable bones as though in enduring stone, like the creatures of that prehistoric day that were too grandly conceived and executed either to exist very long or to vanish utterly when dead from an earth shaped and furnished for punier things. (FD 4)

These past traces denote an artistic monumentalism bequeathed to the present in the figure of an "ornately carved" pipe. Faulkner invests the scene with implicit Romantic overtones by relating the Colonel's act of self-fashioning – "he had left the very print of his ineradicable bones as though in enduring stone" – to a vast series of natural adaptations that culminate in this present scene with Bayard in his office "while the business of the bank went forward in the next room" (3).

Faulkner establishes the continuity of the planter institution through creative acts of adaptation that go back into deep time. The setting is not a degeneration of a past edifice, moreover, for it originates in the postbellum world of the South. The Merchants and Farmers Bank is the leading financial institution for the whole county and is centrally located in the Courthouse Square of Jefferson. As its founder and president, Bayard is both a laborlord, to use Wright's terminology, and a vital artery of finance through which other landowners administer their plantations in the New South. Colonel Sartoris hovers above his kin because he is the progenitor of this postbellum institution. Faulkner goes to great lengths to depict the patriarch's acts of self-fashioning as violent and creative exploits of post-bellum expansionism, and he visualizes the process by which these acts are stored as textual information, embedded and proliferating in the reconstructed order – in the social and mental spaces – of Yoknapatawpha.

Faulkner's opening to the novel thereby establishes a process of information flow in which biology and culture participate in replicating and adapting a planter network of power, privilege, and belief. On one level, there is a subtle self-referentiality on the part of the author himself with Will Falls possessing a paronymic resonance with Faulkner's own name. Yet Will Falls as Faulkner's own narrative proxy is only one participant, for there are interlocking nodes in the flow of information through social space and the evocation of the Colonel's ghost therein. Indeed, the setting of the bank is more than incidental; it is a site of exchange in which commercial and narrative properties intermingle in the circulation of meaning, value, and ideology. The ghost is not strictly speaking disembodied; it is directly associated with the mimetic marks upon the pipe, which in turn establish the idea that information can be at once genetically preserved within the body and encoded upon texts. Here, Faulkner's imagery can help us understand this self-reflexive concept more clearly, for the temporal relationship between past and present is structured in relation to the mouth as the organ that mediates the relationship between ostensible opposites: interior and exterior, personal and social. Falls and Bayard retell the past through this organ, and Faulkner interweaves the ghost into this pattern of communication by emphasizing its present breathing. In one respect, all these voices across time come to hinge upon or are connected to the old Colonel's pipe that Falls has returned to Bayard and that the planter now holds in his hand, tracing the teeth indentations with his fingers: "Holding the pipe in his hand, it seemed to [Bayard] that he could hear his father's breathing even" (3). Here, the mouth with its respiration process is related to the mnemonic surface of the pipe and would simply be an interesting imagistic flourish if not for how Faulkner develops this pattern in his portrayal of the family's manor house. In anticipation of this development, we can begin by stating that the pipe serves to emphasize the coparticipation of multiple agents at once in the production and circulation of information – those that exist within memory and those encoded outside the body in an externally adapted layer of cultural objects.

Associated with the mouth (the organ of speech), the pipe operates as an initial locus of memory or a medium upon which the creative artistry of the past has laid its print, with Faulkner further analogizing this imagery in naturalistic terms, namely, dinosaur fossils captured in strata. The pipe thereby serves as a textual medium upon which history is written, imprinted, and told, a surface on which events correspond to mimetic indentations or information storage. Bayard looks upon the oral inscriptions of his father, which through similitude are constituted in the living act of expression in which old man Falls, Bayard, and the reader participate. As intimated above, this expression crosses temporal and spatial boundaries to replicate information in whole or in part. This single surface of inscription is by no means univocal, moreover, for the pipe is only one surface of representation. Bayard will carry the pipe with him and, at times, touch it as he ascends through his manor house. As a tactile and visual surface upon which a temporal sequence expresses itself, the pipe can be interpreted as an initial rung in a series of heterogeneous associations that allow for the circulation of information. Where Faulkner sets out this symbolic pattern of information flow in the bank, he transfers it onto a more complex architectural surface, the Sartoris mansion itself, which has been "built and rebuilt" (8) and in and through which a planter ideology is made manifest.

With his first depiction of the plantation mansion, Faulkner portrays a process of mnemonic introspection and information preservation in terms of visual media. In aligning Bayard with his father who oversaw the transition from the slave to sharecropping economy, Faulkner begins to explore the reality of what such a hereditary and cultural legacy entails, as he charts Bayard's movements from his bank through his freshly tilled cotton fields to the manor itself. Here, the manor still serves as a vital node of social space, one connected to a now larger and more powerful planter network with its banking, agricultural, industrial, and transportation nodes. In its own right, the manor operates as both a central hub in which the family's movement clusters across time and an arena in which Faulkner identifies a disturbing cartography of institutional consciousness.

In the first chapter, Faulkner prepares the reader for the mnemonic architecture of the plantation house, the interior space of which is made manifest through an interlinking series of associative surfaces. To reach home, old Bayard passes through "upland country," the "viscid shards of new-turned earth glint[ing] damply in the sun," before "descending sheerly into a valley of good broad fields richly somnolent in the leveling afternoon" (8). In what may seem a perfectly harmless depiction of the valley, Faulkner introduces a triadic relationship between light, perceiver, and surface. Here, Faulkner maps this relationship spatially by drawing the reader's attention to the sunlight above, Bayard as observer, and the upturned surface of the earth whose "viscid shards" denote a violence, which will manifest itself in all the various mnemonic loci within the manor. The imagery is complex, denoting not simply violation, as we will see, but also fertility and new life in an uneasy counterbalance of past and present. Indeed, the "new-turned earth" indicates a spring setting with "good broad fields" underscoring the viability of Bayard's lands. On another level of analysis, this descent into the "somnolent" setting intimates that Bayard's journey homeward is simultaneously a movement into the depths of a slumbering consciousness, the "new-turned" earth indicating that we have initiated a process in which the buried interior is now being exposed.

In what follows, Faulkner transposes this "somnolent" setting onto the plantation house itself. Bayard gazes at the "white simplicity of [the manor which] dreamed unbroken among ancient sunshot trees" (8). Since Bayard is descending through the valley, the whole slumbering setting suggests a cognitive interiority or an unconscious domain just beneath – or just beyond – the vantage point of the perceiver. Faulkner continues to embed a self-reflexive dimension into the narrative, moreover, doubling Bayard's own perspective with that of the reader. Like the reader, Bayard beholds a simple white surface – in his case, the exterior of the house – that evokes the two-dimensional flatness of the white page.[7] Like the pipe, this surface exhibits an information pattern that is then reduplicated on every textual surface throughout the manor's interior architecture. There is something violent here about the act of looking, moreover, a hostility (subtly evoked) in the light that falls upon an illumined surface: the trees are "sunshot," attacked, in a sense, by the light that allows them to be perceived.

Faulkner's associative web of imagery assumes greater focus as Bayard draws closer to his home. From a distance, the house and its "sunshot" setting suggest indefinite traces of violence. As Bayard approaches the mansion, the "white simplicity" stages a confrontation that foreshadows a violent paradigm encoded upon all the mnemonic loci within the house. This event is not strictly a memory, but a performance that reflects the memories of murder inside. Growing on a trellis attached to the veranda, a rose bush and wisteria vine are locked in mortal combat, the rose steadily choking the life out of the purple flower and turning it into a commodity:

> Wisteria mounting one end of the veranda had bloomed and fallen, and a faint drift of shattered petals lay palely about the dark roots of it and about the roots of the rose trained onto the same frame. The rose was slowly but steadily choking the other vine, and it bloomed now thickly with buds no bigger than a thumbnail and blown flowers no larger than silver dollars, myriad, odorless, and unpickable. (8)

The foreign rose has been "trained onto the same frame" with the native wisteria, indicating that this presently unfolding violence has been painstakingly nurtured, grafted as it is upon the white simplicity of this architectural and textual surface. With the flowers' buds now "no bigger than a thumbnail and blown flowers no larger than silver dollars," Faulkner implicates the natural setting in a commercial process that connects the Sartoris bank to the manor house, two major nodes of the lien-centered plantation network of Yoknapatawpha. The grammatical construction of the passage also evokes a striking ambiguity. Is it the roses or the wisteria that resembles glass-blown flowers that appear mechanically reproduced like silver dollars? In one sense, roses and wisteria are so violently entangled that both perpetrator and victim are inseparable in producing this silver currency, becoming in the act of violence reflective and mimetic surfaces – first, glass-blown flowers and then, "silver dollars, myriad, odorless, and unpickable."

Although the house initially appears harmless, a mere "white simplicity" asleep, each of its spaces – from its bare exterior to the variable surfaces inside – stages a pattern of domination and bloodshed. In the initial pages of the novel, one finds an imagistic sequence of this violation: the "viscid shards of new-turned earth," the "sunshot trees" around the house itself, and the rose murdering the wisteria on the trellis, each instance intimating that the plantation house and the surfaces that encode its information are entangled in a pattern of assault and exploitation. Whereas, outside the house, the "simplicity" of external surface was tied almost exclusively to natural phenomena, whether dinosaur bones layered in strata or roses feeding off of wisteria, inside, surfaces evoke the prospect of a more sophisticated and curated cognitive cartography, no longer ostensibly dominated by instinct or nature. Within the manor, the first spatial arrangement reduplicates the pattern we saw outside with an additional emphasis upon interior adaptation:

> From the center of the ceiling hung a chandelier of crystal prisms and shades, fitted originally for candles but since wired for electricity; to the right of the entrance, beside folding doors rolled back upon a dim room emanating an atmosphere of solemn and seldom violated stateliness and known as the parlor, stood a tall mirror filled with grave obscurity like a still pool of evening water. (8–9)

Within the architectural structure, we find not disrepair, but a stately room whose chandelier has been adapted to the electric age, candlelight replaced by electricity. We can also observe a new aspect of surface depth. Rather than a simple white surface reflecting light, the "tall mirror" below the chandelier exerts its own mysterious interiority, "filled," as it is, "with grave obscurity like a still pool of evening water" – a surface no longer reflective, but connected lexically to the "grave," a burial motif that Faulkner attaches continually to the mansion. It is interesting to note that in the original handwritten manuscript, Faulkner was evidently working out how to evoke the gradual deepening of surfaces as the reader moves into the house. For instance, he writes that "the white simplicity" of the manor house "dreamed quiet as an unrippled surface of water in the afternoon amid its old sunshot trees."[8] Here, the various surfaces are initially compressed so that the "white simplicity" outside and the "mirror of evening water" appear together in one image. Faulkner later separated them to emphasize the movement inward, from a simple two-dimensional textual surface to a prospective three-dimensional view that compresses a whole family's history into one spatial structure.

With Bayard's entrance into the Sartoris mansion, Faulkner begins to outline a vertically oriented symbolism in which, as we shall see, a proliferating series of textual surfaces structure both the cognitive interiority of Bayard himself and his family across the decades. Faulkner continues his study of deepening surfaces with Bayard's movement upward to the second floor. Climbing the first staircase, Bayard stops between a set of shuttered western windows and an open doorway revealing not simply the "cradling semi-circle of the eastern hills" outside, but another interior space housing a memory of murder. In the figure of the open doorway, Bayard confronts a portal of memory that leads to an event during the Civil War where "a cook who was hidden under the mess stuck his arm out and shot [his uncle, Bayard,] in the back with a derringer" (18). Whereas the white simplicity and the mirror only subtly assert the violent vicissitudes of this interior space, the doorway presents a decisive opening into the collective memory of the Sartorises, into layers of "hidden" violence that will increasingly assert themselves the farther he climbs.

As the possibility of a deeper interiority looms, the resistance to its being perceived also increases. New layers of resistance present themselves to the reader. The perceiver – whether Bayard himself or the reader – cannot simply look within without having to pass through successive layers of material interposition. On the second floor, the doorway is lined with vari-colored glass windows that constitute the deathbed legacy of Bayard's grandmother:

> Bayard stopped again in the upper hall. The western windows were closed with latticed blinds, through which sunlight seeped in yellow dissolving bars that but served to increase the gloom. At the opposite end a tall door opened upon a shallow grilled balcony which offered the valley and the cradling semi-circle of the eastern hills in panorama. On either side of this door was a narrow window set with leaded panes of vari-colored glass that, with the bearer of them, constituted John Sartoris' mother's deathbed legacy to him, which his youngest sister had brought from Carolina in a straw-filled hamper in '69. (10)

On the one hand, one could interpret the imagery as gothic – the gloomy hall in the dim light of sunset emphasizing the arc of an Old Southern family reaching the end of its line. On the other hand, the Sartoris line survives and so does the twentieth-century plantation economy it administers. Thus, this movement into darkness, away from the bright light of day, to the places where light only "seeps" through windows, unfolds as a careful analogy for the movement deeper into cognitive interiority, to the places that are harder to see. Faulkner emphasizes the multiplying of barriers, as the light has to pass through ever more interpositions. As the locus of the pipe served as a touchstone for personal and geological history – layers of strata that uphold the human emergence in time – the open doorway functions according to a similar strategy, locating the "deathbed legacy" of a long-dead Sartoris matriarch, vari-colored windows through which a "hidden" violence, as we shall see, begins to assert its authority over these interior dimensions of self and space.

With Bayard entering into this first memory of murder, Faulkner replays the violence outside, portraying how violent acts structure the cognitive relations within this house of memory and, by extension, within the mind of old Bayard. Within the first memory of violence, the Union officer who shot his uncle in the back seems incidental; indeed, Faulkner intimates that the killer is an exponent of an information paradigm that flows through the memory, a violent interiority now freely asserting itself both within the depths of memory and upon a series of associative surfaces:

> Although there was no more firing and the bugles too had ceased, into the silence, above the strong and rapid breathing of the horses and the sound of their own hearts in their ears, was a nameless something – a tenseness sweeping from tree to tree like an invisible mist, filling the dewy morning woods with portent though birds flashed swooping from tree to tree, unaware or disregardful of it. . . . The glade dreamed quiet and empty of threat beneath the mounting golden day; laked within it lay a deep and abiding peace like golden wine; yet beneath this solitude and permeating it was that nameless and waiting portent, patient and brooding and sinister. (16)

Where, in the first scene of the novel, the dead spirit of John Sartoris "penetrate[s] into the uttermost citadel of silence in which his son lived," here, in the first memory of murder, a "nameless something" enters "into the silence" of the glade. This action of entry, of violation even, is repeatedly echoed, from the first sentence of the novel in which old man Falls "brought John Sartoris into the room with him," to Bayard's entry into the various rooms of the Sartoris mansion, instilling the sense of a deepening interiority where each surface reveals yet another layer of information. As the white simplicity of the Sartoris house dreams among the sunshot trees, the glade "dream[s] quiet and empty of threat," a single surface of representation admitting a trancelike layering of causality, at once peaceful, since the violent act is now over, and yet full of threat, since its submerged memory remains bound up with the material processes of a living consciousness and the economy it administers: Beneath the "mounting golden day" lies the glade, beneath which also lies "a deep and abiding peace," "beneath" which and "permeating it was that nameless" violence – a lower layer "patient and brooding and sinister" that interfuses the whole structure "sweeping from tree to tree like an invisible mist, filling the dewy morning woods."

At first glance, Faulkner's intertwining of memory and social space approximates the normal functions traditionally associated with memory: The house itself has been "built and rebuilt," each new layer interwoven with an older and deeper stratum of history, which the act of looking illuminates and makes present. Yet, from deeper within, "a nameless something" "permeates" these mounting layers of representation. The conscious self is not the primary agent here but simply one node in a proliferating network of agencies, both human and nonhuman. Where Faulkner locates this pattern emerging from within, he also insists upon the vertical height of this "nameless something," upon its precedence as it is "*above* the strong and rapid breathing of the horses and the sound of their own hearts in their ears" (emphasis added). If we remember, the ghost of John Sartoris hovers above Bayard in the bank, even while its bones are left deep in the layers of strata; here again, this "nameless something" simultaneously occupies the apex of spatial relations and is simultaneously beneath and permeating this vision of mnemonic space.

   With the doorway open, Bayard is able to enter briefly into a deeper layer of memory and to recover the details of the murder of his uncle, his namesake, Bayard Sartoris. Yet, inside the mnemonic architecture, these memories are not Bayard's alone; the story is shared, a tale reconstructed by Bayard himself, Aunt Jenny, and the Scottish engineer whom John Sartoris commissioned after the war to rebuild the railroad through the county: "They sat quietly for a time, in the firelight. The flames leaped and popped on the hearth and sparks soared in wild swirling plumes up the chimney, and Bayard Sartoris' brief career swept like a shooting star across the dark plain of their mutual remembering and suffering, lighting it with a transient glare like a soundless thunder-clap, leaving a sort of radiance when it died" (18). *Flags in the Dust* presents several avenues of imagistic correspondence in which the light or "transient glare" of spectatorship apprehends the white simplicity of the page whose two-dimensionality gives way to other surfaces and thresholds – whether the mirror, the open doorway, or the plain of mutual remembering and suffering. However much these thresholds or surfaces of representation may admit a deeper architectonics, they are transient, discontinuous, unstable, and potentially threatening. As with a mirror "filled with obscurity like a pool of evening water," the glade enigmatically "laked" upon itself or a "dark plain of mutual remembering and suffering," the doorway can only remain open for a time, the "transient glare" of narrative memory admitting its traces and once again mediated, the glassy surface that allowed the perceiver momentarily to plumb this interiority continually frustrating consciousness' control over the objects of its perception.

   As the doorway of memory closes and evening descends, that light of vision which momentarily poured through the open door is once again mediated by the deathbed legacy of vari-colored glass paneling: "But the door was closed now, and what light passed through the colored panes was richly solemn" (19). While the movement upward through the house stages a mnemonic pattern of deepening interiority, the observer journeys upward and inward to confront interpositions that frustrate and upend the possibility of a fuller self-knowing. According to a Romantic metaphysics, the light of vision seeks to permeate its object, to sublate it in its upward movement toward cognitive unity. In stark contrast, all these glassy surfaces – the white simplicity with its glass-blown flowers, the mirror of evening water, the vari-colored paneling, the dreaming glade, the glade laked upon itself, the plain of remembering – inculcate a persistent pattern in which the perceiver is unable to apprehend anything directly at all. Rather, this perceiver – whether Bayard within the narrative or the reader who occupies a similar perspectival relationship to the text – is challenged by surfaces that bear potentially dangerous forms of information. In this respect, the page is no longer simply two-dimensional, filled with harmless inscriptions that the perceiver can apprehend at will. Faulkner is welcoming us into the act of reading, while also warning us against it: The movement into a cognitive arena from which the flow of information changes its perceivers and implants them with a "nameless and waiting portent, patient and brooding and sinister."

1.3 The Seat of Consciousness

Faulkner's figuration of the plantation complex offers us a model of selfhood that allows for both the identity formation of a single self and for the construction of that self through many generations – as far back as the memory of that consciousness can go. Old Bayard is, in this respect, a present iteration of a past series of being, and his introspective movements through the house stage a pattern of identity formation in which the architectonics of the plantation house carry the hereditary and cultural information with which this self is encoded. Bayard's identity extends back into his own memory, but Faulkner also makes a surprising move in the first cognitive cartography of his Yoknapatawpha fiction. He indicates that individual consciousness is nestled in social space, a reservoir of information that extends beyond the subject. As much as that self can inform the created order that surrounds it, the plantation encodes a pattern that appears independent of the self's cognitive processes. Faulkner emphasizes the adaptability of the plantation system as the preservation of an information pattern outside the body, one that exceeds the selves that participate in it. In the symbolic language of the Sartoris plantation house, as we will see, the Colonel's epiphany the night before his death involves placing his own mirror image in the principal vertex of social space – into a site where it will outlast the mortal body and be replicated by the greater behavior of the social body across time.

Imagining the self in this broader, more capacious sense complicates the depictions of the individual characters of the novel. Old Bayard may be innocent of the past crimes of the plantation system, yet he reconstitutes its behavior and expression in social space. As Bayard moves upward into the manor house and deeper into his own memory, Faulkner emphasizes the lack of control that the old man possesses over the spaces inside. As much as mirror, windows, or page admit the beholder's vision, these surfaces gradually assert their own dominion over the self, the theme of mimetic mediation demonstrating the dependency of the subject not only on the objects of its vision, but also upon the cognitive and cultural preconditions for such vision. Where Faulkner portrayed apparently instinctual violence at the base of the plantation house, he soon develops this violence as an institutionalized assault on free expression – first in the symbolic choking of wisteria and, as we will see, in the Colonel's suppression of black voting rights. This systematic attack upon human agency involves more than the dominance of the white plantation class over a perpetual underclass; the farther old Bayard climbs the more the white heirs of the plantation complex are themselves subject to an irresistible power that is encoded in every spatial relationship around and in them – a power that is eventually located in the seat of consciousness itself – in the architectural apex of the manor or, the term I repeatedly employ throughout this book, the vertex of social space. This vertex is much more than a node in the network; it has become a centralized hub or, in the language of a Poincaré map, an attractor creating around it a basin of attraction or a zone of stability – and Faulkner will continue to express this in terms of verticality throughout his entire Yoknapatawpha fiction.

After leaving the hallway and passing by "the room in which his grandson's wife and her child had died" (FD 19), old Bayard reaches one of the deepest recesses of the house yet, his own room. With this continuing movement, Faulkner begins to illuminate the paradigm of planter power in terms of racial supremacy. As Bayard passes from the now-closed doorway to his own room, he peers through his window to the backyard below, observing a scene of arrested life: "Then he rose and went in his stockings to the window and looked down upon his saddle-mare tethered to a mulberry tree in the back yard and a negro lad lean as a hound, richly static beside it" (20). Again, Faulkner uses the spatial arrangement of observer and visual threshold with Bayard looking through his bedroom window onto a setting in which the body of "a negro lad" is equated with the "tethering" of a riding animal. Isom, the only son of Elnora Strother, is a member of the primary black family that serves the Sartorises. His "static" black profile, mediated through the upstairs window, serves as another mnemonic locus through which Faulkner stages Bayard's memory of his father before his death. There is also an important racial context here that Faulkner unpacks in the short story "There Was a Queen" (1933), where he identifies Elnora as the daughter of the Colonel, making the young lad upon whom Bayard gazes his nephew.

In this new interior setting, the glassy threshold of the window and the black body as inscription provide another locus through which Bayard recounts the second memory of murder, his own father's death and, with it, the reorganization of a system of racial subjugation and black labor during Reconstruction. The later familial context of "There Was a Queen" (1933) adds a rather painful context to this scene, since the two families, white and black, living side by side, one in the white manor house and the other in the old slave cabin behind the house, are in fact one family, united through blood, although one is bound to the authority of the other. After gazing upon his black kin below, Bayard sits down upon his bed to look at the pipe, again hearing "old man Falls' voice in roaring recapitulation" (FD 20). With the novel's first visual locus of memory reemerging, the reader learns that Falls has kept the pipe for years, returning it to Bayard with the pronouncement that John Sartoris' bloody fate was sealed the moment he began taking life, the moment he began murdering other men:

> "That'us when hit changed. When he had to start killin' folks. Then two carpet baggers stirrin' up niggers, that he walked right into the room whar they was asettin' behind a table with they pistols' layin' on the table, and that robber and that other feller he kilt, and with that same dang der'nger. When a feller has to start killin' folks, he'most always has to keep on killin'em. And when he does, he's already dead hisself." (23)

In this passage, Falls connects the killing of Colonel Sartoris to the patriarch's own violent suppression of the black vote during Reconstruction, one of the principal ways, as we saw in Section 1.1, in which elite planters compelled blacks to return to labor conditions they had endured before the war.

Falls' statement also initiates Bayard's own recollection of his father sitting in the family's dining room and drinking the family's final deathbed legacy, a bottle of port. The patriarch states emphatically that he is tired of murder and, accordingly, will accept his own death at the hands of another man:

> It showed on John Sartoris' brow, the dark shadow of fatality and doom,
> that night when he sat beneath the candles in the dining room and turned a
> wine glass in his fingers while he talked to his son.
>   "And so," he said, "Redlaw'll kill me tomorrow, for I shall be unarmed.
> I'm tired of killing men. . . . (23)

Within this submerged memory, the reader discovers that the Colonel is
part of a legacy of violence, his own death connected, as we are told by old
man Falls, to the Colonel's involvement in stripping black Americans of
self-expression and the political right of representation.

The varying perspectives, those of Falls and Bayard, converge on a
description that becomes characteristic of Faulkner's portrayal of
Southern dynasties: the masculine "brow" overtaken by "the dark shadow
of fatality and doom." On a most immediate level, Faulkner's depiction of
John Sartoris' shadowed face is conventional, perhaps even gothic. The
picture acquires additional complexity in the context of a further thread of
association. The shadow falling upon the Colonel's brow (the shadow of
the glass of red wine that he holds up into the light and turns in his fingers
to see his own fatal reflection) is part of a series in which the surface object
asserts a precarious and illegible internality, slowly changing from white
surface to black inscription, mirroring the narrative timeline in which day
passes into night and surfaces obstruct perception. In this respect, the
white simplicity gives way to the mirror of evening water, which in turn
transforms into the "somber richness" of the vari-colored door panes at
sunset, then into the "richly static" posture of a "negro lad" attending a
"tethered horse," and into the dark shadow that falls from a glass of red
wine in which the Colonel sees his own reflection. As with the description
of the other Sartoris rooms where the power of light is obscured by the
haunted interiority of an object, in this pivotal recollection, the spatial
arrangement of the candles above and of John Sartoris' face below hints at
the presence of a violence that resists perception, that hides, and is stored
in, the objects of social space.

The locus of this violence is the Colonel himself – not the man, but the
institutional power he represents. Even in death, Colonel Sartoris possesses
a startling, even supernatural power. The Colonel operates as a mystifying
presence, permeating the structure of social space and the cognitive interiority of his kin. Faulkner charts the discrepancy between man and
institution by emphasizing Colonel Sartoris' violent act of self-
transcendence. The act is not part of a positive metaphysics, the moving
on of the soul from the body. Instead, the Colonel has replicated himself

into the "fatal semblance of his dream," thereby achieving a resurrected authority by bequeathing himself into an information pattern that can exist outside the human body in mnemonic loci or textual form:

> And the next day [John Sartoris] was dead, whereupon, as though he had but waited for that to release him of the clumsy cluttering of bones and breath, by losing the frustration of his own flesh he could now stiffen and shape that which sprang from him into the fatal semblance of his dream; to be evoked like a genie or a deity by an illiterate old man's tedious reminiscing or by a charred pipe. (FD 23)

Here, the transference of life into "semblance" or into the mimetic inscriptions on a pipe indicates a type of information flow whereby a pattern can be separated from the interiority of the self and then reconstituted in another's cognitive space. As we saw, Faulkner imagines this in a complex spatial manner so that this "semblance" or "nameless something" prospectively occupies a privileged place above others and simultaneously wells up through all the layers of memory, its designation an impersonal pronoun that could signify either subject or object: "*It* showed on John Sartoris' brow . . . he had but waited for *that* to release him . . . he could now stiffen and shape *that* which sprang from him into the fatal semblance of his dream" (emphases added). Faulkner attributes a perverse artistic power to this pattern of violence. Released from "the clumsy cluttering of bones and breath" and "the frustration of his own flesh," John Sartoris has become the mediating craftsman of the material world, the phallic progenitor freed by his death to "stiffen and shape" future generations. Faulkner's language possesses a subtle sexual underlayer with the craftsman waiting for "release" and "stiffening" in the process of artistic consummation. It is not the man who ultimately possesses this power, however, but the information object he erects into a vertical position of power. In short, the Colonel has become an institution, trading the precariousness of flesh for an "enduring legacy in stone," as we saw at the opening of the novel.

  With the memory of his father's death emergent, Bayard enters into the deepest and oldest layers of his memory, climbing a stairway into an attic of "silence and ancient disused things" (86). Ascending into this final architectural space, Bayard is engaged in a ritualistic effort to commemorate and record the latest deaths in the family: his son, John (named after his father); his daughter-in-law; and their child. In this apex of plantation space, Bayard lights a single bulb above his head and bends down to open a lockbox containing the implements of the death ritual:

> Thus each opening was in a way ceremonial, commemorating the violent finis to some phase of his family's history, and while [old Bayard] struggled with the stiff lock it seemed to him that a legion of ghosts breathed quietly at his shoulder, and he pictured a double line of them with their arrogant identical faces waiting just beyond a portal and stretching away toward the invisible dais where Something sat waiting the latest arrival among them; thought of them chafing a little and a little bewildered, thought and desire being denied them, in a place where, immortal, there were no opportunities for vainglorious swashbuckling. Denied that Sartoris heaven in which they could spend eternity dying deaths of needless and magnificent violence while spectators doomed to immortality looked eternally on. *The Valhalla which John Sartoris, turning the wine glass in his big, well-shaped hand that night at the supper table, had seen in its chaste fragile bubble.* (FD 87; emphasis added)

There is a strange discrepancy, even derangement between actual and imagined space in this pivotal scene. On the one hand, the planter looks down to the lockbox and hears "a legion of ghosts breath[ing] quietly at his shoulder." On the other hand, he imagines a reflective space within the lockbox where the ghosts of the Sartoris dead are lined up behind a "portal" facing an "invisible dais where Something sat waiting." We have seen this "Something" before, as when a "nameless something" asserted itself from above at the dreaming "glade." Here, this "Something" is both within and above, enthroned with the "double line" of ghosts stretching toward the dais on which it waits. We are told, moreover, that this imagined space is the "Valhalla" that the Colonel saw reflected in his wineglass, a site in which he placed his "semblance" or "print" so as to outlast his mortal body.

In the uppermost recesses of the house, the mimetic predicament evoked in each previous room comes into fuller view. The perceiver is bound up in engendering an ideological paradigm of planter power that is at once within a medium and above it, freed, as we saw earlier, "from the frustration of [human] flesh." In this final unsettling relationship, Faulkner introduces one of the most personal items thus far, namely, the Sartoris family's brassbound bible, very similar to the Falkner family bible that was put on display at Rowan Oak in 2005. Old Bayard looks down onto the bible, the flyleaves of which are inscribed with the fading names of the Sartoris bloodline:

> [He] came upon a conglomeration of yellowed papers neatly bound in packets, and at last upon a huge, brass-bound bible. He lifted this to the edge of the chest and opened it. The paper was brown and mellow with

years, and it had a texture like that of slightly moist wood ashes, as though each page were held intact by its archaic and fading print. He turned the pages carefully back to the fly leaves. Beginning near the bottom of the final blank page, a column of names and dates rose in stark, fading simplicity, growing fainter and fainter where time had lain upon them. At the top they were still legible, as they were at the foot of the preceding page. But halfway up this page they ceased, and from there on the sheet was blank save for the faint soft mottlings of time and an occasional brownish penstroke significant but without meaning. (89)

Bayard's ritualistic ascent enacts the apprehension not of the living word of God, but of a dead textual body. As Bayard opens the rosewood box, the family heirloom displays all the attributes of a coffin; both cedar containers enclose the implements of war and a personal bible, traditionally buried with the soldier. Faulkner thus tropes the "blank page" of "fading penstrokes" with a corpse, the "faint soft mottlings of time" providing a terminology for the vari-colored bruises that the body acquires postmortem.

After passing through all the layers of memory mapped within the white simplicity of the Sartoris house, Bayard apprehends the blank extraneous page of a brassbound bible as another mediated surface that exerts a definitive power upon the living. Like all other media in the manor, the flyleaf evokes three-dimensional space, a pattern of cognitive interiority unfolding according to a past pattern of violence and containing a "semblance" of life that seems to possess its own sentience and quasi-agency. Gazing down upon the blank mottled page, Bayard remembers yet another surface he once saw in his childhood during the Civil War when, escaping the Yankee patrol, he came upon a spring and was confronted by a skull peering back at him from out of the water:

Then he crawled forth and went to a spring he knew that flowed from the roots of a beech; and as he leaned down to it the final light of day was reflected onto his face; bringing into sharp relief forehead and nose above the cavernous sockets of his eyes and the panting snarl of his teeth, and from the still water there stared back at him for a sudden moment, a skull. (90)

The perceptual uncertainty here is central to many of Faulkner's most self-reflexive passages. Is the skull a reflection of Bayard or an actual body floating in the depths of the spring? Does the skull represent the unconscious domain, the submerged fear of fatality momentarily surfacing, or is it the symbolic source of a hidden miasma that pollutes this house of memory? Or, again, is it the actual body of a fallen soldier? Importantly, this event predates all the memories of murder and locates their precarious source in a complex act of looking, with the perceiving subject constantly changing, being at once old Bayard, John Sartoris, the identical Sartoris ghosts, and the reader whose eyes inevitably apprehend the white surface of the page.

Instead of the prospect of a face-to-face meeting between the individual and God through the medium of scripture, the visual dynamic that unfolds between Bayard and the family bible involves intractable layers of mediation, further undermining the free expression of the subject. Bayard does not simply see, remember, or inscribe; Faulkner's architectural depiction exhibits a powerful spatial rendering of material consciousness coproducing ideology with a series of associative textual surfaces. This final object exhibits the process as ongoing, expressing an ever-emerging semiotics of power in the genealogy of planter names. According to George Handley, "New World planters turned to genealogy as an instrument of hegemony, 'an ideological and metaphorical tool of exclusion' that helped legitimate and consolidate the 'landowning social power' of the plantocracy."[9] In *Flags in the Dust*, Faulkner imagines this process as an act of consciousness that unites a whole sequence of past activity. In the highest layer of the plantation house, the identical Sartoris ghosts are not necessarily supernatural. These beings, who once bore the hereditary and cultural information of the Sartoris line, are harnessed behind Bayard's head, their vision implicit in Bayard's own as he gazes upon the page. As such, they are facets of an embodied consciousness evoked through a hyperawareness of textual surface and a corresponding three-dimensional imaging of the interiority of the mind.

Faulkner's constitution of space thus evokes a cognitive cartography whose interconnection of parts culminates in the attic, situated above other layers of thought and memory and involved in their activity. In the memory of the spring, the light above is mediated from below, the simple surface of both page and water refracting light onto the face of the onlooker and prospectively transposing information from the depths of the spring onto the perceiving features of the subject – onto the face and forehead specifically, a decisive emphasis upon the prefrontal cortex, the site of higher cognitive function. Importantly, the attic is the one arena in which Bayard exerts himself through inscription. In all the other rooms of the house, the old man is simply a spectator, whose perception draws forth memories of murder. In the attic, by contrast, Bayard writes the deceased names of his kin upon the brassbound bible, a surface that Faulkner depicts as a synthesis of all the locations in the house, a site both regulating these other regions and transformed in turn by them. All of the mediating surfaces, ending with the heaven that Bayard's father, John Sartoris, saw reflected in his wine glass and into which he puts his print, are involved in this act of inscription.

Bayard's act of inscription unfolds not simply as an individual process, but within a prism of past relations that inform and culminate in the present moment. In the terms of network theory, the bible functions as an attractor, which as we saw in the introduction is a special point in space that can attract other objects so that they converge upon it. On the one hand, we are certainly within Bayard's consciousness – within the interior domain of the self. Yet Faulkner indicates that there is a seamlessness of degree between the inner architecture of the self and the larger, intergenerational movement of the social body within and about this planter institution. Indeed, Faulkner's first constitution of the plantation house reveals that the cognitive processes of the self are nestled within the movement and behavior of the social body across time – and that this movement tends to cluster around certain attractors that exert a mysterious, even irresistible power as they transpose their ideological content into the perceiving self. As Faulkner continues to create these trajectories of recurrent movement and behavior in his Yoknapatawpha County, this cognitive paradigm along with its spatially oriented vertex of power serves as blueprint for the greater project of mapping and peopling his fictional county.

1.4   Tyranny of Aesthetic Objects

In Faulkner's first depiction of the plantation complex, we can identify three primary elements in the development of a cognitive cartography: first, the dynamic manner in which culture is coproduced by human and nonhuman agents; second, the way in which information continues to flow through the material culture we produce; and, third, the threat to human wellbeing if that information is coercive and tyrannical.[10] We have seen how Faulkner imagines the plantation system as a series of heterogenous elements that when constituted by the social body into a viable infrastructure allows information to move continuously through it. Faulkner also distinguishes additional coercive features that he identified in the culture of the New South. It matters what information circulates in a network; and if that network is weighted or hierarchical enough, information can gain emergent properties that it might not otherwise possess.

In the symbolic language of the novel, the Colonel realizes that his body will break down and corrupt the information encoded into it and, so, he transposes his image – his "print" or "semblance" – onto a site where this text is most likely to be preserved and thus replicated. He places his reflected image into a heaven above, a center of social relations or, in the spatial imagination of Faulkner, the apex of the plantation, namely, the highest or most privileged space that a network composed of nodes of relations can produce, a site or basin of attraction, to use network theory, in which this information pattern is most likely to be preserved and thereby replicated. The Colonel's "print" is not simply an artifact of the psyche; nor is it just one in a series of proliferating objects. It has become expressly ideological and comes to govern a heterogenous series of objects from the mirror of evening water to windows to the family bible and, in the final chapter of the novel, the print is manifest in a statue that gazes over the entire county.

The Colonel's statue is paradigmatic for the Yoknapatawpha novels to come. In terms of the novel itself, the statue completes the symbolic coda of the plantation manor that opened the narrative. In the final chapter, Faulkner emphasizes vertical mastery in the statue of Colonel Sartoris, the "pompous effigy gazing out across the valley" (117). As the father's ghost hovered "above and about his son" in the first scene of the novel, leaving his "print" in "enduring stone," so now a stone statue of the Colonel stands above the county as a whole. If it were not clear enough before, here the image that the Colonel transposed into the "Sartoris heaven" is still in the process of ruling over the future from its elevated position above Yoknapatawpha County:

> He stood on a stone pedestal, in his frock coat and bare headed, one leg slightly advanced and one hand resting lightly on the stone pylon beside him. His head was lifted a little in that gesture of haughty pride which repeated itself generation after generation with a fateful fidelity, his back to the world and his carven eyes gazing out across the valley where his railroad ran and the blue changeless hills beyond, and beyond that, the ramparts of infinity itself. The pedestal and effigy were mottled with seasons of rain and sun and with the drippings from the cedar branches, and the bold carving of the letters was bleared with mold, yet still decipherable. (FD 399)

Faulkner draws upon his own family history in this passage, for the stone statue of his great-grandfather, Colonel William C. Falkner, is nearly identical to the effigy of Colonel John Sartoris.[11] In both cases, the statue is perched high above the other gravestones in an assertive posture, one leg jutting out before the other, creating an illusion of life and movement. Faulkner emphasizes the vertical mastery of the mimetic statue over the landscape as it looks down upon the railroad network that the living man built in the postwar period. If, in the manor house, this "semblance" of life imposes itself upon the living, so in the cemetery, the stone effigy dominates through the "carven eyes gazing out across the valley," its vision duplicating itself in "generation after generation with fateful fidelity." Here, the family bible with its genealogy of dead planter names reappears as well, for Faulkner transposes the "mottled" names found on the biblical flyleaves onto the "mottled" inscriptions on the "pedestal" of the effigy, which suggest the putrefaction of a corpse.

As before, there is certainly a gothic element in the portrayal of the statue, but the planter network in question is not in a state of ruin. Far from it, Faulkner's depiction accurately implies that these private railroads laid the foundation for the making of the new plantation system, with postwar state governments incentivizing their construction.[12] R. Scott Huffard Jr. (2019) provides an incisive history of the New South's railroads "as a cohesive network" that "integrated the South through a capitalist means" (4). This history is worth reflecting on briefly since Faulkner's cartographies are responding in part to the introduction of a new system, "an interconnected network of rapid circulation that was something new and distinct from what came before" (4). Of course, rail technology arrived earlier in the South when, in the 1920s, South Carolina constructed one of the nation's first lines. The 1850s saw a "burst of construction," yet "vast pockets of the South lacked any rail connections, and the region lagged behind the mileage of the North" (2). This changed dramatically soon after Reconstruction when the railroad became a mighty symbol of technological progress for southerners. From 1880 to 1890, the South experienced a railroad revival with the "mileage of the southern railroads almost doubl[ing], as the network grew at a rate that outpaced the rest of the nation's lines" (2).

The new rail connections diversified the South economically, even while ushering in the establishment of modern corporations and massive conglomerates like the Southern Railway itself. Importantly, the "expanded network reoriented trade, dispersing business to country stores, channeling commerce away from ports to interior rail centers like Atlanta, and supplanting the primacy of rivers and steamboats" (3). Though cotton would remain a principal commodity, rail spurred the growth of the manufacturing sector which came to include textiles, steel and "extractive industries like coal and timber" (3). For Huffard, there is a distinct regional context within the broader U.S. history of industrial modernity, since rail travel initially brought about the mixing of races and classes and thus became a critical site of contestation where Jim Crow was codified through law by white southerners who moved to segregate rail cars in a "wave of new legislation in the 1880's and 90's" (3).

In the figure of the statue propped up above its railroad, Faulkner embeds a socioeconomic symbolism for planter power. In network terminology, the railroad provides the edges or connections that link the nodes of the system in question, allowing both ideology and resources to circulate both within and far beyond the bounds of Yoknapatawpha. As in the manor house, there is a self-reflexive quality to the spatial arrangement of the stone monument and the technological infrastructure that connects it to the world beyond. Indeed, the statue serves as an aesthetic placeholder for this sprawling financial, agricultural, and industrial matrix, and the railroad is implicitly an extension of the statue's "carven eyes" that seek expansion. Faulkner employs the imagery of war, moreover, for these eyes are engaged via the railroad in assaulting the "ramparts of infinity." This is no mere military offensive, but a campaign on the future that comes in the form of information and resource flow and possesses a sinister ideological content. As we have seen, this ideology has been erected upon murder and subjugation and now possesses a strange quasi-agency in its ability both to copy itself and to appropriate the interior domain of the human subject. The impulse to protect this interior domain from such an ideology cannot be minimized or disparaged, following poststructuralist critique, as merely falling prey to the illusion of enclosed essences; rather, for Faulkner, the preservation of the interior realm of the human subject becomes the only form of sanctuary, the only source of agency, in an age of scaling information systems.

CHAPTER 2

A Clock in Place of the Sun

During the late summer months of 1933, Faulkner composed a number of drafts of an introduction for a proposed new edition of *The Sound and the Fury*.[1] Random House never published the limited edition, and Faulkner himself, though he had, in his own words, "worked on it a good deal, like on a poem almost," would later, in 1946, dismiss the introduction as "smug false sentimental windy shit."[2] Among the many revealing elements of the discarded document, the introduction provides a distinctive description of art as a collective endeavor. Artistic enterprise, Faulkner argues, can be most readily perceived in the ways that human beings encode patterns of information into shared external structures: "the indigenous dream of any given collection of men having something in common, be it only geography and climate, which *shape their economic and spiritual aspirations into cities, into a pattern of houses or behavior*" (2; emphasis added).[3] Besides sharing an environment, a group of individuals are united by an "indigenous dream" – an original or native longing – to give shape to "patterns of houses or behavior." These two aspects – behavior and social space – are thereby inextricably linked in Faulkner's imagination and indicate that his classic modernist novel visualizes how such "economic and spiritual aspirations" express themselves in the life of the New South, whether in architecture or, on a larger scale, in the building of cities.

The focus of this chapter is on the growth of these large-scale information systems at the expense of the individuals who enact and maintain them. In *The Sound and the Fury*, Faulkner imagines this transformation socially, economically, and, perhaps most importantly, psychologically, since the growth of complicated bureaucracies entails a change in patterns of thinking, away from free association and holistic contemplation. We must attend particularly to Faulkner's own symbolic shorthand as he came to visualize how human hierarchies emerge out of simpler interaction networks. Where we saw the Colonel's statue occupying the central vertex of the cognitive cartographies of *Flags in the Dust*, in *The Sound and the*

43

Fury, Faulkner expands his repertoire of imagery to examine how the information that humans store in social space, at a certain level of complexity, acquires its own quasi-agency – a hyper-mimetic ability to replicate itself through surfaces and selves. Among the many objects and surfaces that exhibit this mimetic agency, two images – the clock and the statue – lie at the center of Faulkner's cartography of the postbellum plantation system. Tracing these images through *The Sound and the Fury* brings us to the heart of Faulkner's diagnosis of the modernization of the planter system, not simply as a scaling social order, but as a coercive flow of ideology in the era of Jim Crow ascendency that jeopardizes the human beings embedded in it.

In Sections 2.1, 2.2, and 2.3, I consider the price exacted upon Benjy and Quentin Compson, contextualizing my argument within the rich history of scholarship on the novel. Faulkner's portraits of Benjy and Quentin powerfully develop the dilemma that we explored in the first chapter. Benjy is subject to a proliferating series of surfaces that constrict and control him across time and, in Quentin's section, this struggle becomes a patently ideological one. For many readers, the heirloom watch that Quentin carries with him will be most recognizable as a talisman or token of a social order that jeopardizes his very being. The iconic image of clock time may appear to evoke a purely existential tension between the individual and technological modernity, but Faulkner, I show, portrays the theme of planter heritage in terms of male-line primogeniture, namely, the transmission of legacy and property from one generation to the next. In this context, Faulkner imagines this legacy as a social force that invades the psyche, vertiginously scaling through a series of mimetic surfaces and sustaining itself through the mind of the subject. Try as he might to gain self-authorship, Quentin utterly succumbs to a cognitive cartography of his plantation heritage that finds ultimate expression in a site of financial power: Grandfather Compson's desk, the node through which the information and resource flows of the family plantation were directed and a node explicitly connected to the statue of Colonel Sartoris.

In Section 2.4, I conclude with an analysis of Jason's violent surveillance culture as another modernizing feature of this plantation network. While some scholars have minimized Jason as a petty failure, a would-be bureaucrat and failed banker, I argue that Faulkner presents Jason as heir to the postbellum plantation system that Colonel Sartoris erected in Yoknapatawpha. As the Sartoris family navigated the transition to the new plantation system through banking and rail, Jason similarly shifts his focus to modern finance, away from the production of cotton to the role of bureaucracy in managing the flows of capital and resources through the county. Throughout this chapter, I thereby interpret Benjy's narrative as a preparation for Quentin's dilemma of authorship and for the iconic conclusion of the novel, which powerfully repurposes the cognitive cartographies of *Flags in the Dust* to depict how the principal vertex of social space in Yoknapatawpha County supervenes upon the selves who encircle it. At the center of relations, high above the individuals who recurrently move about it, the statue of the Confederate soldier enacts a process of self-replication. The mimetic semblance is not alive certainly, yet a commonality of plantation culture is enacted between this information object and those who are forced to endure its imprint, to become mimetic surfaces robbed of depth and immanent life.

2.1   A Self Composed of Surfaces

Faulkner's early novels explore the dangers that information can pose in highly centralized social networks. As we have seen, Faulkner repeatedly associates such information with textuality. Scholarship has certainly understood that self-reflexivity is a key element of Faulkner's modernist achievement and, for some, this came to entail a postmodern acceptance of language as the primary constituent and determinant of human experience.[4] Few scholars, however, have commented on Faulkner's attention to the dangers of textual self-reflexivity when it becomes the sole measure of the self and its environment. This is a strange omission, since *The Sound and the Fury* presents textuality not only as an exponent of centralized and tyrannical social systems but as a bearer of ideology that can erase other avenues for self-knowledge and community. In the character of Quentin Compson, we see the psychological profile of a young man who has given up his very personhood to textuality, equating mimetic surfaces with that strange quasi-agency that we observed in the preeminent information objects of *Flags in the Dust*. Jaron Lanier (2010), the computer scientist and philosopher who coined the term "virtual reality," is helpful here in articulating the conflation of information with our own being. In his claim that "information is alienated experience," Lanier pushes back against the popular notion of information as alive and independent of human cognition, a thesis which Lanier perceives as devaluing human beings. Instead, he emphasizes the relationship between an information object and the retriever of that information as a process of de-alienating experience (28–9).

In Faulkner's earlier Yoknapatawpha fiction, the process by which the stored energy of alienated experience is released is of paramount importance. When during the course of the later introduction Faulkner comes to describe his original vision of *The Sound and the Fury*, he emphasizes this process of de-alienating information. As with the vertices of cognitive and social space in *Flags in the Dust*, so in the long introduction Faulkner identifies the elevated positioning of Caddy Compson and imagines the perspective of those who look upward, both mediated by, and dependent upon her. Faulkner describes "the muddy bottom of a little girl climbing a blooming pear tree in April to look in the window at the funeral" (10) and Caddy's three brothers standing below, looking up at her and depending on her to relay information from the funeral inside.[5] Faulkner also recounts this vertical relationship at another site, at the creek bottom with Benjy looking up at a soaking Caddy. Here is another crucial moment in time, the loss of which forms the principal tragedy of Benjy's existence:

> I saw that peaceful glinting of that branch was to become the dark, harsh flowing of time sweeping her to where she could not return to comfort him, but that just separation, division, would not be enough, not far enough. It must sweep her into dishonesty and shame too. And that Benjy must never grow beyond this moment; that for him all knowing must begin and end with that fierce, panting, paused and stooped wet figure which smelled of trees. That he must never grow up to where the grief of bereavement could be lessened with understanding and hence the alleviation of rage in the case of Jason, and of oblivion as in the case of Quentin. (6)

Benjy may change across time, but he will never outlive this perceptual predicament – and the problem for Benjy is that this vertex, which once held a living being, is replaced with a series of flattened thresholds and surfaces that preserve the mnemonic trace, but without the vitality of the genuine interpersonal relationship. Indeed, Faulkner's evocative imagery substitutes the "fierce, panting, paused and stooped wet figure" with the "peaceful glinting" of the creek water which soon becomes the "dark, harsh flowing of time." Information, in other words, has been severed from flesh-and-blood contact to be mediated by reflective surfaces that become deeply antagonist to the original experience. Benjy, of course, experiences this predicament existentially, for he cannot comprehend the cultural order in which he is set, but Quentin comes to apprehend it as a plantation legacy bequeathed to him through mimetic or mechanical surfaces, through clocks, texts, statues, among many others.

We could relegate this paradigm to a singular flight of fancy on Faulkner's part if not for how meticulously the author stages it. Benjy's cognitive architecture is fundamentally akin to that of old Bayard in *Flags in the Dust*. He too is set amid a proliferating series of textual surfaces and loci that structure his being, even while being unable to process this information in any advantageous fashion. As in the earlier novel, these surfaces possess a determining power, serving both as threatening textual media that constrict the agent in question and as psychic thresholds through which information may pass.[6] The opening of Benjy's narrative initiates this sense of constriction with representations of architectural and geographical space. Benjy looks "through the fence, between the curling flower spaces" (SF 1) to the land his father sold for Quentin's tuition money, associating the land beyond with Caddy. There is still an opening in the fence that permits Benjy and Luster to move beyond the parameters of the Compson plantation. This crawl space serves as the first mnemonic portal in the novel, permitting a perceptual movement back and forth in time. Yet such mnemonic transitions are by no means seamless. As Luster scolds Benjy, "Cant you never crawl through here without snagging on that nail" (2). The perceptual surface is threatening; it both mediates that which is beyond and threatens to injure the perceiver, initiating a paradigmatic form of violence that Faulkner associates with surfaces throughout the novel.

André Bleikasten (2017a) astutely interprets Benjy's spatial predicament as one that circumscribes him in a "space of enclosure," serving as "a prefiguration of the state asylum at Jackson behind whose bars he will eventually be confined" (64). Like the fence with the crawlspace, the front gate of the Compson Place is another visual threshold, which both confines Benjy and promises him access to that "other world" (65), a mnemonically composed landscape intertwining Caddy and nature. According to Bleikasten, Benjy "resents being fenced in and constantly tries to break barriers. When he is in the house, he wants to go outside; when he is in the yard, he runs down to the gate" (65). Here, Faulkner succeeds in fusing together institutional confinement with narrative confinement, a metafictional claustrophobia that evokes a modern form of self-reflexivity, the crisis of becoming an aesthetic object embedded within textual space. Scholars, moreover, have increasingly come to interpret Benjy's narrative not as a realistic depiction of disability, as earlier criticism tended to do, but in the overarching context of modern literary form. James Berger (2014) puts it best when he writes that the "language of Benjy's section is not at all some supposed inner language of a cognitively impaired person. It is the language of literary modernism" (82–3). Here, we can see a self-reflexive ethos that connects the four narratives of the novel and implicitly questions the institutional–linguistic order in which the characters are set. Berger interprets the "totalizing and degenerate forces of modernity" in terms of a patriarchal language system and sees self-care and compassion as the necessary counters to these forces (84–5).

In privileging the surface over the observer, or the word over the agent, Faulkner, I contend, is not attacking a faulty metaphysics of presence, which poststructural critics and their heirs have upheld as a supposedly degenerate feature of Western thinking. Rather, Faulkner is thinking in terms of complex human hierarchies, whose artificial modes of memory storage strikingly transform the way in which information flows through the self and the social body. There are of course great advantages to these modes of storage that Faulkner himself acknowledged; as we saw in his introduction, they are the expression of a people's "economic and spiritual aspirations." The author, however, is invested here in articulating what happens when these systems of information are appropriated by an impersonal and corporatist form of plantation modernity that operates at the expense of the self. What is poignantly at stake for Faulkner, I submit, is the very integrity of personhood, the cognitive interiority of the individual and the immanent dimension that gives it value. When a complex human system fails to uphold this value, then that system tends toward totalitarianism, and Faulkner's guiding insight as a critic of modernity, and as anti-ideological thinker, is to anticipate the rise of such totalisms on the world stage through an artistic meditation upon his own heritage.

When Benjy observes that "I could still hear the clock between my voice" (SF 67), Faulkner points to the encroachment of mechanistic technology upon human interiority. In symbolic terms, the mechanistic object is no longer a prothesis for, or aid to, the human being; rather, it has come to occupy interior space – to express itself "between" our very self-expressions. Thus, Benjy's seeming detachment from his own activities can be interpreted as a consequence of this inner effacement. Benjy repeatedly observes that his own "voice was going loud every time" (67), yet this detachment – being forced to watch from outside – underscores a violation of selfhood that Faulkner expresses in Benjy and then develops assiduously throughout the novel. Quentin, as we will see, intensifies Benjy's perception of the clock being "between" his voice and imagines a clock at the center of all cosmic relationships, a principal vertex of cognitive and social space supervening upon him and proliferating everywhere so that there is nothing outside this predicament.

With William Sowder's superb observation that the visual field in Benjy's section is constituted in two-dimensions, instead of three, we already have a sense that Faulkner is problematizing the possibility of depth and thus the possibility of constituting the integrity of Benjy's cognitive interiority. This "field," Sowder (1988) writes, which "should have been constituted in depth . . . is given in one dimension, a figure on a flat ground" (68). This flatness is perhaps best symbolized by Benjy's inability to recognize his own shadow and his mistaken belief that it is a portal that will permit escape. Benjy repeatedly apprehends his shadow, comparing it in a number of instances to a doorway: "Luster turned on the light. The windows went black, and the dark tall place on the wall came and I went and touched it. It was like a door, only it wasn't a door" (SF 69). The "dark tall place on the wall" offers a portal of memory, similar to the opening in the fence at the beginning of the narrative, yet it is one that constrains him. This shadow on the wall – the flattened mimetic imprint of the self – acquires a particular prominence in the novel, since it also evokes a metafictional reading and, as a result, a crisis of the self in social space that is only strengthened in Quentin's subsequent narrative.

What Benjy cannot know, even in the midst of his emotional pro-testations, is that he too is a flattened surface upon which something is being inscribed. The conclusion of his narrative reasserts this imagery with Benjy innocently apprehending a shadow/doorway that evokes a shared, familial dilemma: "Father went to the door and looked at us again. Then the dark came back, and he stood black in the door, and then the door turned black again" (86). With the closing of the door, Benjy is paradox-ically united with his family in a final, shadowy enclosure, all the voices of the household rising in a host of discordant, vertiginous sensations: "Caddy held me and I could hear us all, and the darkness, and something I could smell" (86). While Benjy is remembering a lost moment, his own temporal dislocation is also intensified through a strange form of textual totalitarianism. The final lines of the narrative emphasize these characters' entrapment within the text, separated even from the world of nature – the smell of trees – that exists on the other side of the window, which in this case is synonymous with the textual surface: "And then I could see the windows, where the trees were buzzing" (86). In this moment, without fully knowing it, Benjy is experiencing his own relegation to a powerless aesthetic object, his being acted upon by a strange, indeterminate activity on the other side of an aesthetic barrier.

Faulkner's visualization of Caddy upon the pear tree with which we began this section helps to elucidate the conclusion of Benjy's narrative. As we saw, Faulkner writes of the imagery that initially inspired the novel, describing a vertically oriented cartography that determines the mediated individuals who cluster under it. At the conclusion of the first section, Faulkner re-employs the imagery of the pear tree and intensifies the visual dilemma of its branches asserting themselves from without, buzzing and scratching upon the windowpane. As Benjy and his brothers once looked up from below toward Caddy braced on the limbs of the pear tree, here, he is similarly placed in a mediated posture, as a passive recipient of information. He remains dependent upon the glassy surface, trapped within the visual field, a mimetic imprint hungering for release and for the authorial power that the branches of the tree represent. What is established in this spatial reversal of agency is the absolute authority of the mediating surface – the surface that acts as a medium for a still obscure, yet pervasive quasi-agency that exerts itself upon the individual. If we read this spatial rendering in self-reflexive terms and it is difficult not to in the context of the narrative as a whole, we may interpret Benjy as the inscription, trapped within the mimetic delineations of the text. Yet this predicament is not simply a metafiction of the absurd. In the three narratives that follow, Faulkner employs Benjy's dilemma to imagine the human being's place in a complex network of relationships that clusters concentrically in social space. As with the plantation manor of *Flags in the Dust*, these visualizations narrativize the manner in which an overarching social power administers and controls the cognitive interiority of individuals, becoming so powerful in its scope that in the case of Quentin he mentally recreates its places of power even when he is over a thousand miles away from home.

2.2   A Clock in Place of the Sun

The first two sections of *The Sound and the Fury* explore how information comes to structure our perceptual awareness and identity. Indeed, once we begin to think entirely in the mode of consciousness that these systems of modernity allow, we tacitly accept flattened textual space as the measure of our own inner life. In this early period of authorship, Faulkner repeatedly stages this spatial relationship with violent and destructive consequences for individuals. Benjy and Quentin Compson are unable to distinguish themselves from their own field of vision. Instead of acting upon objects, they become surfaces subject to a powerful and all-encompassing social force. It matters little if this seemingly omnipotent force is at root an imagined one. A collective fiction is intersubjective and, at a certain scale, it is no longer merely a fiction. In fact, to call it so and to imagine it as a collection of signifiers is to mistake its expansive power. Once it is physically embedded in the structures around us, in our architecture and aesthetic inventions, a fiction no longer exists simply in our minds.

Paramount in the second section of the novel is the vertiginousness manner in which cultural heritage and social space become entangled in the cognitive interiority of the self. Quentin's obsession with Caddy – especially her premarital sexual experiences that bring dishonor upon the family – is just one facet of an ideology of Southern aristocratic honor that Quentin has internalized. In the opening of the second section, Quentin is essentially struggling with the full weight of his own heritage as heir to the Compson plantation. In the first paragraph, Faulkner establishes this notion of genealogical and ideological transmission with the imagery of mechanical time, since, as eldest son, Quentin has already assumed one aspect of his inheritance, the heirloom pocket watch handed down from grandfather to father to son. This watch is no mere keepsake, evoking as it does the nihilistic musings of Quentin's father, Mr. Compson. However, the clock's symbolic meaning in the section cannot be explained by the weight of philosophical nihilism. To be sure, the clock seemingly possesses a marked metaphysical power, for it is an object that "can create in the mind unbroken the long diminishing parade of time," a parade that precedes the perceiving subject, extending all the way back through "long and lonely light-rays" to "Jesus walking," as Mr. Compson told his son upon bestowing the object (SF 87).

In the last chapter, we saw a similar overlapping of tradition and modernity in the imagery of the Colonel's statue. On one hand, the likeness appears as the original stone monument placed in the midst of the plantation network. On the other hand, the statue is not an artifact of the past, but the imposition of a new cultural order supported by, and linked to, other networks through the technology of the railroad. In similar fashion, *The Sound and the Fury* represents planter legacy – the bridging of the antebellum and postbellum periods – with what is perhaps the most iconic image of modernity itself: the clock. Mark Smith (1997) provides historical context for why the clock was so vital to the antebellum modernization of the South. By the 1830s, the case against the slave system was made primarily by northern free-wage-labor advocates who contended that it was "immoral, archaic, and out of step with nineteenth-century liberal capitalist forces" (4). The planters were thereby caught in a dilemma on how to "modernize slavery so that it still satisfied the old capitalist-planter concerns with profit maximization, the preservation of strict social hierarchy, and their claim to modernity without inviting the dangerous democratic tendencies associated with modernization into their society" (5). One of the solutions was to embrace clock time, since "the obedience and regularity it inspired among workers and their managers were, after all, among the litmus tests of modernity in all industrialized, free-wage-labor, capitalist societies" (5). By adopting clock time, planters bolstered their claim to modernity without necessitating that they abandon chattel slavery itself.

In the novel, the timepiece sets the stage for the overarching claim of Southern heritage on the young planter heir, made all the more powerful since it is articulated in the very technological language of modernity itself. Faulkner powerfully reinforces this theme of ideological transmission in the overarching spatial dynamics of the scene. Not only do the light-rays of the watch extend across time to spiritual origins so as to create an illusion of planter continuity; they also pierce through the curtains into the interior dimensions of Quentin's room, turning the entire space into a sun clock: "When the shadow of the sash appeared on the curtains it was between seven and eight oclock and then I was in time again, hearing the watch" (SF 87). The heirloom watch is no mere object, therefore, for Quentin already resides within its spatial dimensions. He can read the time because of where the shadows from the curtain fall within the room, even while he listens intently to the heirloom watch ticking against the collar box. Quentin thereby confronts the dilemma that tormented Benjy, except here its spatial topography assumes clearer delineations as an ideological and mechanistic assault upon the wellsprings of the self. As Faulkner concluded Benjy's narrative with the branches of the pear tree scratching from without upon the glassy medium of the window, he begins Quentin's with a similar spatial arrangement – with the sun outside refracted upon the window and projecting shadows into the interior reaches of the room.

Both brothers struggle, therefore, with a pronounced epistemological claustrophobia. Whereas Benjy finds himself constrained within a series of mimetic surfaces, Quentin finds himself subject to an invasive force that is at once embodied in the figure of the timepiece and linked, as we will see, to the bureaucratic surfaces and monumental architecture of his planter heritage. On one level of interpretation, this spatial relationship will involve Quentin's fatal desire to regain authorship of his own being, an attempt to secure the vertex of his own cognitive architecture, which is here located not within the self, but on the other side of the mediating threshold.[7] Thus, from the first, Quentin is compelled by an external social force that imposes itself upon him. To be "in time again" (87) is not just to listen to the watch; it is to accept the transmission of ideology and the identity that accompanies it, for in listening, the young man is forced to accept a hereditary claim on his personhood. In the process, he must give up other states of consciousness that conflict with these demands, whether they be sleep, dream, or the interpersonal bond he feels toward his disgraced sister, Caddy.

There is an idiosyncratic logic at work in these opening pages, moreover, that implicitly juxtaposes two paradigms of authority. According to the dictates of the clock, to be in time means to be awake, to be subject to mechanical time, and to accept a planter genealogy that stretches back seemingly unbroken to Jesus Christ. But this clock paradigm threatens the deeper, interpersonal sources of the self, since this genealogy does not include Caddy. We are told twice, after all, that Jesus himself "had no sister" (87). Yet, as we saw last section, Caddy possesses a preeminence in the minds of her brothers. She serves as an alternative paradigm of authority, associated with verticality and depth and expressed in the imagery of nature, whether the blooming pear tree in April or the creek bottom where they played together as children. Such a sisterly power is now absent, effaced by that other antagonist paradigm that Quentin associates with the clock and soon begins to scale through a variety of flattened surfaces. Thus, Faulkner visualizes Quentin's Cambridge dorm room as a clock, with the window being the glassy medium through which the real and mimetic interact, a medium that is substituted by a mirror in which the memory of Caddy cannot be fully established:

> *In the mirror she was running before I knew what it was. That quick her train caught up over her arm she ran out of the mirror like a cloud, her veil swirling in long glints her heels brittle and fast clutching her dress onto her shoulder with the other hand, running out of the mirror the smells roses roses the voice that breathed o'er Eden.* (93)

Here, Quentin remembers Caddy's wedding, but there is an implicit dilemma that is compounded by the mimetic power of the mirror. As imitation and copy, Caddy's reflection only retains the impression of a spiritual authority. As a result, the living principle can no longer fully constitute itself; it is thereby "running out of the mirror," fleeting and insubstantial "like a cloud" and now hidden behind a "veil." Faulkner employs, moreover, the metaphysics of an Episcopal hymn (*"the voice that breathed o'er Eden"*) to qualify the power that Caddy as memory has come to assume. To be sure, the fleeing form of his sister channels the power of immanent nature itself (*"roses roses"*), which Faulkner imagines vertically as God's creative self-expression as it infuses the cosmos beneath it with vital life. The *"voice that breathed o'er Eden"* explicitly designates authorship as the touchstone for all these perceptual states.

The problem that emerges is that this alternative interpersonal site which registers such spiritual, natural power cannot be sustained. Caddy's vital, ensouling voice is lost, the mirror incapable of holding her or her smell for long. More tragically still, as the first in a series of information objects, the watch has usurped the power of the voice and continues to assert itself through acts of violent authorship. The initial perceptual context of the section therefore serves as a persistent spatial dilemma. Quentin, the perceiving subject, looks outward upon the objects before him, but instead of achieving the power implicit in vision, he is actually being structured by a paradigm of planter power that he perceives as profoundly antagonistic to his wellbeing. Quentin only half-comprehends his predicament, moreover, not properly understanding that it is he who projects the ideology of the plantation culture onto the spatial relationships around him, at once performing this ideology and, in the process, internalizing its preeminence and power. He looks out of his Harvard dorm room window, but he is not the agent of his own phenom-enological ground. Instead, the curtains are blown inward upon him: "I stood at the window the curtains moved slow out of the darkness touching my face like someone breathing asleep, breathing slow into the darkness again, leaving the touch" (201–2). Whereas the *"voice that breathed o'er Eden"* has fled the mnemonic mirror, now another breath takes precedence and the glassy medium it governs is a threshold that mediates Quentin's own person. Here, Faulkner parodies God's creation of Adam, the living breath not arising from within, but emanating from without to fall upon Quentin's face: "Then the curtains breathing out of the dark upon my face, leaving the breathing upon my face" (203). The subject does not look actively through the window, but is rather invaded by a powerful, godlike force that authors from without and above, touching Quentin's face with an infusion of breath.

No matter where Quentin goes, the overarching spatial dimensions of the heirloom watch take precedence. As the young man walks through Harvard campus, for instance, the setting gives way to the sundial-like placement of Quentin on the ground, and Faulkner continues to inter-weave the clock imagery with an emphatic imagery of authorship: "The chimes began again, the half hour. I stood in the belly of my shadow and listened to the strokes spaced and tranquil along the sunlight, among the thin, still leaves" (116). The chimes of a clock figure "the strokes" of a pen whose inscriptions are placed on "thin, still leaves." Quentin is prospec-tively an inscribed shadow on a textual surface. Standing in "the belly of [his] shadow," he hears the "strokes" of the clock, an imagery that at once suggests an absurdist, metafictional dilemma even while suspending the subject in the dislocating position of never being absolutely present anywhere or in any time. The stroke of pen and clock writes him – just as the breath that blows inward through the window to brush against his face with shadow infuses him with an identity that the young man intuitively attempts to resist.

Quentin's narrative thereby opens in the midst of a mimetic crisis that is quickly transposed from the window onto a host of variable surfaces. Quentin finds himself within the dimensions of a clock, his being composed of a cluster of signs and entangled images, at once the mechanical ticking of time and the pen that is violently authoring his shadowy fate. These scenes invariably involve the imposition of an external authorship onto the creative self – with the imagery of an authorial breath upon Quentin's face part of a pattern to which Faulkner repeatedly returns in the latter stages of the narrative: "I stood at the window the curtains moved slow of the darkness touching my face like someone breathing asleep, breathing slow into the darkness again, leaving the touch" (202); "the curtain breathing out of the dark upon my face, leaving the breathing upon my face" (204). But what is this agency that shapes Quentin from without? Faulkner imagines its power in a variety of ways, for this breath moves through the threshold of the self with the ability *to touch* and *to shape* the young man's cognitive interiority: "*hands can see touching in the mind shaping unseen door Door nothing hands can see*" (203).

Importantly, Quentin does not simply concede to this invasion of his selfhood. Rather, he seeks to resist it, though acting only within the paradigm and unable to conceive of himself outside of it. Indeed, Quentin pursues mastery over objects through acts of violence, with the pocket watch serving as the first site of his failure to achieve such authority:

> I went to the dresser and took up the watch with the face still down. I tapped the crystal on the corner of the dresser and caught the fragments of glass in my hand and put them into the ashtray and twisted the hands off and put them in the tray. The watch ticked on. I turned the face up, the blank dial with little wheels clicking and clicking behind it, not knowing any better. . . . There was a red smear on the dial. (92)

Quentin effaces the mechanical heirloom, pulling the hands off of it and smearing blood upon the clockface. His failure to master the watch and, in the process, to reject the planter legacy being imposed upon him is definitive. Even without hands, the clock continues to click – and Quentin realizes that he cannot administer control over the object in question. Faulkner reinforces this dilemma with an emphatic imagery of replication. The pocket watch is already everywhere, having even usurped the preeminence of the sun itself: "There was a clock, high up in the sun" (95).

Instead of establishing control over the temporal surface, Quentin finds himself situated below an authorial power that has become an all-encompassing vertex of cognitive and social space. This is, of course, a paradigm that we have examined in Chapter 1 and one that Faulkner recreates with ever-greater ease and assurance. As the immanent architecture of the self is displaced, a coercive cartography of consciousness is erected at its expense. For the two brothers, Caddy represents that alternative paradigm of spiritual and natural power, but one that has been effaced and lost due to the conventions that uphold the social mores of the planter aristocracy. For the brothers, this interpersonal loss is definitive. Without this lost paradigm, Quentin has no other means to resist the planter pocket watch, becoming simply another surface clustering about an authorial vertex that demonstrates its power by replicating itself every-where and in everyone. Indeed, once the sun-clock gains preeminence, these authorial surfaces multiply and proliferate. Quentin enters a jewelry shop to fix his watch, confronting a room of clocks of which the proprietor serves as proxy: "There was a glass in his eye – a metal tube screwed into his face" (96). The object over which Quentin sought control has been replicated and, in multiplying everywhere, it assumes a power that is both above and within, at once seated in the sun and twisted into the human face.

In this context, Quentin's earlier perception of a "sparrow slant[ing] across the sunlight, onto the window ledge" (90) serves to foreshadow this pattern of invasion and the appropriation of the natural, creative depths of the self. Like the face of the jeweler, the bird enacts a process of informa-tion flow wherein an artificial power asserts its dominion through a network of relationships. Traditionally associated with the soul or indwell-ing vital spirit, the bird has lost these spiritual or natural associations: "His eye round and bright. First, he'd watch me with one eye, then flick! And it would be the other one, his throat pumping faster than any pulse. The hour began to strike" (90). The bird's eye is round like a clockface – and even its breath is predicated upon a machinelike correspondence to the striking of a clock. Here we can also anticipate an interpretation that will have more explanatory power in the novels to come. In Faulkner, birds act as purveyors of information within a system, agents of mimicry or mimesis, spreading and replicating forms of behavior throughout social space, moving from surface to surface, agent to agent until the information they carry comes to define the greater movement of the social body.

2.3 "A Still Higher Place"

Although this pattern of self-mirroring is more ambiguous here, we can nonetheless observe that Quentin is in the midst of a self-replicating mimetic crisis that jeopardizes the very integrity of his cognitive interiority. Quentin repeatedly strives to re-appropriate the vertex, violently attempting to assume that privileged place around which everything clusters across time. In one key scene, he rehearses his own suicide by drowning. Quentin leans over a bridge and looks down upon the reflective surface of the water below, imagining that he has "tricked" his shadow by appropriating the "blotting" power of authorship and "holding [his shadow] until it was drowned":

> The shadow of the bridge, the tiers of railing, my shadow leaning flat upon the water, so easily had I tricked it that it would not quit me. At least fifty feet it was, and if I only had something to blot it into the water, holding it until it was drowned, the shadow of the package like two shoes wrapped up lying on the water. Niggers say a drowned man's shadow was watching for him in the water all the time. It twinkled and glinted, like breathing, the float slow like breathing too, and debris half submerged, heading out to the sea and the caverns and the grottoes of the sea. (103)

Kristin Fujie (2019) insightfully argues that "this passage uses [Quentin's] pause on the bridge to showcase the internal architecture of his mind. Whereas Benjy's mind moves horizontally between the present and past (as though wriggling through a fence), Quentin's moves vertically, sinking over the course of this passage downward into memory and the levels of his psyche that lie far below immediate life" (424). The spatial relationship of a subject looking downward upon a textual object in order to control it repeats Quentin's effacement of the pocket watch, except Faulkner makes it clearer now that Quentin's violence is focused upon himself. The pocket watch may reflect the perceiver upon its glassy surface, but here the spatial relationship is explicitly textual, since Quentin seeks to "blot" his shadow in the water.

By the latter stages of the narrative, Quentin's failure to identify with the authorial figure above has become definitive. In one pivotal passage, Quentin remembers his childhood picture book and imagines his family trapped in the pages with "a single weak ray of light" illuminating their faces. It is Caddy who expresses violent outrage at the idea of their confinement within the book. As we have observed, she represents an alternative vertical paradigm to which Quentin has lost access. For his part, the prospect of transcending the page and assuming the preeminence of light seems impossible. Instead, he visualizes the two-dimensional surface of the page as a multi-leveled "dungeon" with him in the depths "without even a ray of light":

> When I was little there was a picture in one of our books, a dark place into which a single weak ray of light came slanting upon two faces lifted out of the shadow. *You know what I'd do if I were King?* she never was a queen or a fairy she was always a king or a giant or a general *I'd break that place open and drag them out and I'd whip them good* It was torn out, jagged out. I was glad. I'd have to turn back to it until the dungeon was Mother herself she and Father upward into weak light holding hands and us lost somewhere below even them without even a ray of light. (SF 202)

James G. Watson (2000) visualizes the book in question as "a Compson family photograph album" that at once offers an "inner reality" and an "image of abandonment" (53–4). We may add that Faulkner stages these inner architectonics upon a frustrated metaphysics of light, for this passage visualizes a "ray of light" emanating downward and illuminating mimetic beings trapped in darkness below. Caddy may escape into the light, yet Quentin has already associated the light-rays as proxies of the heirloom clock that entraps everything within it. Mother and Father walk "upward into weak light holding hands" but, by the end of the sentence, they too are similarly dispossessed "without even a ray of light."

Toward the close of Quentin's narrative, Faulkner explicitly grafts the principal cognitive cartography of *Flags in the Dust* onto *The Sound and the Fury*. In detail, we examined John Sartoris' creation of a mimetic semblance and visualized the spatial dynamics of how the plantation patriarch places his "print" high up in the principal vertices of cognitive and social space. Here again, Faulkner returns to this carefully constructed spatial paradigm to identify the ideology that is violently imposing itself on Quentin:

> we used to think of Grandfather's desk not to touch it not even to talk loud in the room where it was I always thought of them as being together somewhere all the time waiting for old Colonel Sartoris to come down and sit with them waiting on a high place beyond cedar trees Colonel Sartoris was on a still higher place looking out across at something and they were waiting for him to get done looking at it and come down Grandfather wore his uniform and we could hear the murmur of their voices from beyond the cedars. (SF 206)

Faulkner erects the cognitive cartography of the Sartoris plantation house upon the surface of Grandfather's desk. In the earlier novel, the vertical positioning of the mimetic semblance above the living entailed the present flows of information and capital through the plantation economy. As we saw, *Flags in the Dust* begins with Bayard sitting at his office desk in the bank, and the pattern culminates for this character in the attic of his manor as he looks down upon a genealogy of planter names inscribed upon the flyleaves of the family bible. A similar pattern appears in the passage above, for the desk is an administerial site upon which the business of the Compson plantation was directed. In both texts, Faulkner emphasizes the relationship between the two-dimensional surface and the three-dimensional cognitive structure that rises out of it. To be sure, the pattern is stored on textual surfaces and in the mind – and in the dynamic interaction between text and perceiver, an institutional ideology is made manifest. The Compson children dare not touch this administerial site, moreover; it possesses such institutional power that they need only "think" of Grandfather's desk and the whole cognitive pattern begins to assert itself from above, the vertex of the plantation order – that monumental stone semblance of the Colonel – coming down to abide with the members of the family.

Faulkner is also symbolically presetting the conclusion of the novel which entails a description of movement across time around the statue of the Confederate soldier in Jefferson Square. In the passage above, the vertex of this cognitive cartography is occupied not with a living man, but with a statue, an effigy that, in *Flags in the Dust*, stands high above the county in an aggressive posture of warlike assimilation with its rail serving as its ideological conduit to the world. In that previous novel, the Colonel shuffles off the finitude of the flesh to place his "semblance" or "print" in the vertex above. Here, the same pattern is at play with a semblance of life achieving a sinister type of transcendence. Faulkner uses precise language to mirror the earlier plantation prototype where an idea achieves an "apotheosis" and thus becomes "symmetrical above the flesh": "you are still blind to what is in yourself to that part of general truth the sequence of natural events and their causes which shadows every mans brow even benjys you are not thinking of finitude you are contemplating an apotheosis in which a temporary state of mind will become symmetrical above the flesh and aware both of itself and of the flesh it will not quite discard" (208). Quentin's confusion here repeats the insistence of the previous novel. The "temporary state of mind" that has achieved this seemingly transcendent power above the flesh is simultaneously bound to the flesh, for it must replicate itself or be replicated in others to survive.

Quentin is undeniably baffled by the cognitive cartography that arises about and within him, so mystified that he attributes agency to the mimetic semblance that stands in the vertex of cognitive space; he projects godlike powers upon it and imagines its dominance above and within him. This confusion is much more understandable to us who enjoy a retrospective gaze upon the history of the twentieth century with the rise of totalist ideologies on the world stage. Here, Faulkner creates a symbolic language to explain what it means to internalize an ideology at the expense of one's own individual well-being. We may assume the poststructural perspective of Weinstein who asks us not simply to question, but to reject the notion that "ideological inflections ... distort some deeper reality." From Weinstein's perspective, there is no "non-ideological core" to distort. Rather, the self is simply a process of interpellation, an internalization of our culture's ideologies. But Faulkner's imagistic insistence remains whether we choose to characterize it as modernist supposition or a refraction of an earlier desire for spiritual autonomy – for the suffering of Benjy and Quentin entails having to endure an ideological superscription that permeates the self so deeply and thoroughly that only a surface remains. Their tragedy is precisely this: the self is robbed of its natural depth, left as Benjy is, hopelessly mediated by his visual field, or in Quentin's final gambit, drowning himself in his own mimetic reflection.

2.4   Invasive Violence and the World Within

Scholars have long interpreted the Compsons as a plantation family doomed to postwar decay, the family that helped to found Jefferson now a gradually diminishing skeleton of its former glory. This traditional reading of Faulkner's great Southern family in decline, though perhaps attractive, is not entirely accurate. While Faulkner imagined its individual members beset with difficulty, he did not see the family simply as a deadend. Faulkner's 1945 *Appendix* paints a very different picture of Jason as a capable man who "competed and held his own with the Snopeses who took over" Jefferson (SF 379). Thus, Jason overcomes his financial difficulties by educating himself in accounting and is subsequently able to rise in the plantation economy from mere "clerk" to "own[ing] his own business as a buyer of and dealer in cotton" (379). The Compson man becomes a wielder of commissary ledgers, minutely engaged in the lien-credit system that was so central to the sharecropping of the New South. In this earlier novel, Jason is not yet this person, aspiring for power through the machinations of unscrupulous finance. I submit, moreover, that whereas Benjy and Quentin are jeopardized by the ideology of the plantation system, Jason is its explicit proxy, representing the perils of financial modernization in the New South.[8] The last two narratives of the novel develop therefore the cognitive cartography of plantation culture from a very different perspective, describing not the failure to constitute personhood in the face of overarching ideology, but the eager willingness to enforce a system of social control. In this final section (2.4), I argue that Jason Compson serves as proxy for the invasive force we have seen thus far.

The third and fourth sections of *The Sound and the Fury* find Jason in the midst of reinventing himself, abandoning the farming of cotton to take up finance. The fact that the word "bank" appears in his section twenty-one of the twenty-four total occurrences in the novel indicates Jason's obsession not simply with money, but with the larger financial system that links Yoknapatawpha to the banking hub of New York. Indeed, in explicitly anti-Semitic overtones, Jason articulates a far broader economic order at play, the postbellum cotton farmer a dupe of the speculators who reap the bulk of the profits which flow, as he repeatedly laments, to a "bunch of dam eastern jews" (224). For his part, Jason conceives of himself heroically, both as a guardian of his mother and of the Compson estate itself, his mission being to "hold on to what little we have left" (242). At this point in his career, he has not yet risen in the new economy, as his long-hoped for job in Herbert Head's bank never materialized. Angry and embittered, the Compson man carries on nonetheless, compensating for his perceived losses by embezzling the money that his sister Caddy sends to her daughter. Jason steadfastly guards this money in a lockbox in his bedroom, faithful counting it once a day as a clerk would in a bank. This overzealousness extends to the rest of the household as well. As we will see, it is his very eagerness to encroach upon, and monitor those around him, that allows him to administer control over his environment.

Jason certainly possesses the skills to navigate the social order of the New South advantageously. Unscrupulous and tyrannical as he is, his narrative also displays his intellectual sensitivity to the ways in which information and resource flow occur. His overweening surveillance of his family's movement allows him to deduce their behavior and manipulate it to his advantage. As such, Jason's mode of agency operates with much greater complexity than his narrative stream of consciousness would suggest. Yet his self-interested pursuit of advantage also betrays a complete blindness to his own unthinking obedience to the demarcations of power in his social world, which Faulkner constructs both in obvious and more subtle ways. Jason's belief in the patriarchal and racist maxims of his culture is clear from the start. His internal monologue begins by visualizing his niece's subjugation in social space, a fantasy that involves sending her to the kitchen below to work among the black servants: "I says she ought to be down there in that kitchen right now, instead of up there in her room, gobbing paint on her face and waiting for six niggers that cant even stand up out of a chair" (SF 211). Here, Jason's desire to administer power is initially imagined in terms of vertical elevation and soon expresses itself violently as domination and invasion.

In his first interaction with his niece Quentin, Jason physically over-powers her, breaking the cup she holds and unsettling her robes so that her flesh beneath is exposed for all to see: "I grabbed her by the arm. She dropped the cup. It broke on the floor and she jerked back, looking at me, but I held her arm ... Her kimono came unfastened, flapping about her, dam near naked" (215). The only other instance of the kimono appears in Quentin's earlier narrative where it is associated with Caddy's head or voice: "*her head kimono-winged the voice that breathed o'er eden*" (122). In this previous depiction, the kimono-winged head and voice possess an elevated position breathing over and incarnating the natural world below. As we observed, the "*voice that breathed o'er eden*" offers another paradigm of power associated with spirit and nature that was under assault in the first half of the novel. This is an important intra-textual context for Jason's violence, since his actions symbolically denote a shattering and simulta-neous appropriation of the sacrosanct dimensions of his niece's private world which are explicitly related with Caddy and, by extension, to Benjy and their brother Quentin. In the above passage, Jason grabs his niece and the cup she holds shatters upon the ground, an imagistic prelude for him exposing her, forcing her across the threshold of the dining room and pushing her against the wall. While we may read this in a perfectly realistic manner, Faulkner has already preset the spatial architectonics and symbolic logic of this narrative world – and thus we may also interpret Jason's actions as an explicit repetition of the violence of the previous narratives in which an interior space is overwhelmed and transformed into the two-dimensional flatness of a mediating surface.

In relation to Benjy and Quentin who are overrun by a force from without, Jason is a proxy for this controlling, invasive force, subjecting his niece to a violence that exposes her interiority and seeks to strip her of depth. As he does with other characters, Faulkner employs the mimetic paradigm of birds to reinforce the spatial paradigm of Jason's violence. Even Jason's idle thoughts about how he would deal with the pigeons, swallows, and sparrows in the town square of Jefferson underscore this pattern of invasion in terms of assimilating and effacing the depths within living things. Jason inwardly laments how his taxes are spent on cleaning the courthouse clock when the most logical solution is not seasonal upkeep, but poisoning the birds so as to rid the town and its monuments of such a "nuisance" for good: "If they'd just put a little poison out there in the square, they'd get rid of them in a day" (292). Jason's attention to the movement of birds and his fantasy of killing them are indicative of the greater pattern of his behavior and thinking. For the aspiring petty tyrant, the birds represent an uncontrollable pattern of movement, "flying back and forth" (290) and "swarm[ing] in the trees . . . [to] swirl around in sight above the roof, and then go away" (291). Jason's fantasy of exterminating birds in the town square hinges once again upon interior space, in this case the physical ingestion of poison, so as to maximize control over the town's principal social matrix.

This paradigm of invasive control also associates Jason with the mechanical and denaturalized social order that threatened his brother. In Quentin's narrative, the clock serves as a symbol of the triumph of surface over the possibility of depth with the clock appropriating sites traditionally associated with transcendence and immanence. As we saw, the mimetic statue and the clock are the elevated icons of this social order, symbolically reigning supreme either up high above the cedars or in place of the sun – and Faulkner uses the movements of a bird as a mirroring device for this pattern, since the bird's interiority is subsumed, its very heart pumping according to the mimetic and mechanistic dictates of the sun-clock. Whereas Quentin apprehends this as a violation of the sacrosanct depths of his being, Jason relishes his position in this paradigm, imagining the court-house clock sterilized of the unsettled surging of natural life.

Jason's surveillance of his niece replays this paradigm of the invasion of inner space. The uncle perpetually seeks to control the thresholds of movement in the Compson Place and thus the interior lives within these thresholds, hyperaware as he is of the comings and goings of the household and cognizant especially of the only room barred to him. Jason himself ritualistically employs the implement of lock and key about the house, carefully guarding his own room and the money he has incrementally stolen from his niece, which he keeps in a lockbox in his closet. Since he guards his dominion so carefully, he monitors anyone who would protect their own privacy, registering this action as a violation of his sovereignty. Toward the close of his narrative, Jason repeatedly thinks about Quentin's locked door. As he reads his paper, he listens intently to the communication of his mother and niece in the rooms above: "I heard her climbing the stairs. . . . I heard [Quentin] at Mother's door, then she went back to Quentin, like the door was locked, then she went back to Mother's room and then Mother went and talked to Quentin. Then they came down stairs. I read the paper" (302). Quentin constantly locks the door after each and every exchange, asserting a means of protecting her own interior space against the prying surveillance of her uncle. When she joins the family for dinner soon afterward, Jason continues to perceive his niece as a surface concealed from him: "Quentin was sitting with her head bent. She had painted her face again. Her nose looked like a porcelain insulator" (302). Jason interprets Quentin's use of makeup as a veillike protection; to unpack the analogy more directly, we can observe that her makeup is visualized as a means of insulating her from the environment around her which is subject to Jason's control. Unlike a conductor that allows electric current to flow freely, an insulator restricts the force of this flow through it. It is no wonder in Quentin's case, for Jason is as persistent in his game of cat and mouse as ever, continuing his invasive surveillance that assumes, as it did at the opening of the section, shades of sexual violation. After dinner, he listens intently as she locks her door above – "Then I heard the key in the lock, and Mother went back to her room" (310) – and later spies on her through her "empty keyhole."

In the fourth section, this paradigm of invasive violence reemerges with the image of the clock. As the clock took the place of the sun in Quentin's section, in the final section a clock has symbolically secured the site of immanence within the Compson Place. Faulkner anthropomorphizes the manor house and visualizes the ticking of the clock as "the dry pulse" within, and self-expression of, the entire architectural structure:

> "You know whut I bet?" Luster said. "I bet he beat her. I bet he knock her in de head en now he gone fer de doctor. Dat's whut I bet." The clock tick-tocked, solemn and profound. It might have been the dry pulse of the decaying house itself, after a while it whirred and cleared its throat and struck six times. Ben looked up at it, then he looked at the bulletlike silhouette of Luster's head in the window and he begun to bob his head again, drooling. (335–6)

As he did with the Sartoris plantation house, Faulkner visualizes the Compson manor as a cognitive cartography with the mechanistic clock securing preeminence in the vertex of the structure and about which various selves cluster across time. Faulkner's anthropomorphization intimates that Jason's violence – "I bet he beat her. I bet he knock her in de head" – has become part of the self-expression of the manor house itself. As Luster articulates Jason's violence, Benjy looks up at the clock and then visually reenacts the violence, perceiving a flattening of visual space upon the surface of the window: "the bulletlike silhouette of Luster's head in the window." The description is consistent with the functioning of Faulkner's cartographies. Luster and Benjy may not willingly serve the dictates of Jason's mechanistic social control, but they are part of its self-expression, its ability to preserve and replicate itself as culture. Jason may be its principal proxy in this novel, but he does not need to be present for this to occur. This is precisely why, when Luster speculates about Jason's violence, Benjy visually projects its consequences before him and, for him as with his dead brother before him, its self-expression is a violation of depth and three-dimensionality. Like Quentin who stood at his dorm room window with the shadows blowing upon his face, Luster now appears as a mimetic being superimposed upon a similarly styled textual surface, his very head described as "bulletlike," a symbolic echo of Jason's violence.

Here again, Faulkner imagines the cognitive cartography of the plantation system in shorthand, as one in which a vertex supervenes upon its constituent parts, transforming its agents into mimetic surfaces. If we recall in *Flags in the Dust*, Faulkner immediately superimposed this spatial paradigm upon the white simplicity of the Sartoris manor with bloodred roses choking wisteria into stamped silver dollars, the flattened surface of which was reduplicated all the way up to the attic above. As the roses and the various surfaces inside that manor house were proxies for a pervasive, unseen quasi-agency, so too Jason serves the dictates of a paradigm of social control that secures a mystifying agency in the minds of the selves who participate in it. To be sure, Faulkner visualizes how this order occupies the vertex of cognitive and social space – in minds, statues, clocks, and a host of other mimetic surfaces – seeking to control, coerce, and replicate its information, stored as it can be outside the body, but dependent upon living and breathing agents to engender it anew. What makes Faulkner's vision of this pattern so germane to us who live in complex systems through which hyper-mimetic information flow occurs is that the pattern is not dependent upon any one person or object; rather, everyone participates at different levels of agency and self-awareness.

This vision of networked space and information flow culminates in the novel's much discussed finale in which Jason, Luster, and Benjy travel around the statue at the center of Jefferson and Yoknapatawpha. The Compson Place may be diminished as plantation hub, but it too is connected to a greater socioeconomic system whose vertices are ever-proliferating, storing culture, and disseminating it in the movement, behavior and thinking of its many proxies. As Benjy apprehended the mimetic branches scratching upon the windowpane and Quentin's narrative spatially extended this pattern of superscription with the imagery of a sun-clock above the city and the statue of Colonel Sartoris high above Grandfather's desk, the finale of *The Sound and the Fury* brings this paradigm to a decisive climax by mapping it upon the literal center of town and county. In this context, Quentin's heirloom watch can be understood to reproduce the courthouse and its encoding of power, for here we are in the very center of Faulkner's County. In this principal vertex of social space, moreover, the clock and the statue are united in a compound image. In 1964, Maurice Bassan was the first scholar to propose that "Faulkner's picture of the courthouse 'square' is really circular, and reproduces visually and symbolically Quentin's watch-without-hands" (48). From this vantage point, we can begin to unpack the complex imagery of the final scene by noting that "the courthouse circle is the circle of time," evoking a temporal dilemma that has spurred a variety of interpretations, to which we briefly turn.

Bassan's reading provides a necessary starting point interpreting the recurrent movements around the statue as a blurring of symbolism and realism. Believing himself unobserved, Luster takes Benjy to the left of the statue of the Confederate soldier, moving clockwise and symbolically proceeding with the stream of time into the future. Here, we can add that Luster's decision is at once an act of novelty and a violation of the route that Benjy is accustomed to take, the counterclockwise path indicating for some critics the power of the past over the present. Later critics similarly interpret the final scene as a touchstone for the thematic concerns of the entire novel. Bleikasten (2017a), for instance, argues that "the scene is a powerful and poignant echo of the violence and disorder we have been witnessing all along, a condensed representation of all that has been presented before" (131). He states moreover that there is connection between the "arbitrary stop to the action" and the "utter meaninglessness" that pervades the Compson world. For Bleikasten, the "ironic effect of contrast" that results from juxtaposing "the final glimpse of peace" with "Jason's outburst of violence" (131) is central to the uneasiness of Faulkner's vision. Other critics share Bleikasten's sense that the novel concludes suddenly by emphasizing juxtaposition and striking contrast.

In Nathaniel Miller's words, it is the encounter between life and death that structures "the anti-climatic non-resolution of the novel" (2005: 39).

Other critics have argued that the conclusion of the novel involves the way in which the tragic history of the Old South continues to haunt the present. Daniel Singal (1997) sees this in the tense relationship between the statue of the soldier and Benjy: "By dint of ritual, the carriage always goes around the square counterclockwise; that way, keeping his head locked to the right, Benjy can entirely avoid seeing the soldier." From this point of view, the ritualistic pattern around the statue prevents Benjy from seeing the object, but Luster's interruption of this movement jars Benjy so that the "heroic past looms directly before [him], staring down to remind him of how far the white South has fallen" (141). Benjy's anguished protest thereby forms "a sensory bond between author and reader at the most profound level of understanding, capturing in a reverberating instant the anguish that welled up inside Faulkner whenever he contemplated the history of his region and that would now supply the motor force for the balance of his career" (142). Miles Orvell (2007) similarly observes that "Faulkner is setting up a tension here between the immobility of the Confederate soldier – impassive, unmoving stone, regardless of 'wind and weather' – and the fragility of Ben, lacking in equilibrium, exploding into rage and grief, subject to externalities that control his responses" (117). This tension gives way to a shared characteristic, Orvell concludes, since both are given the same eyes, indicating "an unsuspected kinship here between the soldier and this ruined Compson, innocent victims both, it would seem, of the tragic history of the South" (117).

All of these readings help to place Faulkner's complex vision within an illuminating historical and literary context. Interpreting this iconic scene as a cognitive cartography clarifies what is at stake. We see neither an arbitrary halt to the action nor a scene primarily concerned with the heroic past. Rather, the final scene powerfully completes the symbolic coda of the novel that first began with Benjy looking upon a surface that begins to release stored information. Here, Benjy's perception is paramount once again and the critics above are correct to emphasize an "unsuspected kinship" between the disabled man and the statue above. But what these interpretations overlook is the extent to which the passage explicitly underscores a process by which the culture of the plantation system is being replicated in the present moment, in the movement, behavior, and thinking of those who encircle it. As with his other cognitive cartographies, Faulkner emphasizes the statue as a vertex of cognitive and social space and the individuals who concentrically cluster about it as its proxies. They may enact or resist the dictates of the information object above them, according to their individual predilections, but by the final sentence, they all resemble the mimetic object they circle, as though its features have been reproduced in them.

The implication is that this paradigm is being replicated in us, for we, as readers, are similarly involved in de-alienating the information object before us. Nor is this information object innocuous. The stone statue is explicitly active, "gazing with empty eyes beneath his marble hand in wind and weather" (SF 377). The soldier is much more than a landmark around which people pass; it is a compression and culmination of every invasive surface we have seen thus far. It is the coalescence of Quentin's sun-clock and the Colonel's mimetic semblance, a centralized or weighted node in a network of relations "gazing" now with authorial power and extending into, and inscribing itself onto, the life around it. At the same time, the statue is not alive; its gaze is "empty"; it does not possess an authentic animating life, for its immanent power resides in a textually oriented confusion on the part of the characters and ourselves.

In this final scene, we do not simply have another cultural artifact. While the monument to the Confederate soldier may be similar in function to the Colonel's statue as well as to the heirloom watch and biblical planter genealogy, here at the Courthouse square, we find ourselves at the legal hub of Yoknapatawpha County itself. The other information objects are obviously linked to it, but they operate in terms of the cultural, financial and transportation infrastructure of the plantation system and aim to ensure the genealogical transfer of power within the aristocratic planter families. Here, the statue of the soldier stands before the courthouse itself and, thus, is interwoven with the rule of law in the New South. There are a number of historical and biographical underlayers to Faulkner's fictional representation that must be unpacked in order to understand the functioning of the statue of the finale – not just how it circulates ideology, but also what kind of ideology is being replicated.

First and foremost, the erection of Confederate statues in the beginning of the twentieth century was a highly organized endeavor to disseminate the ideologies of the Lost Cause and white supremacy throughout the South. Adam H. Domby (2020) recounts the origins of this movement in North Carolina with "a series of increasingly vicious white supremacy campaigns run by Democrats in the 1890s [that] culminated in 1900 with their takeover of the state government, the disenfranchisement of most African Americans, and the institution of one-party rule. Shortly thereafter, Confederate monuments increasingly began appearing in front of city halls, courthouses, and other publics buildings" (16). The dismantling of Reconstruction was quickly accomplished with wave after wave of Jim Crow legislation being passed in southern states, followed by the erection of Confederate statues that was, according to Roger C. Hartley (2021), part of a "systemic assault" directed at black Americans at the turn of the century that included, but was not limited to, "disfranchisement, spectacle lynching . . . and the flooding of Southern public schools with text-books teaching white supremacy and the inferiority of African Americans" (255).

Jim Crow had myriad parts, therefore, not least of which was a unified strategy that instituted the myths of the Lost Cause in public spaces all across the South. No group played a larger role in this endeavor than the United Daughters of the Confederacy (UDC) who erected hundreds of Confederate monuments on public land to "advance the ideology of White supremacy and relegate Southern African Americans to a position of 'otherness' in Southern civic and political life" (Hartley 2021: 55). Karen L. Cox (2003) clarifies the crucial role that the UDC played in inventing, preserving, and disseminating Confederate culture. The Sons of Confederate Veterans worked in concert with the UDC, but these men "were more committed to their own business and political success than to the success of the Confederate tradition." The UDC thereby became a "driving force" of ideologically devoted social elites that were primarily responsible for the speed at which these monuments were instituted in public space (5). According to a 2019 report by the Southern Poverty Law Center, there are at least 1,503 symbols of the Confederacy in public spaces, with over 700 of these being Confederate monuments (10). The vast majority of these were instituted in two periods: the first and, by far, the largest spike during Jim Crow in the first two decades of the twentieth century and the second emerging as a means to resist the civil rights movement in the 1950s and 1960s (11).

As with the majority of Confederate monuments, the two statues of the Confederate soldier went up in Oxford some forty years after the Civil War during the era of Jim Crow ascendency (1895–1915), the first at the university in 1906 and the other at the courthouse in 1907. The details in Oxford are much the same as in hundreds of other places around the South, although in this case Faulkner's own family was involved. In 1900, a local Oxford chapter of the UDC was founded, but during the fundraising, the members became divided as to the placement of their proposed monument. Faulkner's own grandmother, Sally Murry Falkner, led a "dissenting faction . . . to memorialize all the county's Confederates with a monument on the square" (Doyle 2001: 330). When the women ultimately voted to place it in the university, "Sally Falkner resigned from the chapter and led a fundraising campaign on behalf of the United Confederate Veterans, Camp 752, to erect the monument that stood in front of the courthouse" (330–1). When the funds had been secured, disagreement broke out again. This time, Sally Falkner would prevail. Whereas one group wanted the statue placed on the north side of the courthouse and facing north, "she and her faction insisted that the marble Confederate soldier stand at the south side of the courthouse, armed, with his back defiantly to the north" with an inscription below that proclaimed that he had fought for a "just and holy cause" (331).

Faulkner would in time mock the southward facing direction of the courthouse statue in his later work, *Requiem for a Nun* (1951), while removing personal culpability from any agent. In the work, the placement is simply a laughable oversight, demonstrating a collective postbellum blindness on the part of everyone involved: "because apparently neither the U.D.C. ladies who instigated and bought the monument, nor the architect who designed it nor the masons who erected it, had noticed that the marble eyes under the shading marble palm stared not toward the north and the enemy, but toward the south, toward (if anything) his own rear" (189). While Faulkner presents the placement of the statue as an unplanned folly, twenty years earlier in *The Sound and the Fury*, his idiosyncratic and undoubtedly brilliant portrayal depicts the monument as a self-replicating information object placed in the center of social space. Even in its relation to the two Oxford statues, this Yoknapatawpha monument is a compression of characteristics, taking composite form, at once situated in the courthouse square and resembling the university monument, since it depicts a gaze that looks out from under a marble hand.

This broader historical context reveals, moreover, the nature of the ideology being transmitted through the social body. As we have already seen, Jason is an active proxy for this invasive cultural force that, here, explicitly unfolds as a violent and racial form of domination, at once erasing Luster's agency and reinforcing a past form of movement, behavior, and thinking in social space. Importantly, it is Jason's violent intervention that enables the statue to dominate the space around it from its preeminent position in the vertex above. Luster's movement leftward, clockwise with the normal flow of time, is implicitly an act of novelty and defiance, and Jason who is also in the square quickly reinstitutes family convention with brutal violence:

> With a backhanded blow he hurled Luster aside and caught the reins and sawed Queenie about and doubled the reins back and slashed her across the

hips. He cut her again and again, into a plunging gallop, while Ben's hoarse agony roared about them, and swung her about to the right of the monument. Then he struck Luster over the head with his fist. (SF 377)

Jason thereby redirects the carriage counterclockwise around the statue. Jason's violence is much more than a singular or individual activity; he is engaged in protecting the color line so fundamental to the legal framework of Jim Crow segregation in the New South. This is a color line that has already been formulated at the opening of Jason's section where the Compson man meditates upon the whites living above the black servants below and entertains the fantasy of sending his niece to live amongst them. Here, the victimization of Luster and the horse takes on a symbolic and cultural complexity; Jason subjects them to a demeaning public display of violence so that indentured black man and animal are effectively interchangeable.

Consequently, Luster's own instinctual desire to deviate from family convention is brutally repressed – and, worse still, he is forced to become an accomplice in Jason's violence. Once Jason jumps from the cart, it is Luster who takes the reins to "hit Queenie with the end of them" (378). Benjy's relationship to Jason's violence is also telling; like Luster, Benjy is a victim, since Jason strikes Benjy and breaks his flower stalk before jumping off the cart. Benjy, however, does not react as one typically would to a beating; instead, he quits the "unbelievable crescendo" of his wailing protest, quieted by the very violence that he himself must suffer. What becomes powerfully apparent is how the violent, mimetic crisis at the heart of this scene begins to affect every element with which it comes into contract. In an explicit way, Faulkner parallels the empty stare of the statue which opened the scene with Benjy whose "eyes" are "empty and blue and serene again" in the final sentence of the novel.

This is more than simply a symbolic presentation of how the past continues to structure the present. Rather, we see a dissemination of ideology through the nodes of networked space. The immobility of the statue of the Confederate soldier maps itself onto every facet of the narrative – with Faulkner forcefully implicating the formal order of his own writing in the closing movement which flows from "left to right" only to assume a fixed and ordered position both in the narrative and on the page before us: "The broken flower drooped over Ben's fist and his eyes were empty and blue and serene again as cornice and facade *flowed smoothly once more from left to right*, post and tree, window and doorway and signboard each in its ordered place" (378; emphasis added). The return of objects to their "ordered place" corresponds with the perceptual structure of the reading process. Each of these supposedly real objects – post, tree, window, and doorway – can be interpreted as metaphors for textuality, especially the signboard, the final item in the series, which signals that we are prospectively dealing not simply with literal referents, but with signs themselves. From this vantage point, Faulkner violently blurs the literal and figurative so that the narrative events themselves are inseparable from the visual dimensions of the text. The reader may interpret this funneling of meaning into visual stasis in one way or another, but as an observer, he or she also participates in the striking transformation of every supposed living element into an immutable textual sequence and is, on some level, complicit in the de-alienation of this stored information.

In conclusion, it is essential to detect Faulkner's underlying Romantic indignation at the imposition of the statue with its seeming ubiquitous and ever-replicating system of signs. Some critics, as we have seen, would have us believe that the metafictional structure of the novel is an end in itself, the pièce de résistance that the novel challenges us to decode and perceive without flinching. From this point of view, we must accept the poststructural view that we cannot pass through the language of the text, but that the language of the text constitutes the very world around us. I have indicated another possibility altogether, one that implicitly questions this epistemology of textual space and laments the ways in which individuals are subjected to its influence. Indeed, Faulkner goes so far as to implicate his own text with the ideology that has secured cultural preeminence in the structures around us. Like Faulkner's characters, we too are compelled to accept an irresistible dictation without fully comprehending how such a process takes place. And the consequence of accepting the mimetic gaze of the statue is no less than everything, for once textual space and our subjective depths have been conflated, we have no other means to resist that insistence from without. We may even believe that it arises from within and that it is our own deepest wish and desire.

CHAPTER 3

Invasions of Interiority

This chapter explores the development of a distinctive Faulknerian ontology in relation to the information paradigm we have explored. In the Yoknapatawpha novels *As I Lay Dying* (1930) and *Sanctuary* (1931), I examine the author's meditation on coercive mimetic surfaces and the way they proliferate information into and through selves. I show that Faulkner's portrait of the human subject within the modern landscape is no simple matter of despair – and, here, I broaden the scope of this self. No longer analyzing the identity of the planter heirs alone, I include a number of other individuals who live within the plantation economy. While we have seen characters so often destroyed attempting to navigate the overlapping claims of heritage and modernity, I begin in Section 3.1, by exploring two characters from *The Sound and the Fury* who provide a paradigm of autonomous personhood that is able to survive within a coercive social network of the plantation economy. Both Dilsey and Miss Quentin, I show, possess a robust interiority capable of resisting and even disrupting the hegemony of ideological surfaces. In Section 3.2, I extend this analysis to Darl Bundren in *As I Lay Dying* – a hybrid character who explicitly embodies two sides of the mimetic crisis and introduces us to an entirely new socioeconomic milieu: the rural working class.

Though, like Quentin Compson, Darl is aware of the textual nature of the world, he is initially able to harness and internalize this knowledge in becoming a contemplative subject. However, Darl's narrative arc also vividly evokes the perils of mimetic selfhood through its tragic depiction of just how fragile our mimetic nature really is, especially when the possibility of sensuous or emotional access to others is compromised. Here, Faulkner anticipates a major theme in a number of his later novels, namely, alienation as a facet of modernity. We saw a variation of this alienation – along with its attendant nihilism – in the struggles of Quentin, but, in *As I Lay Dying*, Faulkner examines the disruption of the traditional

73

bonds of family and community as a consequence of a world in which human beings are destabilized and uprooted by the modernization of the New South. I analyze this, first, in Addie's ideological fascination with nihilism and then, in Darl's eventual mental health crisis.

In Sections 3.3 and 3.4, I demonstrate how *Sanctuary* articulates this mimetic dilemma both in the rape of Temple and on a larger social scale, in the hyper-mimetic quality that information can possess when allowed to flow unimpeded through the self and the social body. Although *Sanctuary* was published after *Flags in the Dust*, *The Sound and the Fury*, and *As I Lay Dying*, the novel is among the earliest Yoknapatawpha efforts, initially arising out of a prose poem that Faulkner wrote in 1925 during a six-week stay in Paris. While it may lack the coherent social commentary of the other works, *Sanctuary* can be considered nonetheless an extremely fertile experimental novel in its study of the hyper-mimetic quality of information flow through complex social systems that rely more on abstraction than on sensuous interpersonal bonds. In this respect, *Sanctuary* offers a significant variation on this theme of information flow. Faulkner explores not the dynamics of ideological invasion as he did with the planter heirs, but a systems view of information flow capable of connecting human subjects from very different parts of the social hierarchy and, more insidiously, capable of self-organizing into a murderous mob.

In *Sanctuary*, the mimetic circulation of information is, I argue, the lynchpin for Faulkner's maturing ontological understanding of the self within networked space. As one seemingly random action self-organizes into a behavioral sequence, the emergent pattern carries out an implicit aim that eventually cascades into an all-encompassing, omnipresent mode of behavior that replicates without the individual nodes in that network having to come into direct contact. Nor do these individuals need to carry out this directive knowingly or willingly; according to their individual capacity and place in the network, they replicate a coercive information pattern that appears to be greater than any self – to be godlike in its power to shape and thus to possess the very depths of our cognitive interiority.

3.1   A Vertex unto Oneself

At the conclusion of Chapter 2, I analyzed how Luster's act of novelty – his attempt to direct the Compson wagon clockwise around the monument in the town square – was met by Jason's vicious reprisal. The final cognitive cartography of *The Sound and the Fury* thereby plays out a violent paradigm with Luster required to obey family convention and, more insidiously, forced to adopt a pattern of behavior he would not choose otherwise. What I left unremarked is that Luster's act of novelty under-scores a key facet of Faulkner's humanist and liberal vision. As dominant as the statue appears, situated as it is in the principal hub of social space for the County, its power is not absolute. While Jason as proxy might reinforce certain trajectories of behavior, novelty – in this case, spontane-ous individual movement – is an eventuality in any complex system and brings with it the possibility not just of variation, but of genuine change. Luster may be overpowered in this one iteration, but his intuitive desire for free movement and expression underscores a potential answer, however partially realized at this stage in Faulkner's writing, to the ideological dilemma of becoming textually circumscribed.

Though suppressed in this instance, Luster's act of novelty is connected to a larger pattern of behavior that cannot be stamped out or controlled. Faulkner initially establishes this counterforce in Caddy with a pro-nounced symbolism of verticality, depth, and nature, and he reaffirms it in his description of Dilsey at the beginning of the fourth section. Similar to Luster's desire for novelty, Dilsey's movements in these opening pages underscore an emerging moral arc in Faulkner's fiction that affirms indi-vidual agency beyond hegemonic social control. On an immediate level, Dilsey provides the labor and compassion that at once sustain the symbolic order of the plantation network and make it habitable. As critics have long understood, Faulkner's positive characterization of Dilsey undoubtedly reflects his own admiration of, and love for, Caroline Barr, the black caretaker who helped raise him and to whom the Falkners referred as "Mammy Callie." Onto the figure of the matron, Faulkner projects his own Romantic values, so that readers encounter a well-developed person-hood fully capable of spiritually and physically resisting powerful social forces that seek to dominate the world within.

This upspringing resistance against an external social force is the singu-lar insistence of the opening pages of the fourth section. The spatial symbolism of the past three narratives informs this opening characteriza-tion of Dilsey. Thus, Faulkner immediately establishes the external envi-ronment as a surface seeking to invade the depths of the self:

> The day dawned bleak and chill, a moving wall of gray light out of the northeast which, instead of dissolving into moisture, seemed to disintegrate into minute and venomous particles, like dust that, when Dilsey opened the door of the cabin and emerged, needled laterally into her flesh, precipitating not so much a moisture as a substance of the quality of thin, not quite congealed oil. (SF 312)

The external environment is imagined as a "moving wall" that transforms into an invasive force that needles into Dilsey's flesh. Whereas the two Compson brothers are unable to prevent this type of surface from over-whelming them, Dilsey can protect herself; indeed, she can physically exert herself against such pressure. Besides the multiple layers of clothing she wears like protective shells about her, "her myriad and sunken face lifted to the weather" (312). Dilsey's very visage asserts itself upward against the moving wall needling into her, and Faulkner quickly develops this with a complex imagery denoting indomitable interiority. He depicts, for instance, her "hand flac-soled as the belly of fish" (312), thereby expressing another spatial arrangement in which Dilsey is compared to a being residing in watery depths.

This initial symbolism insists upon the kindly matron as a vertex unto herself. She may serve the Compson family and occupy a spatial position of service located in the kitchen, a floor below Mother Compson, the hypochondriac, but Faulkner reinforces Dilsey's interiority as a counter-force capable not simply of resisting external pressure, but of asserting itself from below:

> She had been a big woman once but now her skeleton rose draped loosely in unpadded skin that tightened again upon a paunch almost dropsical, as though muscle and tissue had been courage or fortitude which the days or the years had consumed until only the indomitable skeleton was left rising like a ruin or a landmark above the somnolent and impervious guts, and above that collapsed face that gave the impression of the bones themselves being outside the flesh, lifting into the driving day with an expression at once fatalistic and of a child's astonished disappointment, until she turned and entered the house again and closed the door. (312–13)

This evocative description insists upon Dilsey's physical resistance to the external environment as one that hinges upon a well-developed interiority. Nor is this inner power simply the product of a compassionate simpleton, a charge sometimes made in Faulknerian scholarship. Dilsey's face is described as "myriad," and she possesses both the "fatalistic" view that Quentin possessed and the qualities of a "child." Time itself cannot break her interiority either, for as the flesh collapses, the "indomitable skeleton" within is capable of "rising" and "lifting" into the "moving wall" or "driving day." Instead of being invaded by a surface from above, she thereby asserts herself from below, her very being ascending upward so that she becomes her own "ruin" or "landmark," that is, her own vertex of cognitive and social space.

As a consequence, Dilsey is not imprisoned within mediating surfaces as Benjy and Quentin are. She provides a symbolic paradigm that at once affirms the possibility of free movement in social space and makes of it a foundation for authentic personhood. Importantly, such a personhood does not involve a self-contained individualism; rather, it offers an inter-subjective form of care for others that James Berger (2014) has rightly argued is a "counter to modern totalization" (89). The accompanying imagery of birds reinforces this portrayal, since in these opening para-graphs, Dilsey's movements through the threshold of her cabin parallel the free flight of jaybirds into and out of the mulberry trees beside the Compson house. This motif of free movement – and its accompanying bird symbolism – also sets the stage for the victory of Caddy's daughter, Quentin Compson, who not simply subverts, but strikingly destabilizes Jason's power, which helps to explain the tyrant's rage at Luster in the final scene.[1] We saw in Chapter 2 how Jason subjects his niece to an invasive violence, symbolically associated with a mechanical and denaturalized social order. Although Jason bolts Quentin in her room and effectively imprisons the entire household within a system of mediated thresholds and locks, Quentin triumphantly evades his measures of control. She is able to thwart Jason by taking back the money he has gradually stolen from her.

Apart from the "broken lock" on the metal box that Jason keeps in his closet (the most obvious sign of Quentin's dissent or resistance against metallic containment), the larger scene abounds with motifs of free move-ment that resonate with the description of Dilsey above. Because the narrative does not directly relate Quentin's escape, readers must intuit the event through Jason's discovery of the theft – and thus we find that Faulkner juxtaposes Jason's petty tyranny with Quentin's ability to break free from confinement, which connects her to Dilsey and to her absent mother. At first, Jason opens the door to his niece's room, once again serving as that invasive principle with the door swinging "inward" and the oppressor initially mediating the threshold so thoroughly that those who stand behind him cannot see into the room: "The door opened, swung inward. He stood in it for a moment, hiding the room, then he stepped aside" (332). While he keeps giving orders to those about him, Jason's control over these thresholds has been disrupted. To reinforce this point, Faulkner restages the imagery with which he closed Benjy's stream-of-consciousness narrative. Whereas the cognitively impaired man hears the branches of the pear tree scraping against his bedroom window, denoting his absolute separation from the natural world that he associates with Caddy, in this scene, Jason walks into a bedroom, the window of which is wide open with the pear tree "driving" through it and bringing in the odor of the world outside: "The window was open. A pear tree grew there, close against the house. It was in bloom and the branches scraped and rasped against the house and the myriad air, driving in the window, brought into the room the forlorn scent of the blooms" (332). Quentin's escape is thereby connected to Caddy's pear tree and the prospect of an unmediated threshold through which natural correspondences are once again possible.

As we saw, the pear tree is a vital symbol in the novel and a counterforce to both the heirloom watch that enforces the demands of planter legacy and the statue of the Confederate soldier that is an ideological exponent of the Lost Cause ideology and Jim Crow. Faulkner himself claimed that the whole novel grew out of the imagery of "the muddy bottom of a little girl climbing a blooming pear tree in april to look in the window at the funeral" (10) and her three brothers standing below.[2] With her daughter's escape, Caddy's pear tree blooms once more and pours through the window to convey the restoration of free movement in social space. Faulkner strengthens this prospect of natural flourishing and free move-ment for, in the moment that Jason finds the broken lock on his metal box, the jaybirds fly free outside his bedroom window:

> Then he upended the box and shook it too and slowly replaced the papers and stood again, looking at the broken lock, with the box in his hands and his head bent. Outside the window he heard some jaybirds swirl shrieking past and away, their cries whipping away along the wind, and an automo-bile passed somewhere and died away also. (SF 333)

The flight of birds possesses personal significance for Jason, since he previously fantasizes about social spaces cleansed of such feathered crea-tures. By stark contrast, the jaybirds are free in this scene, and their movement underscores Quentin's victory over Jason and suggests a more hopeful prospect for those who live within ideologically saturated social systems. Onto this, we may add another level of analysis. Birds, as we have begun to see, so often serve a mimetic formulation in Faulkner's fiction, by mirroring and disseminating a pattern of behavior outside the confines of an individual's immediate social relations. In this case, the flight of the jaybirds implies that Quentin's free movement in social space is not hers alone. The jaybirds implicitly align Quentin's escape with Dilsey's robust interiority, and they evoke the continuing prospect of spontaneous, agen-tive movement in social space. Once expressed, such novelty is mirrored by the jaybirds and carried beyond our immediate spatial frame through an additional symbolic inference in the figure of "an automobile" that passes out of hearing.

Faulkner thereby answers the dilemma of the second section of the novel when a bird in flight is subsumed within the machinic logic of invasive surfaces, its "throat pumping" according to the dictates of a sun-clock. The bird prospectively mirrors and transmits a pattern of behavior beyond our immediate frame of reference or interaction network into the broader society. The second section of *The Sound and the Fury* certainly upholds this motif of birds as purveyors of coercive information that replicates itself everywhere. The fourth section, by contrast, indicates that these mimetic lines of information transmission can disseminate another pattern altogether, for here spontaneous action and free movement can utilize the same mechanisms exploited by coercive information patterns. As much as the social body clusters across time to enact hierarchies and instill them with ideology so that they are more likely to last, the self is capable of being its own vertex and, in turn, can transmit information through the nodes of the greater system.

In Faulkner's characterization of Dilsey, we find the first touchstone for free, autonomous movement. Although Dilsey may serve the Compson household, she is nonetheless an agent in the proper sense of the term – and just as importantly, her paradigm carries over to Quentin's escape from confinement. Years later in 1945, when Faulkner reimagined *The Sound and the Fury* for his *Compson Appendix*, we can see how important this theme of disruptive, agentive movement was to him. He concludes the Compson family genealogy with a direct description of Quentin's escape, emphasizing above all her ability to break through every mediation:

> Who at seventeen . . . swung herself by a rainpipe from the window of the room in which her uncle had locked her at noon, to the locked window of his own locked and empty bedroom and broke the pane and entered the window and with the uncle's firepoker burst open the locked bureau drawer and took the money . . . and climbed down the same rainpipe in the dusk and ran away with the pitchman who was already under sentence for bigamy. (379)

Enamored with his new take on his most famous novel, Faulkner instructed his publisher to "print the *Appendix* first in all new editions of the novel," as was done in the edition that Random House published in 1946, though "in subsequent decades . . . it was relegated to the back of most new editions of the novel, and omitted entirely from some."[3] Whereas in the novel Faulkner chose to understate the possibility of autonomous subjecthood through a subtle, intricate intra-textual symbolism, in the *Appendix*, he emphasizes Quentin's active movement and daring escape. The two versions provide variant narratives that effectively unfold the same idea, one which appears more hopeful than many traditional readings of the novel that uphold an angst-ridden modernist experiment about the insurmountably cursed and declining plantation culture of the Old South.

3.2   Upon the Surface of the Self

Darl Bundren of *As I Lay Dying* provides a striking illustration of Faulkner's thinking on the process of individuation, on how a mimetic relationship between self and world can give rise to a vibrant form of immanence, on the one hand, or reduce the self to a powerless inscription, on the other. The initial portrayal of Darl's robust interiority aligns him with characters like Dilsey and Quentin. The man's eventual tragedy, however, underscores the central dilemma of Faulkner's Yoknapatawpha fiction: the susceptibility of interiority – even of robust interiority – to social forces outside the self. Here, we lay out a different socioeconomic context, since Darl's case does not fully map onto the Compson brothers. While these other characters are clearly heirs to the aristocratic plantation culture, Darl and the Bundrens represent another Yoknapatawpha network altogether – the white rural working class.

At this point in his career, Faulkner had not yet intently explored either the sharecropping system or the extractive lumber industry, both of which figure so prominently in his later fiction. *As I Lay Dying* situates the Bundrens within the context of rural precarity and the victory of the New South ideology of industrialization. After the Civil War, the South's continuing dependency upon agriculture and cheap labor locked the region into cycles of economic stagnation. Industrial advocates saw agrarian life as the albatross preventing economic independence and prosperity in the region. In the first few decades of the twentieth century, the "all-out pursuit of industry became a regional obsession," so much so that this "New South ethos conquered the countryside in the 1920s and 30s" (Cobb 2004: 34). The widespread acceptance of this industrial ideology "resulted both from rapid expansion of the urban South and from the economic decline in the rural areas and small towns, especially in the Deep South, where worn-out soil and the invasion of the boll weevil combined to undermine the cotton production and processing that was the mainstay of the economy" (34).

As I Lay Dying was composed in the midst of this deepening malaise regarding agrarian life, reflecting the modernization of the South and the massive demographic upheaval that it involved. Cheryl Lester (2005/2006), for instance, interprets the novel in terms of "Southern diaspora" (32), situating the Bundrens within "the spatial and social dislocation" of the "Great Depression and the transformative programs of the New Deal" where "millions of Southerners were faced with the struggle of maintaining a way of life that was rapidly becoming extinct or of making the effort to adapt to new and unfamiliar environments, occupations and social orders" (28). In this context, the Bundrens are "rural refugees" whose journey to bury Addie entails "the hierarchical distinction between town and country" (36). Instead of confronting the ideological perils of heritage, the Bundrens face quite another dilemma that involves the "dynamic juxtaposition of the old and the new" as the family "moves from the residual complex of life of the Southern countryside to the dominant complex of life in modern cities and towns" (37). Their journey is made all the more difficult as they belong to neither social order. Unlike the Sartorises or the Compsons, the Bundrens have no family legacy – illusory or otherwise. They possess no clear alignment with either the rural or urban, since Anse is a farmer with no family roots and Addie's kin are from Jefferson and are all buried in the cemetery there.

With Darl, then, we are addressing not simply the remaking of planta-tion culture, but the dynamics of a self profoundly unsettled by, and displaced within, a series of intersecting networks – from the rural to the urban and, beyond that, to global modernity. While these overlapping networks inform each other, they provide no underlying sense of rooted-ness or community. This theme of alienation is nowhere better illustrated than in Addie Bundren's only narrative point of view, which provides a poignant touchstone for how to assess both Darl's later struggles and the family dynamic as a whole. Addie's narrative articulates a pronounced tension between town and country, for although we find her living in the country, rural life is completely foreign to her. Addie's family are all dead, and her only significant memory of her father is a nihilistic aphorism that is repeated twice in her narrative: "My father used to say that the reason for living is getting ready to stay dead" (AILD 69, 72). Addie's status as an outsider also involves a cosmopolitan way of thinking about existence that does not map onto rural life. Indeed, her sole request – to be buried in Jefferson – both launches the action of the novel and accentuates the tension between two disparate epistemologies: the rural community-oriented life and a modernity that dashes traditional structures and upends the claims of family and community.

Faulkner presets this tension toward the opening of the chapter with Addie employing her education – itself a feature of urban existence – to make a living in a foreign environment. The young woman reflects on her own pervasive sense of alienation while teaching at a rural school among children who have "blood strange to each other blood and strange to mine" (69) – an alienation only temporarily alleviated by whipping the children for the breach of rules:

> When the switch fell I could feel it upon my flesh; when it welted and ridged it was my blood that ran, and I would think with each blow of the switch: Now you are aware of me! Now I am something in your secret and selfish life, who have marked your blood with my own for ever and ever. (69)

The only interpersonal connection Addie feels is in the moment of violent contact, for it is in this moment alone when her mental life is directly connected to the interiority of the child, to the "secret and selfish life" within. Marriage to Anse brings no relief, and bearing children only exacerbates her isolation. Not only has her "aloneness . . . been violated" (70); she begins to replicate a mental variant of the violence above on her husband and children.

What complicates Addie's personal dilemma is her firm resistance to any narrative that might enable connection to others. She feels little relation to other human beings and realizes that language only serves to deceive people into emotions of intimacy and belonging. As her family grows in size, she begins to believe that words cover over that "lack" at the center of an individual's being: Anse "had a word, too. Love, he called it. But I had been used to words for a long time. I knew that that word was like the others: just a shape to fill a lack; that when the right time came, you wouldn't need a word for that anymore than for pride or fear" (70). For Addie, abstract words like "love," "pride," and "fear" are invasive ideologies. Whereas the whip allows for interpersonal relation, these abstractions are a true violence against the sovereignty of the self, imagined in terms of textual surfaces: "Hidden within a word like within a paper screen" is an idea that strikes her "in the back through it" (70). Here we see a variant of the ideological invasion that the planter heirs faced. Whereas Quentin is overwhelmed by the ideological weight of his own heritage, Addie has no heritage. She perceives the way that language forms connections between selves and communities as mere trickery, which in turn reinforces her alienation from her own husband and children.

During the course of the chapter, Faulkner emphasizes the abstract character of language when formalized as text. Addie explicitly imagines this in spatial terms as a violence "hidden within a word like within a paper screen" (70). She soon visualizes her husband as a dead word or shape, juxtaposing the intimacy of the marriage bed and the cold sterility of text-making:

> Sometimes I would lie by him in the dark, hearing the land that was now of my blood and flesh, and I would think: Anse. Why Anse. Why are you Anse. I would think about his name until after a while I could see the word as a shape, a vessel, and I would watch him liquify and flow into it like cold molasses flowing out of the darkness into the vessel, until the jar stood full and motionless: a significant shape profoundly without life like an empty door frame; and then I would find that I had forgotten the name of the jar. (71)

The inferred context is Addie lying awake after having had intercourse with Anse, an act that connects her "blood and flesh" to the land outside in the birth of sons, but one that she resists mentally by transforming the breathing body beside her into a "shape profoundly without life." While there is presumably some sexual disgust for Anse here, Addie repeats this act of linguistic defamiliarization with her children as well: "And when I would think *Cash* and *Darl* that way until their names would die and solidify into a shape" (71).

There is a complexity to Addie's thought processes that we briefly explored in the nihilism of Mr. Compson. Nor does Faulkner perceive this thought construct as benign, for he reveals its ideological character in the spatial delineations we have seen already, namely, as a vertical power supervening upon the self from above:

> hearing the dark voicelessness in which the words are the deeds, and the other words that are not deeds, that are just the gaps in people's lacks, coming down like the cries of the geese out of the wild darkness in the old terrible nights, fumbling at the deeds like orphans to whom are pointed out in a crowd two faces and told, That is your father, your mother. (71)

Whereas, in the earlier novels, we saw an information object replicating itself from on high, here, the nihilistic thought-construct that Addie has embraced assumes absolute precedence above her. Faulkner thus portrays a cognitive cartography with a "dark voicelessness" or a "wild darkness" descending from above through an information conduit that Faulkner symbolically repeats in novel after novel and here is figured in the "cries of the geese." For Addie, this vertical power blindly dictates human connection in the absence of more genuine familial bonds, for this wild darkness is "fumbling at the deeds like orphans" and arbitrarily self-organizing individuals into a family structure.

Addie's dilemma thereby involves familial and communal belonging – and Faulkner identifies this in the disrupting context of modernization with the themes of alienation and uprootedness. Faulkner's initial portrayal of Darl exhibits a powerful contrast to Addie's alienation but, as we will see, he eventually succumbs to a version of his mother's nihilistic ideology. Indeed, this younger Darl initially represents a decided answer to his mother's experience, for he is intent on developing a cognitive interiority that can correspond to the world outside as well as to other members of his family. Darl has long been associated with interior consciousness by scholars. William J. Handy (1959) was the first to refer to the "Darl of inner consciousness," yet this designation does not really distinguish Darl from a larger cast of characters whose stream-of-consciousness narratives imply similar inward complexity. What singles Darl out, if we look closely at Faulkner's initial rendering of the character's stream of consciousness, is the decisive emphasis upon mimesis in terms of mirroring and correspondences, that is, Darl's awareness of the world as text and his willingness to engage with it on these terms.

Faulkner presets Darl's cognitive interiority with a mimetic symbolism that underscores wellbeing. In *As I Lay Dying*, the mimetic threshold of water initially stages a process of individuation that articulates the organic growth of a self with the imagery of fresh water and nature: "When I was a boy I first learned how much better water tastes when it has set a while in a cedar bucket. Warmish-cool, with a faint taste like hot July wind in cedar trees smells. It has to set at least six hours, and be drunk from a gourd. Water should never be drunk from metal" (AILD 10–11). The underlying implication follows a fairly clear Romanticism, for Darl's early memories entail self-development and the structuring of sense perception, in this case, the experience of drinking fresh water from a cedar gourd. The water tastes of high summer and has gained the scent of the wood container that stores it. Darl even notes that such water should never be stored in metal, subtly indicating that the metallurgy of civilization distorts the sensual enjoyment of this living water.

Faulkner develops this imagery with Darl as a prepubescent boy ingesting the water through mimetic correspondences. The boy remembers how lying in bed, he would wait until the family was asleep and then go to the cedar gourd and look into its reflective darkness to see and enact a correspondence of above and below; the water comes to contain the reflection of stars which Darl then ingests into his being:

> And at night it is better still. I used to lie on the pallet in the hall, waiting until I could hear them all asleep, so I could get up and go back to the

bucket. It would be black, the shelf black, the still surface of the water a round orifice in nothingness, where before I stirred it awake with the dipper I could see maybe a star or two in the bucket, and maybe in the dipper a star or two before I drank. (11)

This activity is an act of individuation, accomplished when all others are asleep. Thus, Darl begins to distinguish himself from his family collective and to engage in acts of self-becoming. Here, Faulkner presents a creation paradigm with Darl actively coming into self-consciousness by leaning over the water below him, which is described with imagery akin to when Yahweh first moves over the deep in *Genesis*. In Faulkner's portrayal, the water is a "still surface ... a round orifice in nothingness" which needs to be "stirred awake." As the boy engages in the process, these primordial waters begin to reflect the stars above, which are then ingested into the self in an act of self-constitution.

This creation paradigm is accentuated only a few sentences later with Darl coming into sexual maturity for the first time: "After that I was bigger, older. Then I would wait until they all went to sleep so I could lie with my shirt-tail up, hearing the cool silence blowing upon my parts and wondering if Cash was yonder in the darkness doing it too" (11). Where before the boy ritualistically seeks out the dark reflective waters so as to ingest their contents, now he produces an organic fluid from within, in the act of masturbation. Again, a type of natural, even spiritual correspondence occurs, as the cool silence blows upon his member and he responds sexually in kind, all the time wondering if his act is his alone or shared by his brother. In other words, Darl has entered into a stage of development where he is acutely concerned with *theory of mind*, aware of his own behavior, while wondering about the internal motivations of others around him.

My reading of mimetic correspondences and self-development diverges from the history of criticism on the novel, which has offered several explanations for Darl's mental unravelling. Until the 1960s, a number of scholars criticized Faulkner's portrayal of Darl, going so far as to state that there is no preparation for Darl's sudden break.[4] Scholars afterward sought to counter this criticism of Faulkner's craft, focusing upon the stages of Darl's mental decline and proposing various psychological diagnoses.[5] Where there is a rich range of interpretative paradigms both for and against such diagnoses, the postmodern turn is of particular interest to us. Beginning in the late 1970s and running through the 1990s, there was a pronounced movement away from previous strategies of diagnosis toward a paradigm that explicitly criticizes a metaphysics of presence and interprets language as différance. Stephen M. Ross (1979) is a notable example, since he challenges the concept of interiority altogether: "Rhetorically the sections are 'interior,'" but "a strict application of the term 'interior' presupposes a metaphysics of consciousness, a metaphysics that the novel challenges" (303–4). Andreas Huyssen (1986) describes the aim of this interpretative paradigm succinctly. "The major premise," he writes, "is the rejection of all classical systems of representation, the effacement of 'content.' The erasure of subjectivity and authorial voice, the repudiation of likeness and verisimilitude, the exorcism of any demand for realism of whatever kind" (54).[6]

Faulkner, I submit, introduces Darl's early development of an inner architecture as a natural activity of making correspondences and producing immanent selfhood.[7] The boy is not overpowered by the information of textual surfaces; he is able to recognize and internalize them willingly, to nurture an inner dimension that borrows mimetically from the external world, but is also able to draw on this internalized information for sustenance. As James Hussey (2015) rightly puts it, "Darl is the centre of intuitive knowledge" within the novel; he possesses an "imaginative intuition that continues describing after vision is lost" (58–9). Darl visualizes the world textually, and this proclivity to understand the world as textual in nature, as a series of surfaces that bear information, is presented by Faulkner as both talent and curse. Just as mimesis can generate developmental interconnectivities in the self, so too can this faculty be used to proliferate an information pattern of self-harm. Addie, as we have seen, perceives the invasive power of abstract language as a violation of her own sense of self – and Darl's tragedy is that he succumbs to this view. Textuality is no longer a site of self-constitution and interpersonal connection; rather, it takes precedence over the self, administering an inhuman control over the natural sources of our being.

Thus, we find that the older Darl, the veteran of total war, perceives mimetic relationships very differently. They are no longer generative; the mimetic relationships that tie us together and found an internal space within the self now transmit a patently destructive ideology, one associated with industrial modernity, imposing itself upon the country setting and threatening to sever Darl from the natural correspondences he made as a boy. As he and his family attempt to cross the river with Addie's corpse, Darl projects godlike agency upon "something" beneath the watery surface. Whereas he once leaned over the water's dark surface in order to nourish his inner being, now the "thick dark current" is imagined as an indwelling power that is simultaneously cut off from, and threatening to assimilate, the self:

> Before us the thick dark current runs. It talks up to us in a murmur become ceaseless and myriad, the yellow surface dimpled monstrously into fading swirls travelling along the surface for an instant, silent, impermanent and profoundly significant, as though just beneath the surface something huge and alive waked for a moment of lazy alertness out of and into slight slumber again. (AILD 56)

Darl is no longer capable of internalizing the external surface, of willingly ingesting it or developing a relationship of correspondences with it. With the loss of this original ability, Darl confronts a "monstrous" power, something imposing itself upon him from without and located beneath the surface.

Faulkner's depiction functions both realistically and symbolically. Darl is in the process of relating the movement of the family from shore to shore, yet this section also reveals his growing inability to assert his own agency or his interpersonal connection to others. Indeed, the dark surface asserts dominion over the whole scene, at first harmlessly clucking and murmuring "among the spokes of the wagon and about the mules' knees" and usurping higher with the branches overhead serving its dictates:

> Through the undergrowth it goes with a plaintive sound, a musing sound; in it the unwinding cane and saplings lean as before a little gale, swaying without reflections as though suspended on invisible wires from the branches overhead. Above the ceaseless surface they stand – trees, cane, vines – rootless, severed from the earth, spectral above a scene of immense yet circumscribed desolation filled with the voice of the waste and mournful water. (56)

This watery surface bears the character of the surfaces we have seen in previous cognitive cartographies. The surface serves as a powerful, albeit temporary hub of social space seeking to subordinate not only the perceiving subject, but all those who cluster around it. Darl thus perceives the "something" beneath the surface exhibiting the centripetal or centrifugal might of a "little gale" to sway all that surrounds it. A natural response might be that we are bearing witness to the unhinged subjective perceptions of mental illness, except that Faulkner's symbolism is too consistent across novels to be the subjective depiction of mental illness alone.

In one respect, Faulkner is engaged here in representing Darl's subjective point of view, the way that the young man projects his own internal conflict upon the topography around him. Yet, in the broader context of his Yoknapatawpha novels, Faulkner utilizes a now well-developed inter-subjective paradigm. As old Bayard perceived himself perceptually chained to a "Something" on a stone dais (that becomes a text and then a watery surface) and Quentin imagined himself invaded by a sun-clock, so Darl comes to admit a similar relationship to a mimetic "something" that usurps his own cognitive centrality. Strikingly, the surface is in the process of overcoming its mimetic subsequence to become vertex and center. As the unnamed *it* "goes through the undergrowth" and about the wagon wheels and higher, all the surrounding objects "sway without reflections." Stephen Ross (1979) argues that Faulkner foregrounds the "perceptual 'surface'" of the text in "the way a cubist painting shatters representational images so that the painting can assert the image of itself" (308). Importantly, this modern shattering of representation is not a victory against a false meta-physics of presence, as Ross' reading suggests. It is an explicit violence against the fragile architecture of the self – encoding a machinic assault upon what are initially depicted as the natural moorings of self-consciousness, the tools by which the individual learns to distinguish his or her innermost being from the social body, to fashion an interior architecture, and then to attribute interiority to others as well.

For Darl, this monstrous mimetic vertex – this anonymous and over-powering external quasi-agency – is not at all natural; rather, it reveals itself to be an exponent of industrial modernity, the same modernity that marshalled a civilization's resources and capital to engage in total war and to which Darl gave his service in the meatgrinder of Europe's trenches, as it was popularly called at the time. This vertex connects everything to it with "invisible wires" and, as we come to the end of the river sections, Darl finally perceives its ultimate dehumanizing machinic power as it severs human meat and dissolves the individual into its "myriad original motion":

> Jewel and Vernon are in the river again. From here they do not appear to violate the surface at all; it is as though it had severed them both at a single blow, the two torsos moving with infinitesimal and ludicrous care upon the surface. It looks peaceful, like machinery does after you have watched it and listened to it for a long time. As though the clotting which is you had dissolved into the myriad original motion, and seeing and hearing in themselves blind and deaf; fury in itself quiet with stagnation. (AILD 67)

Faulkner foils the agency of the characters in the scene with his character-istic conditional style. Jewel and Vernon do not act upon the surface of the river; rather, the surface asserts itself upon them, appearing to have severed them in half, although we can never be fully sure of such agency because of the conditional "as though." This uncertainty is key to the way in which cognition and cartography so often overlap in Faulkner's prose. It is not simply that we project meaning onto the landscape, but that the landscape is already the ideological instantiation of the complex systems – those of language and the infrastructures of meaning they make possible – of which we are a part. In this case, the watery surface provides a provisional vertex through which an ideology overpowers and assimilates.

And what is this ideology that flows into Darl? It is not the ideological flow of the Colonel's statue with the underlying aim of restoring planter power in the New South; nor again the Confederate soldier of the Lost Cause and Jim Crow ascendency imposing its dictates upon Luster. Faulkner offers yet another face of modernity, to use Jay Watson's expression, a paradigm of power implicitly connected to industrial modernity and one that threatens to unmoor human beings so that they are "rootless" and "severed from the earth" (56). Faulkner explicitly maps this dilemma onto Addie with her pervasive sense of alienation in the rural countryside and her gradual acceptance of a nihilistic ideology that offers an overarching explanation for her existence, but fails to provide communal connection. This dislocating form of modernity is what Darl sees in the reflective surface of the river, tied at once to industry and to war. Thus, we come face to face with a modern claim regarding human nature itself, one that rejects the self's interior vitality.

Faulkner's description of writing the manuscript in a coal power plant at the University of Mississippi may be an example of his extravagant mythmaking. Yet, as a biographical context, it helps to clarify both the novel's evocation of industrial modernity and the thematic tension it evokes between authentic human creativity and the imposition of instrumental and mechanical reality upon the creative element:

> in the summer of 1929[,] I got a job in the power plant, on the night shift, from 6 P.M. to 6 A.M., as a coal passer. . . . I had invented a table out of a wheelbarrow in the coal bunker, just beyond a wall from where a dynamo ran. It made a deep, constant humming noise. There was no more work to do until about 4 A.M., when we would have to clean the fires and get steam again. On these nights, between 12 and 4, I wrote *As I Laying Dying* in six weeks, without changing a word. (ESPL 177–8)

In no uncertain terms, Faulkner indicates his own victory over his industrial working conditions. Used to cart coal from the bunker to the boiler, the upside-down wheelbarrow serves as a makeshift writing desk upon which a manuscript flows out without any need of alteration. As hyperbolic as it may appear, the passage powerfully denotes Faulkner's own investment in the Romantic notion of a creative self.

Faulkner's victory also makes Darl's defeat at the hands of an industrial ideology that much more poignant. It should be clear that Darl himself believes in the interior architecture of the self; not only do his early experiences exemplify the pattern of its development, but even at the river, in the face of this "machinery" of modernization, he retains his belief in the spiritual underpinnings of personhood. As the watery surface begins to achieve a mystified authority and assumes the position of a centralized vertex by chaining everything to it with "invisible wires," Darl attempts to restore his sense of stability by visualizing the immanent domain within, connecting emotionally with his brother through the organ of sight:

> Cash's face is also gravely composed; he and I look at one another with long probing looks, looks that plunge unimpeded through one another's eyes and into the ultimate secret place where for an instant Cash and Darl crouch flagrant and unabashed in all the old terror and the old foreboding, alert and secret and without shame. (56)

Darl looks into the depths of his brother's being, so that vision "plunge[s] unimpeded" into that immanent domain, but what Darl sees is already an indication of his dilemma and a foreboding of his eventual incarceration. Although he accesses that "ultimate secret place," he nonetheless perceives a reflection which eschews the possibility of viable interiority and inter-personal connection, a reflection that objectifies the information stored there and foreshadows his vision of the river's machinic assault upon the selves clustered about it. Darl thereby looks into Cash's eyes and sees an objectified reflection upon the surface of the pupils. This is reinforced by Darl's pronoun usage. Instead of the first person, the third person – "Cash and Darl crouch" – denotes a split in Darl's conception of himself and underscores a complete loss of control in which the mimetic surface assumes power over Darl and his brother: "*I felt the current take us . . . . What had once been a flat surface was now a succession of troughs and hillocks lifting and falling about us, shoving at us*" (59).

Critics have connected this split in Darl's self-conception to his use of language. Homer B. Pettey (2003) argues, for instance, that "Darl's madness is due to an inability to recognize his own perceptions as a network of symbols that do not convey reality, but displace it and negate it. Darl's modernist tragedy of being is also the dark destructive comedy of representation and language" (27). Yet, as we have seen, a network of

symbols is not necessarily destabilizing. Darl's tragedy is not a failure to
recognize such a network as decentered, as Ross (1979) and Deville (1994)
also argued; rather, Darl succumbs when he loses his connection with the
"ultimate secret place" within the self that he has nurtured since his youth,
an intersubjective dynamic jeopardized by his experience of total war and
by the death of his mother. It is not so much that textual space is
inherently negative in Faulkner's fiction. Under certain conditions, the
proclivity to recognize the world as text gives rise to an inner dimension
and an empathic ability to imagine the inwardness of others. Initially,
Darl's poetic sensibility is a facet of a striking awareness, a combination of
receptivity and agency that underscores *theory of mind* and the possibility
of empathic knowledge of others. But as much as it is a powerful skill,
Darl's predisposition to thinking in this manner also fails him once his
own interiority is destabilized. He comes to understand himself as a
powerless inscription, an object determined by external patterns of information. He seeks for human contact, but finds that he can only approach
others intellectually, as inscriptions on a textual medium, and is therefore
incapable of direct, sensuous interpersonal connection. Darl's very tragedy
thereby underscores a decided ambivalence towards modernity.[8] The
danger lies not in modern rationality per se, but in our increasing reliance
upon the textual mediation of our relationship with others. The increasing
dependency upon such a textual medium provides a clearer reading of
what is involved in Darl's apparent madness. Faulkner is responding not
simply to the unsettling changes that industrialization wrought in the
South, but also to the forms of self-knowing that accompany this shift
toward technological and social complexity.

Not all the characters of the novel are subject to the perils of textual
space in the same manner. Jewel, by contrast, has another means of self-
becoming at his disposal which Darl admires, but in which he cannot
participate. Darl's conception of his brother gives some indication of the
strength implicit in physical movement and the intimacy that tactility can
engender between beings. Where Darl initially sees his brother and his
horse as textual entities, "two figures carved for a tableau savage in the sun"
(4), Jewel is able to overcome this visual stasis through a dynamic intimacy
with the animal:

> When Jewel can almost touch him, the horse stands on his hind legs and
> slashes down at Jewel. Then Jewel is enclosed by a glittering maze of hooves
> as by an illusion of wings; among them, beneath the upreared chest, he
> moves with the flashing limberness of a snake. For an instant before the jerk
> comes onto his arms he sees his whole body earth-free, horizontal, whipping

snake-limber, until he finds the horse's nostrils and touches earth again. Then they are rigid, motionless, terrific, the horse back-thrust on stiffened, quivering legs, with lowered head; Jewel with dug heels, shutting off the horse's wind with one hand, with the other patting the horse's neck in short strokes myriad and caressing, cursing the horse with obscene ferocity. (AILD 4)

This passage describes a way of perceiving that is increasingly foreign to Darl. He can still recognize something life-affirming in Jewel's embrace of his horse, a man united with his animal in an "glittering . . . illusion of wings" so that their "whole body" is at once "earth-free" and returning earthward to move as one. Faulkner emphasizes the sensuous, unmediated relation between Jewel and the animal. Like Dilsey, who resists invasion from the textual surface above by asserting herself from below to become her own vertex, Jewel's relationship with the horse gives him the possibility of a self-directed upward motion, a quasi-divine "illusion of wings" that comes from being "enclosed by a glittering maze of hooves." Jewel may be markedly estranged from his family, but his physical intimacy with this living creature provides him a strength and a mental reliance that Darl – who depends absolutely upon modern epistemologies of textual space – cannot possess. Clearly, Faulkner is not demonizing the ability to see textually, but he is articulating a modern dilemma that emerges in response to our increasing dependency upon an industrial culture of print technology to ensure social cohesion. In the face of trauma, Faulkner suggests, the mental resilience of the self seeks for a greater engagement with others, an unmediated intimacy with other living beings. In the absence of this engagement, the coherence of our very personality is at stake.

Faulkner thereby nestles Darl's narratives within a larger paradigm of sprawling global networks of industry and information flow. We see the fragile boundaries of the self imperiled by a mental reliance on abstract, soulless, technological forms so that the young man can no longer function at all. Darl's breakdown unfolds not simply as a psychological split, therefore, but as an invasion of the self by an external, seemingly godlike ideological force that is – upon close reading the ultimate despair of modernity itself – the nihilistic dilemma of human isolation and meaninglessness. In *As I Lay Dying*, the "flat surface" of the river ties everyone to it with "invisible wires" and consequently overwhelms the perceiving subject, both literally as flood waters and figuratively as an industrialized assault through textual space. While Darl's tragedy is certainly a modernist one, it is not his failure to deal with the instability of language that dooms him, as prominent poststructural critics once claimed, but an inability to resist the insertion of a coercive ideology into the self. As Faulkner himself articulated at the University of Virginia, Darl "got progressively madder because he didn't have the capacity not so much of sanity but of inertness *to resist* all the catastrophes that happened to the family" (FU 110; emphasis added). It is the self's resistance that must be emphasized here, since it denotes an architecture of interiority – and its modes of perception – that can either challenge, or succumb to, ideologies that seek to control it.

3.3   Virality, Hyper-mimesis, and an End to Immanence

A predominant feature of modernity, for Faulkner, is the machinic proliferation of images that overpowers the organic sources of the immanent and the interpersonal. This proliferation of images and textualities at once allows our complex social systems to cohere, but it introduces a greater dilemma. As the image is divested of the immanent domain that gave it life, it becomes more subject to ideological contagion and can become the bearer of a hyper-mimetic information pattern. *Sanctuary*, perhaps more than any other novel in the Yoknapatawpha canon, explores this problem simultaneously at the level of the image and at scale, depicting the transmission of information through an assemblage of surfaces and selves until that information has attained a quasi-agency of its own, at once dependent upon the nodes of a given network and free from any particular person. Ideology, as we explored it through the first two chapters, can be understood as a free-floating bearer of cultural information that is at once unmoored from the immanent self and seeks nonetheless to substantiate itself within the human being. With *Sanctuary*, Faulkner explores another aspect of information flow in the context of modernization. Where the statues of the Colonel or the Confederate soldier disseminate the ideology of particular regimes of power, there is no equivalent paradigm in *Sanctuary*. Popeye's rape of Temple is undoubtedly the determining event at the center of the novel, informed by ideological aspects of the culture pertaining to masculinity, but the rape itself is not a self-contained ideology like the ones we have analyzed thus far. What preoccupies Faulkner most is the way information flows through and across networks – and how this information is adapted and changed by individuals as it circulates.

In other words, *Sanctuary* expresses a dynamic vision of networked social space, anticipating information flow as virality, namely, the rapid circulation of information within and across networks as it adapts itself to new configurations and forms. We can begin to illuminate this emphasis upon rapid information flow with Peter Lurie's identification of two overlapping, but conflictual strands of modernity in the composition of *Sanctuary*. Lurie (2004) employs Theodor Adorno's aesthetic theory to articulate a "non-identical" struggle whereby "modernist art resists commodification" (3). From this point of view, "modernism derives its identity (and its aesthetic and cultural value) from its opposition to the simplistic, escapist pleasures and commercial impulse of mass art" (3). For Lurie, *Sanctuary* adopts these two contrasting positions at once, both the strategies of commercial fiction and the modernist opposition to them. These two strands of modernity do not just operate in dynamic tension with each other; they indicate Faulkner's "larger ambitions with the book, his interest not only in imitating consumer culture but in examining or testing it" (32). Devan Bailey (2020) argues, moreover, that Faulkner's self-reflexive examination of mass culture emphasizes circulation, since the narrative of *Sanctuary* internally configures "the passage of [Faulkner's] body of work into commercial composition and circulation" (82). As a result, "hardly a moment passes in the narrative without its calling attention to the circulation to which the novel directs itself" (83).

Beyond its compositional history, *Sanctuary*'s singular vision of networked social space also reflects the forces of modernization in the South and the profound upheaval of rural life that they entailed. Where *As I Lay Dying* expressed this in terms of migration, *Sanctuary* develops this theme in the figure of Popeye, the disfigured criminal whose rape of Temple is one in a series of events that interlink networks up and down the social hierarchy. While the character's motivations remain opaque, he is nonetheless related to a dislocating form of modernization that blurs hierarchal distinctions and social demarcations. Yet there is also a complexity to Popeye's functioning that resists straightforward social critique.[9] On the one hand, he is an iteration of the gangster antihero which rose to prominence during the Depression, denoting resistance to new modes of industrial and bureaucratic complexity. On the other hand, he personifies and embodies the emergent industrial character of the New South and is consistently associated with an imagery of mechanized, denaturalized processes that upend traditional structures.[10]

Faulkner eventually frames Popeye with a backstory that relates him to the turbulent, mercurial life of the city and industrialization. Readers learn that Popeye's father was a "strike breaker hired by the street railway company to break a strike in 1900." In his first exchange with Popeye's mother, the father boasts that he bears no loyalty for the company and could work for any other: "I don't care a damn who is running the car, see. I'll ride with one as soon as another" (S 303). The mother immediately relates this to herself, and rightly so, since the man's lack of loyalty to any company or organization extends to his own family. As soon as the strike in Memphis ends, the father abandons Popeye to a childhood of illness and institutionalization. The undersized, disfigured boy consequently adopts a penchant for violence, which Faulkner articulates with two principal emphases: first, Popeye's ability to move across thresholds and barriers; and second, the boy's threat to interior spaces. We find this first expressed in Popeye's escape from his mother's apartment: "The window was open. It gave onto a lower roof from which a drainpipe descended to the ground. But Popeye was gone. On the floor lay a wicker cage in which two lovebirds lived; beside it lay the birds themselves, and the bloody scissors with which he had cut them up alive" (309). Although Faulkner never reveals Popeye's motivations, he does provide a history for the character that involves not simply a broken family structure related to modernization, but also the crossing of thresholds with invasive violence being the signature expression of such transgression. Popeye functions as a pernicious variation of the ability to move freely in social space, which we saw positively portrayed in Miss Quentin who also escapes confinement through the open window. In the passage above, by contrast, this ability to cross barriers and thresholds does not affirm or protect an immanent domain within the self. Popeye's first act of violence does precisely the opposite, for the effacement of the lovebirds inside the cage locates the threat as one to interior spaces.

Faulkner provides this backstory very late, yet it highlights the paradigm of violence in the novel: a transgressive form of violence with Popeye as both catalyst and proxy and one that disseminates itself by exploiting a cultural epistemology dependent entirely upon vision and textual space. Popeye himself is subject to the same mechanisms of transmission as the other characters. He has no interior world because he has been robbed of it and, in turn, he replicates the mode of his effacement onto others. Temple's rape may be the ultimate expression of an invasive assault upon the sacrosanct dimensions of interiority, but Faulkner does not directly portray this assault; rather, he intimates it through a vertiginous form of hyper-mimetic self-mirroring. In short, *Sanctuary* repurposes the cognitive cartographies we have seen thus far, but with commercial mass culture and modernization as two explicit frames of compositional and historical reference.

The opening scene of the novel – the meeting of Popeye and Benbow next to a spring in rural Mississippi – employs an imagery of self-reflection and mirroring to preset this paradigm of hyper-mimetic information flow. Devan Bailey (2020) insightfully interprets the spring in terms of a "medium of exchange," a "liquid form through which commodities circulate" (82). While the symbolism of the spring has received critical attention, it has not been noted that the spring has its direct antecedent in *Flags in the Dust*.[11] Faulkner, in fact, directly repurposes the reflective imagery of the spring from the first cognitive cartography of his Yoknapatawpha canon. As we saw in Chapter 1, at the top of the Sartoris manor, Faulkner depicts a planter family genealogy as a decisive information object to which all the intergenerational behavior of the family is tied. Not only does it possess a privileged place *above* the family, but also it is stored *within* a lockbox of treasured family heirlooms. When Bayard opens the flyleaves of the bible to gaze upon his family's genealogy, he visualizes the pages as a spring which possesses identical features to those in *Sanctuary*. The spring is close enough for someone to hear the main road, yet also hidden from it. Bayard hears the "crash" of the Yankee patrol on the main road – and Horace Benbow, years later, listens to the sound of automobiles from the "invisible highroad" (S 6). In the Sartoris attic, moreover, Bayard remembers "a spring" that "flowed from the roots of a beech" (FD 90) – and in *Sanctuary*, Faulkner gives nearly an identical description: the "spring welled up at the root of a beech tree" (S 3). Both depictions present the spring as a mimetic surface that stores information and replicates it into the selves that peer into it.

Where *Flags in the Dust* presents this visual relationship within the context of one single institutional network, *Sanctuary* presents this on a larger scale, not simply in one expanding institution, but across social groups and classes. The plantation with its well-developed symbolism initially frames the threat, but the underlying problem of the novel is that the information pattern in question has no sure origin and can spread anywhere without check. Similar to Darl's experience by the river, the meeting of the lawyer Horace and the criminal Popeye exhibits a shattering of clear correspondences, even in the very act of constituting them in the interlinking of nodes and networks. The spring as a natural source is replaced by an emphatic imagery of jumbled interconnection – "the broken and myriad reflection" and "the scattered reflection" (4). Here, in this first scene, high and low society are the first to intersect as Horace and Popeye meet for the first time, so that Horace's youthful, handsome countenance is mixed into the features of Popeye whose disfigurement is explicitly mimetic: "His face just went away, like the face of a wax doll set too near a hot fire and forgotten" (5). Popeye is a warped mimetic object explicitly associated with violent inscription and industrial reproduction: "He had that vicious depthless quality of stamped tin" (5). Popeye's very features paradoxically possess no depth, no sign of natural interiority; instead, Popeye is a vicious metallic text, which implies that he is not merely an aggressor, but a surface upon which someone or something else has violently written. This imagery is reinforced a page later with "Popeye's eyes" which "looked like rubber knobs, like they'd give to the touch and then recover with the whorled smudge of the thumb on them" (6). Faulkner's description thus emphasizes the self as a surface which can be decisively shaped with the organ of the eyes being the cognitive medium through which this violent writing takes place. Throughout the first half of the novel, Faulkner repeats the cognitive cartography of the reflective spring in the threat of Popeye, characterizing him with a hyperbolized range of mimetic imagery and proceeding to portray the stages by which surfaces overwhelm and invade the self's interiority.

Faulkner's shadow symbolism can also be interpreted as an expression of the mimetic paradigm that he initially epitomized in the imagery of the spring and in the person of Popeye. As he did in *The Sound and the Fury*, Faulkner employs "the shadow" – the *locus classicus* of mimesis – to portray an emergent, but not yet consummated violence. Before Temple is raped with a corncob, an object imitating a phallus, she sees shadows threatening the symbolic locus of interior space in the Old Frenchman's Place: "The shadow of the stove fell upon the box where the child lay.... A thin whisper of shadow cupped its head and lay moist upon its brow" (66). Thus, shadows proliferate within the plantation house, falling upon the medium in which Ruby's baby lies and even invading within to caress the child. Nor do Temple's fears belong to her alone. Benbow later affirms her apprehension that some mimetic force threatens to appropriate all interior spaces. He similarly thinks "of the first time he had seen [the baby], lying in a wooden box ... of Popeye's black presence lying upon the house like the shadow of something no larger than a match falling monstrous and portentous" (120–1). Benbow's stream of consciousness thereby parallels Temple's cognitive experience and reinstates the threat as one staged upon the edifice of sanctuary and, as becomes undeniable in Temple's rape and subsequent transformation, upon the possibility of an inner architecture.

In the plantation house, this mimetic paradigm threatens the inhabitants and simultaneously unsettles the intricate web of hierarchal differences that protect the young Temple. Indeed, the young woman projects her own danger onto the baby and implicit in this transference are her assumptions about the nature of power and the hierarchy of distinctions they maintain:

> Crouching she drew the box out and drew it before her. Her hand touched the child's face, then she flung her arms around the box, clutching it, staring across it at the pale door and trying to pray. But she could not think of a single designation for the heavenly father, so she began to say "My father's a judge; my father's a judge" over and over. (51–2)

With this threat to interior spaces, Temple's ability to maintain an intricate hierarchy of value is thrown into profound confusion. She loses the ability to identify a transcendent godhead and attempts to console herself with a powerful substitute, her father the judge. The imitative acts of violence at the plantation entail, therefore, the dismantling of Temple's interior being and the mores that protect it. But it is not simply Temple succumbing to violence, societal order falling victim to chaos, that occupies Faulkner in the novel; the author is attempting to visualize a whole social order from its institutions to its precarious criminal under-belly as an interdependent and dynamical system. What appears initially as violent chaos and disorder spreads and self-organizes, so that the whole interconnected system of networks, clusters, and nodes begins to reflect this one event of invasive rape.

With Temple, Faulkner individualizes the mimetic processes by which this one behavioral paradigm begins to replicate. Indeed, he minutely depicts the stages of Temple's transformation, emphasizing, above all, the process by which Temple's inner self is overwhelmed through the flow of a hyper-mimetic information pattern through surfaces and into the self. In this respect, Temple's rape is not an isolated event, for the novel gradually reveals how one individual pattern of behavior passes into one being and, from there, reverberates through the entire social body. Even the central violation of the novel – the rape of Temple with a corncob – unfolds as a grotesque, but supplemental act. Importantly, the cob itself is another mimetic displace-ment. As John T. Matthews (1984) insightfully argues, the cob is a phallic "substitution" that covers over the elliptic absence at the heart of the narrative (260). Nor does Faulkner directly describe the violence of this pivotal scene. Rather, he characterizes the event as a growing void that swallows up everything around it: "'Something is happening to me!' ... 'I told you it was!' [Temple] screamed, voiding the words like hot silent bubbles into the bright silence about them" (102). Temple's expression is already "voided," becoming a series of evanescent "bubbles" and assuming the character of all the effacements we will shortly see: irreparably empty and polluted.

Once the rape occurs, Faulkner depicts the triumph of mimesis in direct proportion to the loss of the victim's sense of interiority. Portraying Temple after the rape, Faulkner suggests an ominous connection between Temple and Ruby's baby: "[Ruby] stood beside the road, carrying the child, the hem of her dress folded back over its face" (137). As Popeye and Temple speed by, Temple notices that Ruby has folded her dress over the baby's face. Because Temple has connected herself with the internal positioning of the baby in the box, its concealment provokes a dilemma that immediately begins to grow in intensity and scope. Faulkner's description of the May morning underscores the growing divide between that lost interiority and a mimetic pattern now assuming dominance: "It was a bright, soft day, a wanton morning filled with that unbelievable soft radiance of May, rife with promise of noon and of heat, with high fat clouds like gobs of whipped cream floating lightly as reflections in a mirror, their shadows scudding sedately across the road" (137–8). The May morning paradoxically evokes blooming sexuality that is "wanton," "rife," and "filled with promise," but these associations are quickly overpowered by mimetic "reflections in a mirror" and "shadows" on the road.

In chapter 18, Faulkner explicitly depicts the ongoing conflict between Popeye and Temple as a mimetic effacement of interior space. Temple desperately searches for some kind of referent to express the violation of her body. Yet she is in shock, unable to process the rape so that "the hot minute seeping of her blood" at first elicits only the "dull" repetition of "I'm still bleeding" (137). Temple nonetheless resists, using her mouth to voice the violated interiority of her body. Her "mouth round and open like a small empty cave" powerfully denotes the vestiges of interiority, which are, as much now as during the rape, under attack. Popeye reacts definitively to Temple's "mouth round and open," brutally effacing this new sign of interiority with the mimetic externality of the mirror: "Then he gripped her by the back of the neck and she sat motionless, her mouth round and open like a small empty cave. He shook her head. 'Shut it,' he said, 'shut it;' gripping her silent. 'Look at yourself. Here.' With the other hand he swung the mirror on the windshield around and she looked at her reflection" (138–9). Faulkner replays this conflict between Temple and Popeye again, one side exposing the interiority of the mouth and the other effacing it with the mirror:

> Again, the bitten sandwich in her hand, she ceased chewing and opened her mouth in that round, hopeless expression of a child; again his hand left the wheel and gripped the back of her neck and she sat motionless, gazing

straight at him, her mouth open and the half chewed mass of bread and meat lying upon her tongue" (141–2).

Temple's open-mouthed gesture frequently emerges, and Popeye counters it, his weapon that of the mirror. This evocative image takes on special significance in the context of Faulkner's cognitive cartographies in which, as we have seen, mimetic surfaces exert a quasi-agency upon the beings that are trapped within textual space, flattening them into inscriptions and robbing them of their inner depth. Popeye continues to use this mimetic implement until Temple's mouth loses the ability to voice its experience and expresses instead a type of contamination with "the half chewed mass of bread and meat upon her tongue."

Where Temple's mouth denotes the abject site of Popeye's transgression, with her imprisonment in the brothel, Temple hears this pollution voiced everywhere, issued forth from the very breathing of her new jailors. She hears her door being guarded by two dogs that climb "into Miss Reba's lap with wheezy, flatulent sounds, billowing into the rich pneumasis of her breast" (143). As Miss Reba's diseased breath mingles with the "wheezy, flatulent sounds" of her dogs, Temple loses "the secret whisper of her blood" in "a hundred conflicting sounds" (148). The previous struggle between Popeye and Temple is effectively over. Temple's inability to listen to the "secret whisper of her blood" is accompanied by a complete loss of perspective. Popeye's repeated use of the mirror appears again in this new setting as a definitive mimetic mediation: "In a dim mirror, a pellucid oblong of dusk set on end, she had a glimpse of herself like a thin ghost" (148). Temple's intuitive relationship with her own body has been jeopardized and, with this loss, her epistemological dependence on the mirror is complete. She is "a shadow moving in the uttermost profundity of shadow" – a mimetic shape in the final stages of losing any animating feature. Faulkner portrays this dismantling process as the triumph of mimesis over interiority. As Temple loses connection to her secret blood, the violent authority of the mirror assumes control. Even the doctor who arrives in the brothel to monitor Temple's bleeding becomes its proxy. Reaching "down her body, below her thighs," he assumes control over her secret blood. The mirror of the previous scene reappears in the image of the doctor's glasses that reveal no immanent depth, only cold mechanical processes which are now internalized "behind" and within: "Behind the glasses his eyes looked like little bicycle wheels at dizzy speed; a metallic hazel" (150). As the mirror had reduced Temple to a mimetic shadow, now the doctor's glasses permit her to peer into another person to see a completely dehumanized and mechanical interiority.

Oppressed by a host of mimetic media (mirrors, photographs, and glasses), Temple is finally overwhelmed by the reflective power of a broken clock. As with all its previous incarnations, the clock's glass face reveals an effaced interiority: "The glass face, become mirror-like, appeared to hold all reluctant light, holding in its tranquil depths a quiet gesture of moribund time, one-armed like a veteran from the wars" (150). The clock is a grand elaboration of all the reflections and mediations thus far: its glass face is "mirror-like," it entraps light and, at its heart, the hands do not move, but remain unalterably in place to signal 10:30. The very center of the mechanical apparatus thus parodies an indwelling spiritual power: instead of an indwelling agency, however, a one-armed disfigurement occupies this center of relations.

René Girard (1979) is helpful for understanding Faulkner's text here, since he clarifies how violence achieves metaphysical status in the minds of victims. Religion, he writes, "protects man from his own violence by taking it out of his hands, transforming it into a transcendent and ever-present danger to be kept in check by the appropriate rites" (134). Hypermimetic expressions particularly imperil these cultural rituals, so that such rites no longer work. Among all the differences that break down, one "that tends to disappear in the course of tragedy is the seemingly indelible distinction between man and god" (134). In *Sanctuary*, violence emerges in human acts, but seems too pervasive to be merely human. Faulkner's expression of this crisis takes a very particular form: he depicts the process by which violence successively effaces every guardian of sanctuary until it has completely appropriated the immanent architecture of the victim. The tragedy of *Sanctuary* can be located not only in Temple's physical violation, but also in her gradual acceptance of the mimetic authority of the mirror, which assumes absolute preeminence and becomes a vertex to which she must submit herself. "Half past ten oclock," Temple thinks repeatedly – and, with this, the mimetic flow is triumphant both in transgressing the seeming intractable boundaries of social class and appropriating the cognitive interiority of the victim.

With the immobile "veteran from the wars" *within* the clock, Faulkner signals the supremacy of a violent pattern both to mediate and overwrite identity. Temple can no longer identify Popeye's violation of her, for the mystifying face of the clock – godlike in its precedence and ubiquity – dominates her consciousness:

> She watched the final light condense into the clock face, and the dial change
> from a round orifice in the darkness to a disc suspended in nothingness, the
> original chaos, and change in turn to a crystal ball holding in its still and
> cryptic depths the ordered chaos of the intricate and shadowy world upon
> whose scarred flanks the old wounds whirl onward at dizzy speed into
> darkness lurking with new disasters. (151)

Temple sees a "final saffron-colored light" "consumed" by shadow. This
final victory of mimesis over light is accompanied by the replacement of
her previous gesture, the round and open mouth, by another "round
orifice in the darkness." This new orifice effaces all distinctions to become
the "original chaos," a crystal ball containing in its depths a grand apotheosis of externality, a shadowy world known only through scarred inscriptions seeking to write "the old wounds" again. Temple thus sees what Darl
saw on the "flat surface" of the river when he is subsumed into the water's
"myriad original motion" (67). Temple succumbs not simply to the
brutality of one man, but to "the original chaos" that occupies the "cryptic
depths" of the self but which, in this case, is located outside the self. The
seemingly indelible distinction between man and god thereby collapses
completely and, like Darl in *As I Lay Dying*, Temple confuses the mimetic
surface for the original wellsprings of being and, in the process, gives up
her very being to a coercive ideology from without.

3.4   A Sourceless Self amid the Social Body

Sanctuary experimentally develops the cognitive cartographies of previous
novels to visualize how information flow occurs in complex social systems
that possess various and varying paradigms of power. Mystification plays a
vital role in this process of rapid circulation, for it is not simply human
beings transmitting information, but also surfaces and objects that aid in
its circulation. As before, such information objects must be imbued with
metaphysical power in the minds of those who perceive them.
In *Sanctuary*, this confusion is the reason that information flows so freely
into individuals who mimic and adapt patterns of behavior they might not
otherwise adopt, even those that jeopardize the inner life, as is so clearly
the case with Temple Drake and Horace Benbow. *Sanctuary* draws lines of
connection, moreover, between individuals that exceed the personal, interpersonal or familial; the various social networks that interact in the novel,
sometimes in the most peripheral manner, are drawn together through the
mimetic modalities within the self, but the speed at which these networks

interact is clearly a modern phenomenon that the novel registers in terms of visual culture and virality. Faulkner's experimentation points to a disquieting realization about modernity itself: The mimetic modalities that bind us together can be hijacked by pathological – and potentially totalitarian – behavior, so that one tragic act ripples through the greater social body and transforms it permanently. Temple's rape is the horror at the center of the novel certainly, but Faulkner is not so much interested in the act itself as upon the effect that it has upon the victim who does more than simply mirror the act; the victim opposes and transforms the information before passing it on, as we will see. Writ large, one event manifests at scale, disseminating its information and transforming into a collective paradigm enacted by the greater social body.

Sanctuary thus imagines social hyper-connectivity as a threat and the immanent wellsprings of the individual – those idealist and Romantic sources of the self – as the sites most threatened. As Temple is gradually overcome, the very idea of sanctuary, that indwelling domain within the self, loses its viability, but it does not disappear completely. Instead, a new form of authority assumes its place, rewriting the self through underlying mimetic mechanisms that allow for personhood in the first place. Temple's later conversation with Benbow at the brothel shows how thoroughly she has internalized a pattern of mimetic superscription. Temple tells him of her experience sleeping on the mattress of corn shucks. "Whenever I breathed I'd hear those shucks" (216), she says, tying her own pattern of respiration to the external coverings of the corncob used to violate her. As breathing became a sign of pollution in the brothel, Temple relates the interiority of breath to a phallic and mimetic effacement:

> That's because breathing goes down. You think it goes up, but it doesn't. It goes down on you, and I'd hear them getting drunk on the porch. I got to thinking I could see where their heads were leaning back against the wall and I'd say Now this one's drinking out of the jug. Now that one's drinking. Like the mashed-in place on the pillow after you got up, you know. (216)

As we saw, in the novel's opening scene, Popeye is the first character to be associated with this type of violent superscription. Popeye's features paradoxically possess no depth; he is simply a vicious metallic text, at once stamped but revealing no trace of how this impression came to be (5). Temple now desires to participate in this violent writing, to "fasten [herself] up" with an "iron belt" that has "long sharp spikes on it": "I'd jab it all the way through him and I'd think about the blood running on me" (217–18).

Here again, René Girard's notion of mimetic desire is instructive, for the participation of the victim escalates the mimetic rivalry. Indeed, the "victim of this violence," Girard argues, "strives to master it by means of a mimetic counterviolence" (1979: 148). Temple's descriptions of her rape follow this logic, for she now recalls the experience as a violent reversal in which her plundered insides are fastened up to take on the proportions of phallic instrumentality: "Then I thought about being a man, and as soon as I thought it, it happened. It made a kind of plopping sound, like blowing a little rubber tube wrong-side outward. It felt cold, like the inside of your mouth when you hold it open" (S 220). As before, the interiority of the mouth serves as a symbolic touchstone. Although the rape goes unmentioned, she relates a moment of penetration that unhinges the precarious relationship between inner and outer. Like her previous confusion regarding breath going down, "blowing a little rubber tube wrong-side outward" is an act that unsettles the fragile thresholds upon which a self is founded and maintained across time.

In accepting Popeye's violence as a supernatural force, Temple has been written over, remade into a new being. When Horace first sees her in the brothel, her once exposed and rounded mouth is "painted into a savage cupid bow" (214), an image that at once emphasizes superscription and foreshadows her aggressive sexuality. In her later encounter with Red, "she sprang like a bow, hurling herself upon him, her mouth gaped and ugly like that of dying fish as she writhed her loins against him" (238). Temple's mouth, that one-time symbol of interior protest, has become an effaced object identified in terms of protrusion, not depth: Red "dragged his face free by main strength. With her hips grinding against him, her mouth gaping in straining protrusion" (238). In these scenes, Temple begins to master Popeye by appropriating his violence. In the dancehall, her frustrated desire at Popeye's impotence is channeled into her aggressive pursuit of Red. Her desire to replace Popeye is a powerful counterviolence which, according to the stipulations of mimetic desire, "assert[s] mastery over the model" so that his "prestige vanishes." If this is so, Girard observes, the model "must then turn to an even greater violence and seek out an obstacle that promises to be truly insurmountable" (1979: 148).[12] Once a sexual proxy for Popeye, Red has become a dangerous player in an escalating rivalry between model and victim. In order to regain the power he once possessed, Popeye must therefore kill him.

By the time of the trial, this mapping of mimetic externality over interiority resonates with a well-established symbolic power: Temple's "face was quite pale, the two spots of rouge like paper discs pasted on her cheek bones, her mouth painted into a savage and perfect bow, also like something symbolical and cryptic cut carefully from purple paper and pasted there" (284). In effect, Temple's face has been plastered over with papier-mâché. True to her adopted identity, Temple will protect the memory of her violation because she herself has participated in the blind machinations of mimetic desire. Temple is not the only subject overwritten, moreover. *Sanctuary* presents the process by which the flow of a coercive information pattern is deified by those who adopt it – a dilemma at once staged upon the immanent wellspring of an individual self while uniting and implicating all the characters of the social body at large.

While critics have commented on the psychological implications of the mirror-like relationship between Temple and Benbow, this symbolic code of mimetic superscription and violated interiority illuminates Benbow's voyeurism as an expression of hyper-mimetic information flow through the greater social body. Eric Sundquist (1985) observes that "the voyeuristic shock" of the characters properly "belongs to the reader" (55), and indeed Benbow serves as the reader's proxy, part of an apparatus of vision that is already subject to the machinations of a coercive information object. As Temple's violation visually culminated in the elevation of mimetic surfaces, Benbow's apprehension of his stepdaughter's photograph similarly engages a mimetic surface and confronts a supernatural agency that appears from "beneath" the flattened dimensions of "dead cardboard":

> As of its own accord the photograph had shifted, slipping a little from its precarious balancing against the book. The image blurred into the highlight, like something familiar seen beneath disturbed though clear water; he looked at the familiar image with a kind of quiet horror and despair, at a face suddenly older in sin than he would ever be, a face more blurred than sweet, at eyes more secret than soft. In reaching for it, he knocked it flat; whereupon once more the face mused tenderly behind the rigid travesty of the painted mouth, contemplating something beyond his shoulder. (167)

Is it Benbow or the photograph that moves? Is there something within the photograph or is this effect the result of the "image blurred into the highlight" above it? Faulkner evokes both possibilities, while underscoring the entanglement of textuality with an already contaminated interiority. Benbow's vomit emerges, in this context, as a tragic reinstatement of pollution. Greg Forter (2015) provides a convincing psychoanalysis of how the "vomit aims in fact to repudiate an 'unassimilated' set of desires that [Benbow] has already internalized" (100). I offer an alternative analysis of vomit as the ultimate indication of interior violation.

As with the original chaos in the glass face of the clock, the photograph achieves a metaphysical power in the mind of the perceiver. Indeed, the face of the photograph is "suddenly older in sin than [Benbow] would ever be," forming a surface that seemingly predates all other relations and disseminates itself through similitude. Accordingly, the "rigid travesty" of Little Belle's "painted mouth" mirrors the effacement of Temple's mouth, a pattern mapped not only onto Benbow in the figure of vomit, but also onto every young woman he sees: "the same identical paint on their mouths" (172). Consequently, Benbow participates in an intersubjective dilemma, the mouth repeatedly emerging as a protest soon to be silenced and overwritten: "He followed them into the day coach filled with snoring, with bodies sprawled half into the aisle as though in aftermath of a sudden and violent destruction, with dropped heads, open-mouthed, their throats turned profoundly upward as though waiting the stroke of knifes" (168). Echoes of Temple's rebellion against Popeye are present: The passengers lie "open-mouthed," awaiting what seems to be certain execution.

In a modernist text like *Sanctuary*, the hyper-mimetic flow of information gradually overwhelms all the major characters. Temple, Benbow, Popeye and others – each repeat this pattern not because the crisis is "beneath" or "beyond." Faulkner's ingenuity lies in showing how individual acts express themselves as a dynamic and ever-changing circulation of a culture unmoored from any sure foundation. This dislocating circulation is, indeed, already underway at the very opening of the novel. If we return to the scene in question, we find that the physical setting denotes a mimetic predicament made manifest through vision. From "beyond the screen of bushes," Popeye initially watches Benbow "kneel to drink from the spring" in a space in and around which "broken sunlight [lies] sourceless" (3). Here, Faulkner establishes the symbolic structure we have seen so far, one in which traditional forms of identity are already effaced. Some act of violence has severed the light from its source and, by extension, mediated the possibility of immanent vision. Like all the surfaces we have seen, the reflective surface of the spring is already contaminated with Popeye spitting into its depths. Faulkner also foreshadows the clock that imprisons light and completely overwhelms Temple's sense of interior space (151). In this first scene, a bird sings, but Faulkner indicates that this expression seems "as though it were worked by a clock" (5). The bird, traditionally a symbol of the winged soul, thus only repeats a mechanized pattern already laid out, becoming simply another machinic proxy for the flow of information into new selves.

With Goodwin's lynching, Faulkner replays the problem of mimetic sourcelessness, leading, in turn, to the godlike ubiquity of violence. Here, the scapegoat cannot appease the crowd, which yearns for more killing (296). Instead of an individual act, the lynching visualizes violence at scale with a social body participating and creating out of Goodwin's very body a cognitive cartography. Corresponding to the round shape of Temple's mouth and of the clock face that secures preeminence over it, another image of circularity obtains haunting ascendency in this lynching scene. Goodwin becomes a mass of fire around which onlookers gather and, as the image of the circle suggests, he is neither the beginning nor the end of the pattern in question, simply a variable repetition of it, spreading even now to engulf the perpetrators: "From one side of the circle came the screams of the man about whom the coal oil can had exploded, but from the central mass of fire there came no sound at all" (296). Benbow hears a furious interiority that has paradoxically transcended sound screaming out of the center of the flames: "Horace couldn't hear them. He couldn't hear the man who had got burned screaming. He couldn't hear the fire, though it still swirled upward unabated, as though it were living upon itself, and soundless: a voice of fury like in a dream, roaring silently out of a peaceful void" (296). As the language moves to conditionality, complicating any sure telling of the event, the mystical authority of violence is ever more certain. In Goodwin's lynching, a voice of fury occupies the inner domain of the circle that has paradoxically become a peaceful void. Faulkner has repeatedly employed this image of the void, depicting it as an emergent phenomenon that follows in the wake of violation, jeopardizes any clear telling of the event, and thereby disarms the community to protect itself in future.

In conclusion, the novel's tragedy and brilliance undoubtedly lie in Faulkner's conception of a complex social system as a series of interaction networks linked together not just through interpersonal human contact, but by mass culture, the dissemination of information through networks of selves and textual surfaces. There is a consequence to imagining the rapid circulation of information in this way, for once the information pattern in question hits a point of cultural saturation, it may assert itself more freely. The lynching scene surely entails this tipping point. We no longer see a drawn-out process of enculturation in which information copies itself from surface to surface, as we did in the earlier chapters. Instead, Faulkner portrays a spontaneous mimetic mirroring that ripples through the social body as it collectively and violently asserts itself on Goodwin. In this,

Faulkner has fully developed a symbolic language for the mimetic mechanisms that allow individual interaction to scale into collective behavior. As we will see, *Light in August* and *Absalom, Absalom!* employ this symbolic paradigm with a much clearer social critique. Faulkner's ostensible distaste for *Sanctuary* as a "cheap idea" which was "deliberately conceived to make money," as he wrote in a 1932 introduction to the novel, may very well have been the novel's rather one-sided view of such hyper-mimetic behavior. In the novels to come, we begin to see how individuals may resist the hyper-mimetic flow of ideology through the self and social body.

CHAPTER 4

When Ideology Wavers

The world that Faulkner's characters create is a world that governs and instructs them. We have seen in detail how Faulkner visualizes his cognitive cartographies as a centripetal clustering of the social body that instantiates and circulates ideology. By ideology, I do not mean an explicit doctrine or belief, but a pattern of information that prompts specific modes of behavior in those who perceive it. This self-enforcing ideology, although invented, is not some fictional yoke or free-floating idea easily assumed or thrown off. On the contrary, as a social force, it is capable of hyper-mimetic dissemination across generations, replicating itself both into the fragile architecture of individual consciousness and, beyond that, into the collective behavior of the social body. Yet this abstract and pervasive cultural force is also by no means omnipotent. Operating without the bedrock of community – the sensuous, empathic interaction of human beings – this system, for Faulkner, can become weakened and obsolete as a result of its own abstraction and escalating incoherency. This chapter examines *Light in August* (1932) and *Absalom, Absalom!* (1936) as Faulkner's first novels to explore the weakening of a cognitive cartography. For the first time in the Yoknapatawpha fiction, these novels specifically address the racial ideology of the South as a key element of this incoherence and begin to consider the larger ramifications of institutionalizing insidious ideologies at the expense of human well-being.

Sections 4.1 and 4.2 explore the unsettling vision of modernity that Faulkner presents in *Light in August*. Readers have a much greater sense of a South in a state of profound change with the rural, agricultural foundations of the culture upended by rapid industrialization, which in turn jeopardizes and imperils the human ability to build and maintain community. The novel also presents a range of responses to these technological changes as characters simultaneously pursue well-being and attempt to evade ideological invasion. The two characters of Lena Grove and Joe Christmas present the poles of this spectrum. Like Dilsey and Miss

Quentin before her, Lena Grove exemplifies the capacity to live fruitfully within the complex assemblages of modernity. Yet the novel is centrally dedicated to the tragedy of Joe Christmas, emphasizing particularly the insidious racial ideology that Christmas both resists and performs. This ideology, Faulkner indicates, can form a powerful and centralized vertex of cognitive and social space, but it is ultimately a destructive force within the South's social order.

The second half of this chapter examines how *Absalom, Absalom!* develops the meditation on racism as ideology that was implicit in *Light in August*. The novel is no longer about the manner in which ideology secures cultural primacy. Certainly, Faulkner figures the power of the planter ideology in the initial success of Thomas Sutpen. Yet the novel is also the first Yoknapatawpha fiction to depict this ideological system as increasingly unstable and incoherent. Whereas the author initially attempted to understand how information continuously flows through a networked system as culture, *Absalom, Absalom!* depicts entropic states capable of undermining and destroying the social order. These entropic states, though perilous to the well-being of many, are not simply to be feared. As ideological surfaces waver in their ability to disseminate cultural directives, there emerges the potential for reorganization and renewal, trajectories of novelty and behavior that gesture beyond the seemingly intractable bounds of social space and the self-reflexive epistemology of textual space that reinforces them.

4.1 From Light to Enclosure

In *The Sound and the Fury*, the redemptive paradigm of free movement was subtly embedded within the much more predominant tyranny of coercive cognitive cartographies. In *Light in August*, by contrast, Faulkner immediately affirms this paradigm in the character and cognitive interiority of Lena Grove. In much the same way as Faulkner's portrayal of Dilsey frames the fourth section and provides a new paradigm for autonomous behavior, Lena offers a spatiotemporal way of thinking that resists the tyranny of textual space and bookends the larger narrative arc of *Light in August*. Like Dilsey, however, Lena has frequently been relegated to the status of well-meaning simpleton. Cleanth Brooks (1969) puts it somewhat mildly when he calls Lena a "very simple young woman" (65). Irving Howe is more pointed when writing that Lena exhibits "a low level of intelligence," echoed, in turn, by Donald Kartiganer (1988) who states that Lena is "barely conscious at all" (32). Carolyn Porter (2007) is more charitable in calling Lena "young and uncomplex" (87), simultaneously affirming her as a vital source of movement in the context of Henri Bergson's influence on Faulkner's artistic development.

In 1957, Darrel Abel was the first scholar to interpret Faulkner in a Bergsonian light and, since that time, a number of scholars have explored the way in which two forms of temporality operate in Faulkner's prose: what can be called pure time, intuitively grasped and flowing indivisibly; and mathematical time, as perceived through intellection, broken up into units of seconds, minutes and hours.[1] Carolyn Porter (1975) analyzes the tension between these two notions of time in the opening of *Light in August*, noting particularly Faulkner's employment of the quintessential Bergsonian metaphor of the string (108). Thus, in one of the novel's opening scenes, Lena, as the positive proponent of Bergsonian "lived time," envisions the motion of the wagon coming toward her as "a shabby bead upon the mild red string of road," an imagery that is reinforced with the road as an "already measured thread being rewound onto a spool" (LIA 8).

What makes Lena's way of thinking a viable alternative to the tyranny of textual space is not just her ability to think and act in terms of Bergsonian duration, but also her capacity for *theory of mind*, to act through empathetic relation to others – the cornerstone of self-becoming, as we saw in Chapter 3, in the most auspicious moments of Darl's early maturation. In the limited pages devoted to her, Faulkner emphasizes Lena's intuitive awareness of, and openness to, other minds in her preference for walking by foot rather than riding by wagon. She is not interested, as her brother believes, in the convenience of the "smooth streets" and "sidewalks" of modern towns; instead, she walks through the towns "because she believed that the people who saw her and whom she passed on foot would believe that she lived in the town too" (3). Her intellectual dexterity entails attempting to perceive through others and prepares for her ability to think outside of the delineations of textual space and to affirm the sensuous immediacy of space and time as the arena in which human relation is made possible. Indeed, Lena's cognitive interiority offers a key medium for resistance and alterity within networks dominated – as we will shortly see – by an instrumental and industrial modernity that upends a traditional agrarian way of life and replaces it with alienation and rootlessness.

Lena's conception of her own movement is therefore distinctive in the Yoknapatawpha fiction. She, like so many other Southerners at the time, is engaged in diaspora, unsettled by the rapidly changing conditions of Southern life in the Depression Era, both the precarity of agrarian life and the proliferation of industrialization. Yet she is not absolutely determined by these conditions, exhibiting an intuitive understanding of the places in which she moves and of the people whom she meets. Faulkner articulates this duality in terms of textuality, for Lena faces the dilemma we have seen before: the self enfolded into textual space without the capacity to think outside it. In the opening chapter, Faulkner interweaves her movement with textual time by mimetically compressing four weeks of her movement from town to town in the metafictional image of the "urn":

> backrolling now behind her a long monotonous succession of peaceful and undeviating changes from day to dark and dark to day again, through which she advanced in identical and anonymous and deliberate wagons as though through a succession of creakwheeled and limpeared avatars, like something moving forever and without progress across an urn. (7)

Here, Faulkner employs one of his principal techniques of temporally compressing movement into static representation. On one level, Lena as an indivisible agent is displaced, fragmented into a series of "avatars." She is thus a textual creation, an inscribed sequence set upon a two-dimensional surface that imprisons the living subject.[2] However, Lena is capable of conceiving of herself and others outside of the mediating tyranny of this textual frame and, by association, the larger social system which demarcates her movement and self-expression. We saw that Jewel also displayed this ability. Although he and his horse appear to Darl as "two figures carved for a tableau savage in the sun," they are able to overcome the dictates of the mimetic frame (AILD 4). With Lena, such an ability is explicit. In her search for the father of her unborn child, she is neither determined nor overwhelmed by the mimetic representation in which she is embedded.

Instead of remaining fixed upon a flat surface, Lena visualizes the road as a string and the successive wagons as beads and then imagines her motion through the sense perception of other selves. Unlike so many other characters who are trapped within their own subjective perspectives, she envisions "the mild red string of road" by looking in such a way that "the eye loses it as sight and sense drowsily merge and blend" (LIA 8). She abandons sight as the primary sense and imagines the perspective of the father of her child hearing her before she comes into his vision: "I will be riding within the hearing of Lucas Burch before his seeing. He will hear the wagon, but he wont know. So there will be one within his hearing before his seeing. And then he will see me and he will be excited. And so there will be two within his seeing before his remembering" (8). She

exhibits a powerful ability to imagine selves interacting in time and space –
and while she is wrong about the good intentions of Lucas Burch, she
nonetheless anticipates a father for her child, Byron Bunch, who in turn
desires to escape the industrial trap of lumber extraction in which he
labors. Thus, Lena's attempts to see into the mind of others are predicated
not upon naiveté; rather, they demonstrate a rich cognitive life that entails
free movement in social space – the kind that we saw embedded in Dilsey's
care for others, realized in Quentin's escape from confinement, and
nascent in Luster's desire for novelty. Lena thereby possesses a creative
power to move among the institutions of modernity, both the industrial
lumber culture and the plantation regime, and yet to imagine possibilities
of experience outside the dicta of those institutions.

Lena Grove develops the trajectories of free movement that we saw
intimated in the earlier novels – and she does so with a symbolic emphasis
on immanence and nature. Whereas light is refracted, broken, or sourceless
in so many of the cognitive cartographies we have analyzed so far, Lena is
the first of Faulkner's characters to offer the possibility of an unmediated
intuition that can revitalize the static inscriptions of textual space – those
"avatars ... moving forever and without progress across an urn" (7).
As Faulkner himself explained at the University of Virginia, the title of
the novel invokes "a luminosity older than our Christian civilization" and,
in the character of Lena, "an older light than ours" (Gillespie 1983: 39).
If we return to Miss Quentin's escape in *The Sound and the Fury*, the
branches of the pear tree hanging in through the window is a fitting image
for the immanent life pouring through the mediating thresholds of sense
and of culture. Lena expresses this type of imagery, as she is associated with
light, nature, and fertility – and when we first find her, she too utilizes the
open window as her primary trajectory of movement, first to see her lover
and finally to escape her brother's house.

Faulkner's Yoknapatawpha fiction indicates that the more dependent we
are upon cultural mediation, upon a proliferating series of textual surfaces,
the more abstract our epistemology becomes. And this mediated,
abstracted way of understanding has a destructive effect on our well-
being. [3] While Lena is able to find a father for her baby in Byron, the
other main characters of the novel are profoundly entangled in ideology
and succumb to it in ways that preclude the possibility of viable community, reflecting the plight of characters from earlier novels. *Light in August*
adopts a similar narrative structure to *Sanctuary*, portraying the New South
as a series of interaction networks that are connected to each other less
through interpersonal relations and more through commonalities of

ideology and culture. Here again, we find a technological acceleration where individuals temporarily cluster together in social space to produce more isolated and splintered centers of industrial textuality.

Lena's personal history reflects the shift from the rural farming life to a landscape dominated by industrialization and the economic precarity of the Depression Era. While she was born on a small farm, the novel begins with Lena in movement, in search of the father of her child and leaving Doane's Mill, a makeshift community that recently emerged and temporarily thrived as an industrial lumber hub before falling quickly into decay. In the first description of the now-defunct mill, Faulkner sets the stage for a cognitive cartography in which individuals collectively cluster in social space to serve institutions that simultaneously uproot them and break their former agrarian relationship with the landscape:

> All the men in the village worked in the mill or for it. It was cutting pine. It had been there seven years and in seven years more it would destroy all the timber within its reach. Then some of the machinery and most of the men who ran it and existed because of and for it would be loaded onto freight cars and moved away. But some of the machinery would be left . . . gaunt, staring, motionless wheels rising from mounds of brick rubble and ragged weeds with a quality profoundly astonishing, and gutted boilers lifting their rusting and unsmoking stacks with an air stubborn, baffled and bemused upon a stump-pocked scene of profound and peaceful desolation, unplowed, untilled, gutting slowly into red and choked ravines beneath the long quiet rains of autumn and the galloping fury of vernal equinoxes. (LIA 4)

While Doane's Mill may currently be a ghost town apart from the "five families" that remain there once "most of the men" are freighted away, the ideology that underlies this community nonetheless thrives, recreating itself wherever there are new resources to consume. Indeed, Byron Bunch, Joe Christmas, and Joe Brown – three of the novel's main characters – actively serve this ideology and, like Lena, they are rootless, without any definite connection to the land. Faulkner's depiction above underscores, moreover, the parasitical and assimilating power of this industrial ideology as it comes to possess the vertex of cognitive and social space. We saw how Darl projected this ideology upon the river, imagining its "ceaseless surface" rising and making everything about it "rootless, severed from the earth" in "immense, yet circumscribed desolation" (AILD 56). Here, Faulkner presents a very similar cognitive cartography of "desolation" as "machinery" marks the landscape with wheels jutting up out of the earth and "gutted boilers lifting their rusting and unsmoking stacks" into the sky.

In the opening of *Light in August*, Faulkner more fully develops the industrial modernity that he evoked in earlier novels. From the outset, the tyranny of textual space is contextualized in terms of a plantation economy intertwined with the ecologically unsound resource extraction of lumber, which bases itself, above all, upon ample low-cost labor. While the clock is an iconic image of modernity, as we saw in Chapter 2, lumber is rarely seen in this light. In his classic *Technics and Civilization* ([1934] 2010), Lewis Mumford argues that the "woodsman" is the prototype for the modern engineer, an agent of mechanization: "The rational conquest of the environment by means of machines is fundamentally the work of the woodsman" (77). The extraction of lumber is thus primary for technical development, "synonymous with power production and industrialization" (79). In Faulkner's oeuvre, this view takes regional specificity. While the political proponents of industrialization in the post-Reconstruction period promised economic independence, the reality was that the entire region was almost entirely dependent upon northern financiers (Cobb 2004: 11–12). With persistent stagnation in agricultural productivity, the industries that grew were funded in large part by northern money. Nowhere was this truer than in the lumber industry where huge tracts of public and private land were sold for a fraction of their value. In this context, the South experienced both explosive industrial growth and economic precarity on a level that far exceeded the rest of the nation.

During Reconstruction and beyond, Southerners "seemed to believe that region's timber resource was inexhaustible, and that the land beneath the forest was of minimal value." In fact, "much of the southern population felt the heavy stand of timber was actually a barrier to the spread of civilization" (Clark 1984: 14). As we saw in Chapter 1, private railroads were key to remapping resource flows, making Southern industry less dependent on waterways and, in turn, bolstering the extensive resource extraction that was already well underway. By the end of the nineteenth century, the central Mississippi pine belt was accessible like never before, and "all the southern railroads were lined with sawmill villages, which supplied both freight and passenger income. In fact, sawmills and planing mills were more prominent in this corridor of the South than were cotton gins, and they produced a far greater volume of heavy freight" (Clark 1984: 18).

In *Light in August*, Faulkner explicitly identifies the "material and conceptual conversion of forest into *polis*" (Watson 2019: 83), a conversion in which these industrial hubs dominate and supervene upon the people who erect and serve them. As with the other cognitive cartographies we have examined, these mills possess a strange form of quasi-agency imagined in terms of vertical height – with wheels "rising" from the ruins of the mill and boilers "lifting" their smokestacks above the landscape, establishing, in other words, spatial vertices of power and belief. Through Byron Bunch's narration, Faulkner soon introduces Joe Christmas and Joe Brown, but it is not simply their stories that Bunch narrates; in his conversation with Mooney, a foreman at the Jefferson planing mill, Bunch reveals the psychological effect these industrial hubs have on those who participate in them: "A man knew that he was just living on the country, like a locust. It was as though he had been doing it for so long now that all of him had become scattered and diffused and now there was nothing left but the transparent and weightless shell blown oblivious and without destination upon whatever wind" (LIA 38). Bunch is speaking about Joe Brown and implicitly about Joe Christmas, but the dilemma that he identifies is undeniably his own: to be rootless, living off the country like a locust imperils the interior architecture of the self, leaving only a "transparent and weightless shell" that has no substance or identification with the landscape.

In a past era, a pastor like Reverend Gail Hightower might provide Bunch and the community such an identification, but part of Hightower's function in the novel is that his religious epistemology has become so abstract and lifeless that it can no longer serve the community. Indeed, his very name, Hightower, indicates a vertex of cognitive and social space, but it is clear that this vertical principle has become lifeless, coupled as it is with dead surfaces throughout the novel. Byron perceives the minister, for instance, as "a forgotten flag above a ruined fortress" (363), and the townsfolk similarly provide a striking depiction: "They told Byron how he seemed to talk that way in the pulpit too, wild too in the pulpit, using religion as though it were a dream. Not a nightmare, but something which went faster than the words in the Book; a sort of cyclone that did not even need to touch the actual earth" (61). In the townspeople's imagination, Hightower's sermons articulate the visual symbolism of his name. Although his preaching is tied to the "Book," it is nonetheless envisioned as a "cyclone," an inward spiraling vortex of wind that has little relation to the earth below.

Hightower thus represents a dead epistemology, an abstraction without any tangible correspondence with the earth. For Porter (1975), Hightower "comes to us a static and drooping figure behind a window from which he rarely moves" (117). It is, I argue, precisely Hightower's perceptual stance behind the mediating threshold that circumscribes his ability to serve his community. He has effectively imprisoned himself in a lifeless epistemology of textual space. Thus, each evening, he ritualistically watches as the light fades outside his window – and again Faulkner depicts this in terms of the coupling of verticality and textual space with the light dying on the inscribed surface and amid the leaves outside Hightower's window. We thereby see the consequence of allowing a system of representation to lose contact with the immanent life within: "So the sign which he carpentered and lettered is even less to him than it is to the town; he is no longer conscious of it as a sign, a message. He does not remember it at all until he takes his place in the study window just before dusk" (LIA 60). Hightower nightly enacts the dying of the light structured absolutely by an epistemology of textual space: "He is waiting for that instant when all light has failed out of the sky and it would be night save for that faint light which daygranaried leaf and grass blade reluctant suspire, making still a little light on earth though the night itself has come" (60). The leaves of grass clearly serve as proxies of the signboard, retaining a little of the now-absent light, but without living meaning and purpose. In this context, readers can understand why Hightower warns Byron not to pursue Lena and only comes to acknowledge her life-bearing value when he delivers her baby.

With Hightower's ministry incapable of offering meaning to the community, the mechanistic ideology of industry appropriates the vertices of power and belief throughout the region. Thus, the novel's divergent, onion-skin-like narratives converge in examining the wellbeing of individuals who live in and serve the nascent assemblages of modernity, whether the lumber industry gradually gobbling up the natural landscape or a cityscape characterized by "sootbleakened" surfaces sheared of any natural associations. In the first paragraph of chapter 6, this dilemma takes on nightmarish proportions as Faulkner relates Joe Christmas' earliest memories of an orphanage in Memphis. Here, Faulkner echoes the earlier imagery of Doane's Mill, imagining a compound set among the looming smokestacks of factories whose very soot stains the windows and thereby obscures the children's perceptual relationship with the world beyond:

> Memory believes before knowing remembers. Believes longer than recollects, longer than knowing even wonders. Knows remembers believes a corridor in a big long garbled cold echoing building of dark red brick sootbleakened by more chimneys than its own, set in a grassless cinder-strewnpacked compound surrounded by smoking factory purlieus and enclosed by a ten foot steel-and-wire fence like a penitentiary or a zoo, where in random erratic surges, with sparrowlike childtrembling, orphans

in identical and uniform blue denim in and out of remembering but in knowing constant as the bleak walls, the bleak windows where in rain soot from the yearly adjacenting chimneys streaked like black tears. (119)

Much can be said about this now iconic passage. For our purposes, I highlight the elements that go into composing a cognitive cartography. In Joe Christmas' memory, we perceive a compound interlaying of imagery that Faulkner has previously employed. As with earlier cognitive cartographies, the adaptive, machinic delineations of modern culture are ascendant – with the children collectively inhabiting what is effectively a "grassless" compound devoid of natural associations. Yet the creative, immanent life (that element that is "before knowing" and "longer than knowing") remains, although it is made to serve this modern assemblage which entraps the children "like a penitentiary or a zoo," even while using them to disseminate its information.

Faulkner thereby presents a cognitive cartography in the midst of replicating itself both upon the landscape and in the minds of those bent to its service. In keeping with his signature technique of compressing histories of movement, behavior, and thinking into social space, Faulkner directs the spatial and cognitive trajectories of many lives through this edifice, which stamps upon each individual a depersonalized, industrial ideology. As before, bird imagery accentuates the way in which ideology can be mirrored and disseminated beyond the confines of an individual's immediate social relations. In this case, Faulkner strikingly interweaves the imagery of sparrows with the movement of the children as they come and go and evokes, as a result, a powerful duality between the cognitive architecture of the self and the physical delineations of social space. To be sure, the children are visualized as birds that fly "in random erratic surges" into and out of the compound. Although these movements may seem erratic or chaotic, they self-organize across time into an information flow that reifies this faceless industrial ideology within the individual so that this self will carry and recreate it.

Faulkner imagines this instantiation of ideology precisely in the manner I have laid out previously. The bird-like movement of children through the compound is simultaneously a motion "in and out of remembering," producing a feedback loop in which consciousness becomes subject to the absolute and definite delineations of textual space. Thus, the sentence ends with a sinister affirmation of ideological surfaces which mediate the individual's ability to think and know: "but in knowing constant as the bleak walls, the bleak windows where in rain soot from the yearly adjacenting chimneys streaked like black tears." While Faulkner offers a sentence of great complexity, evoking the movement of myriad lives through this vertex of cognitive and social space, the overarching sense of determination is all too definite, hinging, as we have seen so often before, on an epistemology of textual space. This epistemology may seem to offer an infinite series of authorships, as it recreates itself *ad infinitum*, but this is only an illusion of plurality. While everything else is in a state of flux, the sentence intractably concludes with the mediating thresholds of this institution, the "bleak walls" and "bleak windows," upon which an indelible pattern of information gradually coalesces to dominate and to control. In Faulkner's spatial imagination, the proliferating vertices of industrial modernity take the shape of smokestacks transmitting a textual pattern from their vertical position above the inhabitants of the compound – and what they transmit are preestablished patterns of movement, behavior, and thought. Here, moreover, Addie Bundren's nihilistic vision of a "dark voicelessness ... coming down" and "fumbling at the deeds like orphans" (71) takes new form. As we saw, her alienation is a response to the modernizing forces of the Southern landscape. In *Sanctuary*, Popeye similarly represents the trauma of this transition with a dislocating world of interlinking networks. *Light in August* takes this troubled vision of modernity to new artistic heights with industry supervening on the landscape, but providing no underlying sense of community or identification. For Addie, it is this dark voicelessness that makes orphans of us all and, in the figure of Joe Christmas, Faulkner locates this disorientating experience not only within a rapidly changing landscape, but also within the abstracted and totalitarian order of the color line of Jim Crow.

4.2   The Insidious Ideology of Race

Faulkner has greatly refined his cognitive cartographies with this regional depiction of the depersonalized industrial assemblages of modernity. Where, in *Flags in the Dust*, Colonel Sartoris placed his institutional "print" up high to preside over the lives to come, likewise, the factory system is visualized as "rising" and "lifting" into the sky to attain a preeminence of power and belief that administers itself through the proliferating surfaces of modern life. This industrial system has achieved a complexity in which it no longer relies solely on an individual network or the nodes within that network; indeed, the abandoned mill in the opening of the novel indicates that the system is already everywhere, consuming, transforming, and employing individuals in its ceaseless machinations. *The*

Sound and the Fury and *Sanctuary* depict mimetic surfaces as the key to controlling and manipulating the interior architecture of the self – and in *Light in August*, we find a very similar pattern in which an institution supervenes upon an individual through sheer scale, so much so that the individual cannot think outside its epistemology with its seemingly intractable mores of identity, race, and class.

Scholars have elucidated the manner in which Joe Christmas' dilemma unfolds, seeing it as a tragedy of metafiction or detailing the ways in which the protagonist psychologically internalizes the conventions of his culture. I argue, moreover, that Christmas' struggles and tragic lynching follow and develop the mimetic crisis we have identified in Faulkner's earlier cognitive cartographies, a dilemma in which an individual may resist, but possesses no other way of knowing than that administered by an institutional epistemology of textual space. But this is not just the consequence of any bureaucratic system buttressed by a scaling social and industrial order. For the first time, Faulkner concentrates on the abstract racial ideology of Jim Crow segregation, exploring how it demarcates social space and insidiously mediates an individual's very self-consciousness. Christmas' tragedy is not simply that of a man being overwhelmed by social forces; rather, we see a drawn-out process in which a specific racial ideology transforms a man against his own will into its bearer and replicator.

Christmas' character arc exemplifies, therefore, the mimetic dilemma that faced so many of Faulkner's earlier characters: The more an institutional epistemology asserts itself upon an individual, the less that individual can think beyond the terms of its mediation. Institutional power functions in terms of its textuality, codifying itself in and through mimetic surfaces. Immediately after describing the compound, Faulkner repeatedly characterizes Christmas as a shadow who lives within the corridors of this institution: "In the quiet and empty corridor, during the quiet hour of early afternoon, he was like a shadow, small even for five years, sober and quiet as a shadow" (LIA 119). The use of this mimetic Ur-symbol recurs frequently throughout Christmas' narrative arc, at once structuring his ambiguous identity in terms of racial duality and underscoring a metafictional dilemma similar to, and as insistent as, the ones with which Quentin, Darl, and Temple struggled.

Joanna Burden strikingly provides an explicit imagery of racial division with her use of shadow imagery, one infused by her religious abolitionist upbringing, but ultimately underscoring a metafictional dilemma of absolute enculturation. She passionately tells Joe that blacks are not so much a people "as a thing, a shadow in which I lived, we lived, all white people"

(252). She describes, "all the children coming forever and ever into the world, white, with the black shadow already falling upon them before they drew breath. And I seemed to see the black shadow in the shape of a cross" (253). In Joanna's imagination, the black shadow takes vertical precedence, exerting itself from above upon individuals before they first take breath. While her vision is shaped by her particular heritage as a northerner living in the South, she reinstates the symbolic logic of the factory soot falling from above to coalesce on the walls and windows of the orphanage. Joanna visualizes this in religious terms with the crimes against African Americans predetermining the future so that "all the little babies that would ever be in the world, the ones not yet even born" are already bound "on the black crosses" (253). Thus, to be bound to a shadow, to be inscribed within one way of knowing becomes the singular insistence not just of Joanna's oration, but of Joe's whole experience. And it is one linked not just to rural life or to the plantation culture or to the industrialization of the New South, but more pointedly to Jim Crow segregation, an ideology that absolutely dictates permissible movement and behavior for black Americans within all these Southern regimes.

This evocation of textual space – the self ceaselessly conflated with mimetic surfaces – thereby possesses both a racial and metafictional context. The depiction of Christmas' face as parchment suggests that the man is at once a product of miscegenation and a surface upon which someone else writes: "His face was gaunt, the flesh itself a level dead parchment color" (34); "his face calm and a little pale beneath the smooth parchment skin" (149). Like Quentin, Christmas seems almost aware of his own metafictional tragedy, a signifier half-conscious of being imprinted from without:

(1)   "He could see it like a printed sentence, fullborn and already dead" (105);
(2)   "He watched his body grow white out of the darkness like a kodak print emerging from the liquid" (107);
(3)   "It was just cold, implacable, like written or printed words" (149);
(4)   "It was not until later that thinking again flashed, complete, like a printed sentence" (270).

These four examples denote Christmas' cognitive reality as one dictated by an epistemology of textual space. Growing up first under the industrial towers of Memphis and then having to submit to McEachern's religious violence, he either sees or thinks in terms of textual space and, in each case, the mimetic surface is already written and in the process of univocally asserting itself. Whereas his black racial identity remains a narrative enigma, Joe and those about him accept it as the determining factor in his life. Like many of the characters we have seen before, Joe is tailored to think through an institutional paradigm to such an extent that, despite his outrage and resistance, he becomes simply a textual surface forced to endure an absolute ideological inscription and, even more tragically, to transmit this pattern onto others.

Faulkner develops this dilemma with the careful employment of the shadow motif throughout Christmas' character arc, reinforcing in turn the dynamic coupling of shadows and mimetic surfaces that we have seen in previous novels. While the instances are too numerous to recount in these pages, a few key sequences indicate the manner in which Faulkner develops this predicament. In our first sequence, Christmas is a youth living with his adoptive parents, the McEacherns. At night, he lowers himself by rope, "passing swift as a shadow across the window where the old people slept" (170). As he leaves the house and embarks out onto the lane, he walks between trees whose "shadowed branches lay thick and sharp as black paint upon the mild dust" (171). At the conclusion of the sequence, it seems to Christmas that "his mind [was] projected like a shadow on a wall" (172). Such a sequence prepares for two other key events in the novel. While readers do not witness Joe murder Joanna, we nonetheless see the buildup to the violent moment as one enacted upon a textual surface. When Joe refuses Joanna's command to kneel and pray with her, Faulkner depicts the outcome in mimetic terms: "But the shadow of [the revolver] and of her arm and hand on the wall did not waver at all, the shadow of both monstrous, the cocked hammer monstrous, back-hooked and viciously poised like the arched head of a snake." Here, Faulkner indicates that Joe pays attention not to Joanna, but to their shadows on the wall: "But he was not watching [her eyes]. He was watching the shadowed pistol on the wall; he was watching when the cocked shadow of the hammer flicked away" (282).

As with Temple's unrepresented rape, the murder of Joanna remains an ellipsis up to which Faulkner slowly builds, interlaying Joe's passive perception with a metafictional emphasis upon an already inscribed sequence of events. As we saw, Temple is similarly beset by a proliferation of mimetic surfaces that ultimately invades her cognitive and physical being. She attempts to articulate this vertiginous textual paradox as her rape unfolds, apprehending it as already inscribed. "'Something is happening to me!' . . . 'I told you it was!' she screamed, voiding the words like hot silent bubbles" (102). As Lisa Hinrichsen (2014) contends, there is a temporal shift from the present (is) to the past (was) that underscores Temple's "inability to place the trauma inside a continuous history – to put the crime within time – and an inability to witness it at the moment it happens" (162). Faulkner thus locates the novel's "central formal and thematic inquiry in the tension between acting and knowing – between ontology and epistemology" (162–3). This tension can also be understood as a metafictional one, so that the event only signifies through its representation.

Christmas himself repeatedly expresses the same phrase: "*Something is going to happening to me*" (LIA 104, 118). As with Temple, he is subject to a mimetic epistemology that circumscribes his being, effacing his interior cognitive architecture and forcing him to watch himself from without. After the murder of Joanna, this crisis grows in intensity and scope. Hailing a passing car, Joe gets into the vehicle, but he takes no notice of the couple's terror and apprehension. He perceives only the outlines of a text being inscribed by mechanical processes: "He saw only the two young, rigidly forwardlooking heads against the light glare, into which the ribbon of the road rushed swaying and fleeing" (284). Faulkner again overlays the event with textual imprintation as Joe prospectively perceives the couple's heads as the ribbon carrier of a typewriter against "the light glare" of the white page. This logic ceaselessly structures his perception, and Joe becomes effectively a vehicle for the transmission of meaning, one that he passively witnesses from without. Thus, at the end of the scene, when he exits the car, he suddenly realizes that he is holding a murder weapon: "Then he discovered that the object was attached to his right hand. Raising the hand, he found that it held the ancient heavy pistol" (286). With Joe passively witnessing the gun attached to his hand with a type of amazement, readers may even suspect that Joe is innocent of the crime. As Randall Wilhelm (2011) shows through close textual analysis, Faulkner never confirms whether Christmas is the killer. Although the sense of predetermination is so strong in the novel, we, the readers, are the ones who fill in this most important of narrative details.

In this context, Joe's lynching provides a powerful crescendo to his narrative arc, closely echoing the crises we have analyzed in earlier novels. In a truly sinister manner, Joe becomes a hyper-mimetic pattern of information that threatens to replicate itself everywhere. His very person, therefore, becomes the site of a cognitive cartography so coercive that it ultimately attains vertical preeminence, escaping its own mediation to duplicate itself in others:

> He just lay there, with his eyes open and empty of everything save consciousness, and with something, a shadow, about his mouth. For a long moment he looked up at them with peaceful and unfathomable and unbearable eyes. Then his face, body, all, seemed to collapse, to fall in upon itself, and from out the slashed garments about his hips and loins the pent black blood seemed to rush like a released breath. It seems to rush out of his pale body like the rush of sparks from a rising rocket; upon that black blast the man seemed to rise soaring into their memories forever and ever. They are not to lose it, in whatever peaceful valleys, beside whatever placid and reassuring streams of old age, in the mirroring faces of whatever children they will contemplate old disasters and newer hopes. (LIA 464–5)

Critics have minutely articulated the totalitarian ethos of the murder – with Percy Grimm's ability to combine racist propaganda and violence to stir the mob to action. Here, we additionally see the spatial forming of a cognitive cartography. The immanent architecture of the self is once again the stage upon which a coercive ideological violence operates to achieve vertical dominion not just in the present, but in the future as well. Like Temple whose mouth offers a striking symbol of interiority at once dismantled and appropriated, Joe lies with his mouth open and a shadow hovering above it. As with Temple moreover, this mimetic image invades the depths of the self and transforms the unwilling victim into a pattern of information that attains the vertex of cognitive space, rushing out of Joe's body "to rise soaring into the [lynchers'] memories forever."

The frightening consequence of this event is the prospect that this pattern of information will continue to structure the cognitive lives not only of those who participated in the lynching, but also of the next generation whose "mirroring faces" become receptive surfaces. Again, the whole violent cartography unfolds according to a textual epistemology that empathizes vertical height and reflectivity. To be sure, the natural moorings of the self are replaced with the mechanistic logic of "a rising rocket," and thus the mimetic shadow which should be simply an imitation of the human form becomes instead a vertex capable of reduplicating itself without impediment. We saw this in the first two chapters with statues asserting themselves into the consciousnesses of those below. Though the process is greatly refined in *Light in August*, the imagistic logic is the same, for this mechanical mimesis soars into the memories of the witnesses, visualized both as a "blast" upward and a dissemination downward into "peaceful valleys" whose "reassuring streams" immediately become "mirroring faces." The mimetic shadow thereby dominates, invading the self to replicate itself "serene" and "triumphant" through the reflective relationships that link together and, therefore, structure the greater social body.

Faulkner reinforces this imagery of ideological transmission with a double emphasis we have unpacked earlier. As this mimetic violence seemingly transforms into pure information, it simultaneously becomes "serene" and not "particularly threatful." We recall that the proliferating surfaces of the Sartoris plantation house exhibited such a sinister tranquility, for they "dreamed quiet and empty of threat ... yet beneath this solitude and permeating it was that nameless and waiting portent, patient and brooding and sinister" (FD 16). Darl also apprehends the "peaceful" surface of the river "like machinery ... after you have watched it and listened to it for a long time" (67). Temple's relationship with the "glass face" of the clock likewise possesses an avowal of "tranquil depths" (150) which presets the conclusion of the novel when the young woman looks from her "compact mirror" to the semicircle in which the "dead tranquil queens in stained marble mused" (316–7). In *Light in August*, the imagistic insistence is similar: "It will be there, musing, quiet, steadfast, not fading and not particularly threatful, but of itself alone serene, of itself alone triumphant." Though it has become "tranquil" in this transformation into pure information, the abstract ideology that replicates itself is aggressively coercive, for it is already implicit in the regimes of Southern life, a legacy of chattel slavery reformulated as Jim Crow segregation which continues to shape both the social reality and cognitive interiority of Southerners, black and white. Thus, this "musing" and "tranquil" pattern of information simultaneously possesses a new power that exploits the self-reflexive structure that underpins it. Faulkner suggests as much with the conclusion of the scene as the "scream of siren" reiterates the actions of the lynching to crescendo and fades: "Again from the town, deadened a little by the walls, the scream of the siren mounted toward its unbelievable crescendo, passing out of the realm of hearing" (465). Faulkner has used this symbolic technique before, as we saw earlier this chapter, with a mirroring paradigm typically employing birds and cars. While the sound may no longer be heard by Grimm and his mob, the siren nonetheless persists, passing on spatially and cognitively, a proxy for a hyper-mimetic pattern of information transmitting itself more readily, freed from the flesh of one individual to assume the ethereal quality of sound itself.

4.3   The Tyranny of Textual Space

Unlike his earlier novels, *Absalom, Absalom!* explores the dynamic that is produced when a cognitive cartography begins to waver, disrupted by an emergent entropy that upends its centrality and epistemology. This is a significant step in the author's development. The only challenge to

ideologically saturated systems that we have seen so far were isolated
examples of individual agency and spontaneous movement. Here, by
contrast, Faulkner is meditating on the entropy produced when these
institutional assemblages fail on a large scale and, with them, the systems
of representation that uphold them. These final two sections (4.3 and 4.4)
explore, therefore, Thomas Sutpen not as a man, but as a coercive ideology
replicating itself through an epistemology of textual space. As forceful as
this plantation ideology initially appears, Faulkner also identifies the
internal contradictions that erode its power and hold over those who
engender it. Though he situates the weakening of this ideological paradigm
during the Civil War, he also suggests that it is not war alone that is
responsible. Rather, we see how regimes of power fail from within – with a
network of individuals increasingly unable to relate to each other, so
mediated are they by the ideological and racial abstractions of the plantation system. Importantly, Faulkner imagines the ensuing entropy in terms
of an express disenchantment with textual signification. It is not simply
existential angst that the characters articulate, but a disillusionment with
the textual epistemology of the plantation system as it enters into a period
of chaos and reformation.

   In *Absalom, Absalom!*, Faulkner significantly reconsiders the role of the
patriarch in the figure of Sutpen, depicting not ingenuity as he did with
Colonel Sartoris, but the manner in which individuals faithfully reproduce
culture.[4] To be sure, this man is no artist. As we gradually learn, his
plantation was erected in order to solve a very basic problem that entails his
autonomous movement in social space. According to Grandfather
Compson, Sutpen came from a mountainous area in North Virginia, a
boy with little conception of the class and racial hierarchy of the South.
When he arrives in Tidewater Virginia, he not only accepts the values of
his new home; readers see a process by which Sutpen comes to internalize
the plantation hierarchy so completely that he will remain true to it even
when this system is no longer viable. Sutpen thereby builds his identity
through imitation, aping the aristocratic class structure that he believes will
allow him agency and free movement. The process begins with a moment
of jealousy involving the shoes of "the man who owned all the land and the
niggers and apparently the white men who superintended the work" (AA
184). Sutpen's desire is not strictly for a valued object but rather for the
social mobility that this object represents. This desire is strikingly reinforced when he is turned away from the front door of the plantation manor
and told to use the back door like the other servants and slaves (188–90).
To his shock, the impressionable youth realizes that he is beneath even the

slaves of the establishment, and he thus seeks to solve his lack of status by faithfully replicating the order around him with him as master.

With the paradigmatic symbolism of a cognitive cartography, Faulkner depicts Sutpen's youthful epiphany in terms of vertical height and mimesis: "It was like that, he said, like an explosion – a bright glare that vanished and left nothing, no ashes nor refuse: just a limitless flat plain with the severe shape of his intact innocence rising from it like a monument" (192). The figurative language closely follows that of previous novels, for Faulkner imagines the construction of a vertex of cognitive space as an explosion upward that prepares for the erection of a mimetic monument. Faulkner repeats this vertical insistence some pages later when he describes Sutpen telling his tale to Grandfather Compson. Sutpen is at his "prime too: beard body and intellect at that peak which all the different parts that make a man reach" (193). This peak is imagined in vertical terms, for it "feels so sound and stable that the beginning of the falling is hidden for a little while – with his head flung up a little in that attitude that nobody ever knew exactly who he had aped it from or if he did not perhaps learn it too from the same book out of which he taught himself the words" (193–4). Again, there is an insistence that this vertex of cognitive space has been replicated from without, that the very possibility of height and thus of power – the "head flung up" – rests upon a mimetic process by which an ideology is individuated and re-constituted in cognitive and then in social space. Yet Faulkner is just as insistent that the stability of this antebellum institution is an illusion. Indeed, the system is already breaking apart, eroded by its internal contradictions, as we will see, but this reality is still "hidden for a little while."

Faulkner thus amends the plantation assemblage that he depicted in *Flags in the Dust* to portray not the survival of a system in new form, but the demise of the slave system itself. Sutpen is simply a node through which its ideology faithfully passes without significant alteration or amendment. This depiction of Sutpen the actual living, breathing man powerfully corresponds with Sutpen the abstract ideology that opens the initial narrative frame of the novel. Sutpen's great error was his belief that replicating the plantation edifice would give him agency and allow him free movement in social space. He would have free rein to come and go as he pleased; in short, no door would be barred from him. His afterlife as an ideological paradigm, freed from the individual flesh, fulfills this promise, but most certainly not in the way he would have imagined while alive. What is most insidious about Sutpen's afterlife as an ideological paradigm is that it masquerades as a form of novelty, when it is simply a reproduction of the failing antebellum social system. Despite portraying the failure of Sutpen's design, Faulkner by no means minimizes the danger of this coercive ideology. Without a doubt, the whole novel hinges upon the subtext that, in Quentin Compson's case at least, it remains as threatening as ever. We have seen such a pattern repeatedly: As the ideological directive asserts itself upon the perceiving subject, that subject loses the ability to see anything beyond the coercive paradigm whose ostensible ubiquity is reinforced by an ever-proliferating series of surfaces.

In the opening pages of *Absalom, Absalom!*, Faulkner draws upon many of the elements he hitherto employed to introduce Sutpen as an invasive ideological paradigm circulating through the nodes of a network and into the interior architecture of the self. The first and most subtle symbolic layer that establishes Sutpen as an ideological transmission into new minds is that of birds which fly in "random gusts" into and out of a "wisteria vine" blooming "on a wooden trellis before one window" (3). Much like the sparrow-like trembling of the children who move in "random erratic surges" through the orphanage in *Light in August*, the "random" flight of birds evokes a striking compression of histories of movement to introduce Quentin's spatial relationship to Rosa Coldfield as she begins to tell the Sutpen narrative: "Sparrows came now and then in random gusts, making a dry vivid dusty sound before going away: and opposite Quentin, Miss Coldfield in the eternal black ... sitting bold upright ... [and] talking in that grim haggard amazed voice" (3). By employing a colon to parallel these two forms of transmission, Faulkner equates the repeated movement of birds outside the window with the narrative exchange on the other side of this glassy threshold. He also intimates the manner in which order emerges out of individually erratic or chaotic activity. Indeed, in both novels, the collective movement of birds and children is described as "random," but because such movement clusters into a network trajectory – the flow of information through social and textual space – these movements self-organize into a predictable pattern of behavior.

With this symbolism of ideological transmission in place, Faulkner then introduces Sutpen as a "ghost" inhabiting the narrative exchange between Rosa and Quentin: He "mused with shadowy docility as if it were the voice which he haunted where a more fortunate one would have had a house" (4). Like the Sartoris ghost or the lynched and brutalized bodies of Goodwin and Christmas, Sutpen appears to possess a sinister tranquility. Despite this initial lack of substance, the ghostly patriarch inhabits Rosa's speaking voice and immediately asserts itself through textual surfaces:

> Out of quiet thunderclap he would abrupt (man-horse-demon) upon a scene peaceful and decorous as a schoolprize water color, faint sulphur-reek still in hair clothes and beard, with grouped behind him his band of wild niggers like beasts half tamed to walk upright like men, in attitudes wild and reposed, and manacled among them the French architect with his air grim, haggard, and tatter-ran. Immobile, bearded and hand palm-lifted the horseman sat; behind him the wild blacks and the captive architect huddled quietly, carrying in bloodless paradox the shovels and picks and axes of peaceful conquest. (4)

Sutpen's activity asserts itself not simply in social space (in Jefferson's Courthouse Square as we learn in the opening of chapter 2), but upon a textual surface in the visual and audible imagination of Quentin Compson. The dead patriarch arises upon a scene that is described as a "schoolprize water color" and, as such, he is at once a static inscription and a vertical paradigm possessing godlike power: "Immobile, bearded and hand palm-lifted the horseman sat." Herman Rapaport (2017) aptly describes Sutpen's appearance as "a seeming act of God [that] bring[s] something into existence" (21). Indeed, the patriarch appears upon the textual surface with his "hand palm-lifted" toward the heavens. The uplifted hand or *hamsa* is an ancient symbol that possesses a rich, intercultural history. Most recognizable in the Judeo–Christian heritage, it is a representation of God's hand, a sign of divine sovereignty connecting the above and the below – and, here it denotes Sutpen's power as one that has transcended the flesh and yet possesses the vertical ability to recreate itself in physical form.

This initial depiction of Sutpen establishes the symbolic coda both for him and his plantation complex. By the novel's conclusion, the Sutpen manor is likewise portrayed as a textual surface that has already violently transmitted its information, intimating that the slave system, despite its demise, continues a half century later to bequeath its ideology upon the living. The manor evokes the novel's opening metafictional imagery of Sutpen leaping out of a painting, except now this "canvas curtain" of "one dimension" bears a tear running perpendicularly across it:

> It loomed, bulked, square and enormous, with jagged half-toppled chimneys, its roofline sagging a little; for an instant as they moved, hurried, toward it Quentin saw completely through it a ragged segment of sky with three hot stars in it as if the house were of one dimension, painted on a canvas curtain in which there was a tear; now, almost beneath it, the dead furnace-breath of air in which they moved seemed to reek in slow and

protracted violence with a smell of desolation and decay as if the wood of
which it was built were flesh. (AA 293)

Certainly, the house conceals the murderer, Henry Sutpen, along with the
fratricidal motivations that Quentin and Shreve attempt to discover in
their narrative collaboration. Yet Faulkner simultaneously develops
another avenue of symbolic discovery, for the torn canvas allows
Quentin and the reader to see through the surface and to perceive a
striking vertical symbolism that aligns the "three bright stars" above with
the "dead furnace-breath of air" below. As Sutpen initially appeared upon a
"schoolprize water color" with his hand raised toward the heavens, here,
the "canvas curtain" of the manor evokes another insidious appropriation
of metaphysical correspondences between heaven and earth. The "three
hot stars" locate the "looming" and "enormous" hierarchical dimensions of
the plantation complex, even while suggesting the kind of inversion that
we repeatedly saw in the deranged correspondence of light and surface in
the Sartoris mansion from *Flags in the Dust*. Instead of guiding the seeker
toward new creation, the stars denote that the institution itself has taken
on an insidious quasi-agency. Indeed, its "slow and protracted violence" is
described sensuously and physically as if the architectural edifice
"were flesh."

   The novel's self-reflexive coda intimates, therefore, that an information
paradigm is already transmitting itself into the perceiver. If we return to
the opening of the novel, we are better equipped to recognize how
Faulkner repeatedly reinforces the way that the Sutpen paradigm asserts
itself upon the cognitive interiority of Quentin, not simply invading the
fragile architecture of the self, but also achieving in the process a robust
tangibility. The ghost is still bound to Rosa's speaking voice and, in this
state, remains "peaceful" and "harmless," an abstraction tied to words, but
its growing substantiality entails more than the delineations of one man,
no matter how fearsome and tyrannical. As an ideology pouring out of a
textual surface, the Sutpen paradigm is physically present, reproducing
itself before Quentin's very eyes:

   the invoked ghost of the man ... began to assume a quality almost of
   solidity, permanence. Itself circumambient and enclosed by its effluvium of
   hell, its aura of unregeneration, it mused (mused, thought, seemed to
   possess sentience, as if, though dispossessed of the peace – who was
   impervious anyhow to fatigue – which she declined to give it, it was still
   irrevocably outside the scope of her hurt or harm) with that quality peaceful
   and now harmless and not even very attentive – the ogre-shape which, as

> Miss Coldfield's voice went on, resolved out of itself before Quentin's eyes
> the two half-ogre children, the three of them forming a shadowy back-
> ground for the fourth one. (7–8)

Faulkner is adamant that this pattern cannot generate itself naturally
("unregeneration"), yet as the perceiver takes in (or de-alienates) the
Sutpen text, he or she accepts a pattern that possesses a "shadowy" power
to reproduce itself. Once again, Faulkner uses the mimetic image of the
"shadowy background," which prepares the reader to visualize Sutpen and
his family as a "fading and ancient photograph" that asserts itself from
"behind and above" the narrative voice:

> Quentin seemed to see them, the four of them arranged into the conven-
> tional family group of the period, with formal and lifeless decorum, and
> seen now as the fading and ancient photography itself would have been seen
> enlarged and hung on the wall behind and above the voice and of whose
> presence there the voice's owner was not even aware, as if she (Miss
> Coldfield) had never seen this room before – a picture, a group which even
> to Quentin had a quality strange, contradictory and bizarre; not
> quite comprehensible. (8–9)

As Colonel Sartoris' print hovers above his son and Christmas' expelled
shadow "soars" forever into the memories of his attackers, the Sutpen
paradigm is a shadowy reproduction that similarly occupies the vertex of
cognitive space. Where Quentin initially envisions Sutpen emerging out of
a painting, here this "picture" hangs "behind and above the [narrative]
voice," its ideological authority fortified through contact with new minds.

It is not one surface alone, therefore, that propagates the pattern in
question. Sutpen is at once an ideological abstraction and a compression of
many surfaces and temporalities into a cognitive cartography. The novel's
second chapter establishes this in variant form. In a superposition of places
and temporalities (Mississippi in 1833, Mississippi in 1909, and Harvard
in 1909), Quentin insists upon the same process occurring continually, so
that he "still breathed the same air in which the church bells had rung on
that Sunday morning in 1833" (23) when Sutpen first arrived in Jefferson.
In this state of spatiotemporal superposition, Sutpen becomes a vertex of
cognitive and social space with the birds wheeling in circles around him
and the Courthouse Square: "(and, on Sundays, heard even one of the
original three bells in the same steeple where descendants of the same
pigeons strutted and crooned or wheeled in short courses resembling soft
fluid paint-smears on the soft summer sky)" (23). As before, the surface of

a canvas prospectively serves as the stage upon which beings move, the pigeons imagined in circular succession so that their intergenerational behavior is visualized as "soft fluid paint-smears on the soft summer sky."

Sutpen's arrival in Jefferson is thereby retold from a different point of view, but Faulkner retains the spatial dimensions of the cognitive cartography that he had evoked earlier. In the first chapter, Sutpen prospectively emerges out of a canvas, his right hand uplifted with vertical command to tear his plantation out of the surface of the earth. Here, he appears in the midst of the community with the sound of the Sabbath bells to intone his arrival. Like the church bells around which the pigeons "strut," "croon," and "wheel," Sutpen is that vertex to which the social body "look[s] up" (23) and who is already "halfway" across the town square and thus positioned in the very middle of Yoknapatawpha's social body. He appears as though he "had been created out of thin air and set down in the bright summer sabbath sunshine" (23). Faulkner alludes to the biblical creation myth, for Sutpen engages in *creatio ex nihilo*, emerging as a vertex unto himself with the power to remake the space around him. Even the birds are circulating his information pattern across space and time. Faulkner strengthens the patriarch's centrality in social space by indicating that the man's appearance is followed by a period in which his name "went back and forth" through the community in "steady strophe and antistrophe" (24). Here again, we cannot absolutely situate this depiction, since we, as readers, are contending not simply with various temporalities, but with various spaces as well, at once multiple Jeffersons and the surface of a text before us as well. To be sure, strophe and antistrophe are the first sections of a lyric poem or the choral ode of ancient Greek tragedy, and they suggest that the pattern in question unfolds just as much textually as within the social networks that comprise a growing community of individuals.

In this respect, Faulkner unsettles his readers, visualizing the behavior of the social body as one that is synonymous with Sutpen's name being audibly voiced through mimicry by the collective body and repeatedly imprinted on a series of surfaces: "*Sutpen. Sutpen. Sutpen. Sutpen.*" (24). After the long sentences which temporally compress the behavior of a community from 1833–1909, Faulkner provides a striking counterpoint with the staccato verbalization and imprint of the planter's name, followed after each occurrence with a full stop. With the power of *creatio ex nihilo*, the planter is his own enclosed ecosystem, his own beginning and end, presenting a circular occurrence out of which the perceiver cannot escape. This is Quentin's fate most of all: to endure the imprint, to think and dream in the demarcations of an ideology that is instantiated everywhere, in the architecture of the town and in the very language that the citizens use to speak about the reality about them. As we move through the novel, moreover, the Sutpen paradigm gains scope and power, becoming much more than a pervasive absence, psychological rupture, or vanishing point at the center of relations, for it is instantiated in social space with the power to invade the cognitive interiority of individuals seemingly at will.

The various narratives entangle Sutpen with his individual family members who are likewise visualized not as real people, but as textual surfaces. Mr. Compson introduces Charles Bon, Sutpen's interracial son, in just such a manner. He tells Quentin that Bon "must have appeared almost phoenix-like, fullsprung from no childhood, born of no woman and impervious to time and, vanished, leaving no bones nor dust anywhere" (58). Father's vision is at once Shakespearean and metafictional. Bon does not age, Father implies, because the man is no longer flesh; like Sutpen before him, he is an information pattern, a textual inscription: "Miss Rosa never saw him; this was a picture, an image" (58). Mr. Compson continues to emphasize this metafictional paradigm with Ellen's fantasy about her daughter and Bon's impending nuptials:

> She postulated the elapsed years during which no honeymoon nor any change had taken place, out of which the (now) five faces looked with a sort of lifeless and perennial bloom like painted portraits hung in a vacuum, each taken at its forewarned peak and smoothed of all thought and experience, the originals of which had lived and died so long ago that their joys and griefs must now be forgotten even by the very boards on which they had strutted and postured and laughed and wept. (59)

Mr. Compson strikingly juxtaposes the real individuals with the mimetic reproduction of them. The "originals of which had lived and died" are forgotten by the very surfaces they touched, but the artificial reproduction still exists with a "lifeless and perennial bloom," visualized, yet again, as a copy fixed at the "peak" and, because of this verticality, retaining a strange and sinister power to disseminate its information into those clustered below.

Similar to Quentin in his initial meeting with Rosa, Mr. Compson conceives of Sutpen and his family as an "almost substanceless" text hovering "behind and above" the flesh. Although dead, this text nonetheless threatens to transmit its content into the perceiver. Mr. Compson's narratives are obsessed with this process by which human information is stored on mimetic surfaces and then transmitted into living consciousness.

As he tells his son, Bon never truly courted Judith. Nonetheless, Bon and Judith as concepts are dynamically interlinked, and Father visualizes this transference from flesh into pure information as a type of cinematic projection:

> There was no time, no interval, no niche in the crowded days when he could have courted Judith. You can not even imagine him and Judith alone together. Try to do it and the nearest you can come is a projection of them while the two people were doubtless separate and elsewhere – two shades pacing, serene and untroubled by flesh, in a summer garden – the same two serene phantoms who seem to watch, hover, impartial attentive and quiet, above and behind the inexplicable thunderhead of interdictions and defiances and repudiations out of which the rocklike Sutpen and the volatile and violent Henry flashed and glared and ceased. (77)

Mr. Compson repeats the spatial dynamics that Quentin expressed in his initial vision of the Sutpen family as a family portrait "behind and above" (9) the narrative voice. Bon and Judith are similarly "untroubled by flesh" and, as mimetic phantoms, they in turn "hover . . . above and behind" the actual event, possessing that "quiet" attentiveness that is the bequest of all such vertical abstractions. Mr. Compson repeatedly imagines Bon in this manner: "He seems to hover, shadowy, almost substanceless, a little behind and above all the other straightforward and logical even though (to him) incomprehensible ultimatums and affirmations and defiances and challenges and repudiations" (74).

Mr. Compson extends this paradigm of coercive textual surfaces not simply to Sutpen and his plantation, but to the greater hemispheric slave system of the Americas. He identifies Charles Bon's seduction of his half brother Henry within the context of the slave system with its flows of information, resources, and capital. By using the mimetic surface as his primary conceptual apparatus, Mr. Compson narrates how Bon attempts to mold Henry to accept his mixed-race mistress and son. The analogy begins simply enough – with Bon corrupting his young friend and half brother as through an early photographic process in which a glass-plate negative is prepared to fix an image: "So I can imagine him, the way he did it: the way in which he took the innocent and negative plate of Henry's provincial soul and intellect and exposed it by slow degrees to this esoteric milieu, building gradually toward the picture which he desired it to retain, accept" (87). This straightforward photographic analogy soon leads into one of Faulkner's longest sentences, one which focuses principally upon the implantation of ideology into selves and surfaces:

> I can see him corrupting Henry gradually into the purlieus of elegance, with
> no foreword, no warning, the postulation to come after the fact, exposing
> Henry slowly to the surface aspect – the architecture a little curious, a little
> femininely flamboyant and therefore to Henry opulent, sensuous, sinful;
> the inference of great and easy wealth measured by steamboat loads in place
> of a tedious inching of sweating human figures across cotton fields; the flash
> and the glitter of myriad carriage wheels, in which women, enthroned and
> immobile and passing rapidly across the vision, appeared like painted
> portraits beside men in linen a little finer and diamonds a little brighter
> and in broadcloth a little trimmer and with hats raked a little more above
> faces a little more darkly swaggering than any Henry had ever seen before.
> (87–8)

The first half of the sentence examines how Bon introduces Henry to "the
surface aspect" of his New Orleans culture, first, to the "architecture,"
which was built not by any particular architect, but more strikingly by the
resource or information flow of slavery itself. Thus, Faulkner offers his
reader an explicit cognitive cartography: The architecture of the city serves
as a textual "surface," a symbolic abbreviation of a drawn-out temporal
process of labor and resource extraction that begins in the "tedious inching
of sweating human figures across cotton fields," continues with cotton
loaded into "steamboats" to be shipped down the Mississippi, and comes
to be expressed in the fine "glitter" of wealth among the elite residents of
New Orleans.

Faulkner thus imagines the mimetic surface as a compression of histories
of movement as they assume the preeminence of vertical space. These
surfaces are everywhere in New Orleans, the architecture and the performance of affluence that similarly take the appearance of "painted portraits," artistic abstractions that are sustained through the resource flow of
the slave system. These painted surfaces are visualized as vertices
"enthroned and immobile and passing rapidly across the vision."
As Sutpen emerged from a surface erected above and behind the narrative
exchange of individuals, so the same spatial insistence is present here in the
decadent slave culture of New Orleans. The black laborers that inch across
the cotton fields in Mississippi, the resources that they produce – this
process is attenuated into a vertical information pattern that is subsumed
visually by the young Henry, a pattern that Bon believes will change his
friend and half brother. Indeed, once Bon introduces the young Henry to
the elite culture of New Orleans and "watch[es] the picture resolve and
become fixed," he begins to insist upon a conceptual verticality erected and
"enthroned" by this slave culture. "But that's not it. That's just the base,

the foundation. It can belong to anyone," Bon tells his friend and half-brother with Henry responding: "You mean, this is not it? That it is above this, higher than this, more select than this?" (88). Bon thereby builds his young friend toward this "higher" (88) conception with Henry repeating the question: "You mean, it is still higher than this, still above this?" (88).

Faulkner constructs his long sentence with clause upon clause toward a "supreme apotheosis," a spatial verticality which is eventually visualized as a doorway, a "façade shuttered and blank" (89), which again assumes a duality between verticality and surface, becoming "the blank and scaling barrier" (89) and then "a wall, unscalable, a gate ponderously locked" (89). And what do we find inside? For Bon, it is the aesthetic and sexual delights that the slave culture provides to the elite, a temptation he believes Henry will not be able to resist: "a row of faces like a bazaar of flowers, the supreme apotheosis of chattelry, of human flesh bred of the two races for that sale – a corridor of doomed and tragic flower faces walled between the grim duenna row of old women and the elegant shapes of young men trim predatory" (89). Throughout the novel, Faulkner depicts Henry as the soft, sensitive Sutpen child. Unlike his sister Judith who can face her father's violence and mastery over his slaves without flinching, Henry reacts in disgust, vomiting and averting his eyes. Similarly, in this new cosmopolitan setting, he cannot accept the proffered delights of this "supreme apotheosis of chattelry," the first in an escalating series of conflicts between the two young men that eventually culminates in fratricide.

In this context, *Absalom, Absalom!* is not strictly about the decline of the planter class. We already know that Faulkner has devoted whole novels to describing how this class survives under new material conditions. Rather, the novel is better understood as a narrative about tipping points in which an institution can no longer bear the tensions implicit in its ideology without fatal consequences. The mutual affection of the reunited brothers Henry and Bon unfolds in this light. Young Henry is enraptured with the handsome and worldly Bon, while Bon gains his long-hoped for access to his father and family. Yet despite the natural and intuitive bonds of family and friendship, the relationship between the two men cannot evade the racial contradictions that this social system has produced. Henry, for his part, cannot understand or accept the inconsistent and widely incongruous ideology of racial identity underpinning the system in which he is set, and Bon forcefully employs that knowledge to try to corrupt the naïve young man. Despite their mutual love for one another, the two men are thus locked in an ideological struggle, each representative of one side of a cultural contradiction that neither young man can resolve.

4.4   Cognitive Cartographies Upended

Absalom, Absalom! identifies the flows of information, resources, and capital that sustain the greater slave system. At the same time, the novel depicts a rising entropy that undercuts this system. In this respect, the novel depicts a greater crisis disrupting the stability of the slave system with the murder of Charles Bon in 1865 and in the mounting disarray of the entire hemispheric slave system from the cotton fields of Mississippi, to the decadent wealth of New Orleans, to the plantations of Haiti. Rather than framing the Civil War's entropy as a matter of North–South conflict, Faulkner depicts the Southern regime imploding from within – as the disruptive force of the conflict between Henry and Bon, two Southern brothers within a single house, indicates. As Faulkner scales this disruptive implosion from the personal to the public, he explicitly employs the archetypal and tragic symbolism of spilled blood, providing an ethical paradigm with which to understand the collapse of slavery throughout the Western hemisphere. In its original Greek sense, the spilled blood is "miasma," a "stain, defilement by murder or the earth colored with stains of blood" (Liddell and Scott 1972: 1132). Faulkner articulates this tragic paradigm in epic terms and identifies the historical violence of a vast institution from its initial stages of revolt and revolution in Haiti to its eventual collapse in the American South.

Thus, we discover that, long before he erected his design in Mississippi, Sutpen administered "a soil manured with black blood from two hundred years of oppression and exploitation" (AA 251). From this soil, Sutpen hears a voice that arises as a seemingly absolute vertex of power and belief: "the planting of men too; the yet intact bones and brains in which the old unsleeping blood that had vanished into the earth they trod still cried out for vengeance" (251). Sutpen thinks that it is the "heart of the earth itself he hear[s]." Certainly, the blood crime of slavery is too great to stage upon any one body alone. Like the void into which Christmas' features collapse and from which the "black blood" soars like a breath into the minds of the perpetrators, the Haitian earth in *Absalom, Absalom!* serves as the medium into which the blood of countless individuals spills and springs forth a sourceless self-expression. The violent pattern does more than haunt the present culture; its dissemination depends upon hyper-connectivity and, thus, it flows through the social body, instantiated in its physical and textual architecture and individuated in the fragile architectonics of the self.

Scholars have fruitfully explained Sutpen's haunting in psychoanalytic terms. Michael Zeitlin (2004) insightfully argues that the "Sutpen tragedy will not remain isolated, fossilized, locked away in some remote, aestheticized space." To be sure, the "fantasy space slowly becomes reified space" (634). I have shown that the symbolic content of this fantasy space is imbued in the aesthetic and physical structures around the characters. As ideology, Sutpen is already a hypermobile carrier of content and, at a certain degree of both cultural saturation and incoherence, it also jeopardizes the very structures upon which it depends for survival. Thus, the stability of an ideological surface – the information flow by which a text is replicated into the inner lives of those who subsume it – is a powerful means by which institutions survive, but it is by no means guaranteed. Charles Bon may employ the power of the New Orleans' slave ideology to pierce Henry's provincial soul, to reveal to the young man that his own inheritance and birthright are bound up in a complex system of labor, capital, and belief. Yet *Absalom, Absalom!* is also the first of Faulkner's novels to examine what happens when these ideological surfaces lose their power, when historical circumstances disrupt the movement, behavior, and thinking of a community, when such circumstances, in other words, unsettle institutional epistemologies and force a community to adapt.

Judith's iconic letter – perhaps the novel's most famous moment – can be considered as a case in point. Judith, in the midst of the war and bravely maintaining the home front, has lost her mother and grandfather and finally received direct word from Charles Bon, her intended, who reports of the imminent defeat of the Confederate cause. She harnesses the surrey with her half sister Clytie and travels to the Compsons to deliver the letter into the hands of the startled matron of that establishment. As she gives the letter to Mrs. Compson, Judith powerfully expounds upon the futile character of all surfaces whether they be the parchment paper upon which Bon's words are inscribed, the greater social "loom" into which we all are woven, or the marble tombstone that eventually marks our demise:

> Read it if you like or dont read it if you like. Because you make so little impression, you see. You get born and you try this and you dont know why only you keep on trying it and you are born at the same time with a lot of other people, all mixed up with them, like trying to, having to, move your arms and legs with strings only the same strings are hitched to all the other arms and legs and the others all trying and they dont know why either except that the strings are all in one another's way like five or six people all trying to make a rug on the same loom only each one wants to weave his own pattern into the rug; and it cant matter, you know that, or the Ones that set up the loom would have arranged things a little better, and yet it must matter because you keep on trying and having to keep on trying and

then all of a sudden it's all over and all you have left is a block of stone with
scratches on it provided there was someone to remember to have the marble
scratched and set up or had time to, and it rains on it and the sun shines on
it and after a while they dont even remember the name and what the
scratches were trying tell, and it doesn't matter. (AA 100–1)

Owen Robinson (2006) argues that the passage provides an "extraordi-
narily illustrative account of the processes that go into Yoknapatawpha's
construction, as well as being a highly moving account of living with and
in those processes" (201). Indeed, this passage strikingly reflects Faulkner's
own sense of complex systems. As much as the social body clusters in social
space to erect and maintain remarkably stable institutions, Faulkner is
simultaneously concerned with adaptation, change, and variation, those
historical pivot points in which institutions and their ideologies are remade
and reconstituted. From this point of view, Judith utters a powerful
articulation of the social body's utter dependence upon imprinting its
information onto the institutions around it. We have seen variations of
this imagery before – invisible strings or chains binding the individual into
a collective cognitive cartography. Here, Judith expressly articulates this
concept in terms of self-expression so that each member tries to "move
[her] arms and legs with strings only the same strings are hitched to all the
other arms and legs." Thus, the individual is inextricably interwoven into
the greater social tapestry, each member of which attempts to instantiate
his or her own reality upon the greater order. Judith's despair emerges
because her own sense of value is deeply intertwined with her faith in these
institutions, their ideologies, and their forms of self-expression. She focuses
all her angst, moreover, upon the character of a constructed surface – page,
loom, and tombstone – as it loses its relevance in the tacitly implied
articulation of Confederate defeat in Bon's letter.

Judith is not just speaking about the nature of signification itself, nor is
she articulating "a classic case of existential angst" (201), as Robinson
(2006) calls it. Rather, finding herself in the midst of war, she observes
that the typical patterns of movement and behavior are being disrupted,
that the social mores that maintain the society no longer hold sway. Even
in her state of despair, the young woman nonetheless fantasizes that such
surfaces retain some power if only they can be passed from "one mind to
another":

And so maybe if you could go to someone, the stranger the better, and give
them something – a scrap of paper – something, anything, it not to mean
anything in itself and them not even to read it or keep it, not even bother to

> throw it away or destroy it, at least it would be something just because it
> would have happened, be remembered even if only from passing from one
> hand to another, one mind to another, and it would be at least a scratch,
> something, something that might make a mark on something that *was* once
> for the reason that it can die someday, while the block of stone cant be *is*
> because it never can become *was* because it cant ever die or perish. (101)

Judith cannot give up completely on the ideological power of the slave
system. Even though it is reduced to a "scrap of paper," "it cant ever die or
perish" as long as its information continues to circulate and is passed into
others. In this respect, Judith is a replicator of the ideology of the slave
system. Her despairing vision offers no challenge to it; rather, she attempts
to reinstate the authority of the Confederacy, even with the knowledge
that this authority is already vanquished.

Faulkner stages her despairing vision by depicting what happens on the
home front as wartime deprivation sets in. The very problem that Sutpen
initially sought to remedy – his own admission through the front door of
the plantation house – has similarly begun to lose its relevance in this
setting. We find, for instance, that whereas Sutpen's tenant, Wash Jones,
had never been allowed through the front door, now the man comes and
goes freely through the whole estate and, indeed, is vital to its maintenance
and very survival. The waning of the ideological power of the antebellum
plantation system is reflected, therefore, both in Judith's despair with
textual surfaces and in Wash's unfettered movement in social space.
Judith and Rosa apprehend this with mounting unease and then outright
despair, for Sutpen's whole design rests firmly upon these two aspects, and
the diminishment of one necessitates the failure of the other.

Although a new system will take its place, Faulkner depicts the Civil
War as a historical pivot point that produces the kind of information
entropy that can upend institutions. For Faulkner, moreover, this large-
scale disruption of the cognitive cartographies of the South is always
individually oriented. Donald Kartiganer (1998) expresses this particularly
well, arguing that "war in *Absalom, Absalom!* is generally peripheral to the
main action." At the heart of the "destruction of the South" is a story
about family: "The white man murders the black man who is his brother"
(641). As large as such a system may be, the incongruities that eat away at
institutions are not simply abstract like the Sutpen text above and behind
the events; they are embodied in the flesh-and-blood relationships between
families and individuals. Henry and Bon's relationship is certainly paradigmatic, and Faulkner depicts this growing contradiction in other

narrators as well, especially as it concerns racial relationships – and he reveals the consequences for those who accept the power of this ideological paradigm without question.

As I argued in the previous section (4.3), those who rely on abstract epistemologies are less capable of establishing viable connection with others; indeed, they relate to others through that epistemology and thus authentic knowledge of other human selves is jeopardized. Rosa's tragedy can be seen in just this context. Rosa may disparage Sutpen as a demon, but she believes in the Sutpen paradigm so completely that her relationships are absolutely mediated by it, none more striking than her confrontation with Clytemnestra, Sutpen's mixed-race daughter and Rosa's own niece through marriage. While the spatial delineations of her vision of the Sutpen paradigm match those of Mr. Compson, Rosa nonetheless upholds a very different view of the tragedy that befalls Sutpen and the South, since her interpretation of the Sutpen paradigm is mediated through her explicit bigotry. Her prevailing sense of class consciousness and racial prejudice are refracted everywhere in her narratives. For her, as with the townsfolk of Jefferson, Sutpen will always be that class usurper who used the Coldfield's good name to attain respectability. She cannot forgive Sutpen's deviation from traditional Southern class conventions and, in her mind, the great blight of war and privation arises as an express punishment for Sutpen's actions. In other words, Rosa cannot fully understand why the regime around her is failing. She mistakenly sees Sutpen as the cause and projects godlike power onto the man.

As she recounts her discovery of fratricide, Rosa endows the Sutpen face with such mystical authority that it comes to mediate all relationships. As she runs into the Sutpen manor house and encounters Clytie at the foot of the grand staircase, Rosa feels that she has entered a cognitive cartography so vast that there is neither an outside nor a time before its existence:

> It was the Sutpen face enough, but not his; Sutpen coffee-colored face enough there in the dim light, barring the stairs: and I running out of the bright afternoon, into the thunderous silence of that brooding house where I could see nothing at first: then gradually the face, the Sutpen face not approaching, not swimming up out of the gloom, but already there, rocklike and firm and antedating time and house and doom and all, waiting there (oh yes, he chose well; he bettered choosing, who created in his own image the cold Cerberus of his private hell) – the face without sex or age because it had never possessed either: the same sphinx face which she had been born with, which had looked down from the loft that night beside Judith's and which she still wears now at seventy-four, looking at me with

no change, no alteration in it at all, as though it had known to the second
when I was to enter, had waited there. (AA 109)

In *Sanctuary*, Temple was similarly overwhelmed by an external ideological
power that she believes to be the original substance of the cosmos, the
prima materia from which all matter originates. Here, Rosa confronts the
Sutpen face, which takes individual expression – indeed, is replicated into a
body or a text – but is far greater than any one individual or surface. Like
Temple with the glass-face of the clock, Rosa ascribes divine qualities to
the Sutpen face, for it was always "already there, rocklike and firm and
antedating time and house and doom and all." Like the glass-face of the
clock or the monumental image of the statue, the Sutpen face transforms
into the original archetype; it exists above time and can take individual
form in the "coffee-colored face" of Clytie who bars the staircase and
becomes an insurmountable surface or barrier that mediates Rosa's experience: "I was crying not to someone, something, but (trying to cry)
through something, through that force, that furious yet absolutely rocklike
and immobile antagonism which had stopped me" (110).

In Rosa's imagination, Clytie is a replica of Sutpen, which "he created
and decreed to preside upon his absence" (110). Thus, Clytie's "presence"
possesses a mystical authority that is projected upward into the air between
the women:

> [it] seemed to elongate and project upward something – not soul, not spirit,
> but something rather of a profoundly attentive and distracting listening to
> or for something which I myself could not hear and was not intended to
> hear – a brooding awareness and acceptance of the inexplicable unseen
> inherited from an older and purer race than mine, which created postulated
> and shaped in the empty air between us that which I believed I had come
> to find. (110)

Here again, Rosa gives expression to the spatial nuances of the cognitive
cartographies of Yoknapatawpha. Between the two women on the Sutpen
stairway, in the "empty air," arises a vertex of power and belief. It is
"project[ed] upward" out of the face of the mixed-race woman, but it is
not a spiritual essence, although it seems to possess a supernatural authority. Rosa has no proper language for it; she deifies this force, this presence,
attributing mimetic and divine qualities to it, conceiving it to be omnipotent, both flesh and beyond flesh, a mixture of human action and a
transcendent ideology. For her, it is replicated in Clytie as well as in the
other children and underlies the very plantation house itself, for when

Clytie warns Rosa not to go upstairs, Rosa perceives that "it had not been she who spoke but the house itself that said the words – the house which he had built, which some suppuration of himself had created about him as the sweat of his body might have created, produced some (even if invisible) cocoon-like and complementary shell" (111).

In this confrontation, Rosa cannot relate directly to the young black woman at all; instead, her relationship with her is mediated through her profound anxiety with the miscegenation of the Sutpen family. She thereby reacts with intense hostility when Clytie touches her. Faulkner's depiction begins simply enough: "Then she touched me, and then I did stop dead" (111). For Rosa, this one act becomes indicative of a profound violation of the class and racial codes that uphold the slave system and without which it would collapse. She indicates that she does not blame Clytie individually, that Clytie "did me more grace and respect than anyone else I knew" (111). Yet Rosa's acute sense of violation, of black on white flesh, is as significant as all the other tragedies befalling her homeland. For her, Bon's dead body on the second floor is as much a punishment for Sutpen's usurping crimes as is the touch of this young mixed-race woman. Thus, when Clytie touches Rosa, the white woman comes face to face with the Sutpen monstrosity itself: "I know only that my entire being seemed to run at blind full tilt into something monstrous and immobile, with a shocking impact too soon and too quick to be mere amazement and outrage at that black arresting and untimorous hand on my white woman's flesh" (111). For Rosa, Clytie's touch takes on a deep and sinister symbolism in which she can sympathize with the black woman, even while hating her as the embodiment of social disruption: "I crying not to her, to it; speaking to it through the negro, the woman, only because of the shock which was not yet outrage because it would be terror soon, expecting and receiving no answer because we both knew it was not to her I spoke: 'Take your hand off me, nigger!'" (112).

This deified vision of the Sutpen face and of the coercive power of textual surfaces is, therefore, endemic to many of the principal characters in the novel. Although Rosa's vision of the Sutpen vertex is informed by her own prejudice, the spatial dynamics attributed to it are intersubjective. For her, the Sutpen face "project[s] upward" and manifests "in the empty air between" her and Clytie (11). Rosa has to speak "through the negro" to the Sutpen face that has grown so large that it occupies every surface, relationship, and vantage point. Because of her own powerlessness in the face of this seemingly ubiquitous paradigm, she lashes out at Clytie, chastising her with racial invective, yet simultaneously feeling kinship with the slave: "The two of us joined by that hand and arm which held us, like a fierce rigid umbilical cord, twin sistered to the fell darkness which had produced her" (112). Theresa Towner (2000) expresses it perfectly when she writes that the touch of Clytie's hand on Rosa's arm "represents the simple fact of common humanity in the midst of the many barriers constructed to deny or restrict that humanity" (15). Indeed, Rosa's vision of the Sutpen face is a fantasy that costs no less than everything. It is a barrier to accessing her common humanity with Clytie, and one can see how the duality of the scene – Rosa's simultaneous hatred for Clytie and her hidden feelings of kinship with her – will come to inform the Jim Crow South that reinstates the class and racial hierarchy that undergirds Rosa's outrage at a black woman touching her white skin.

In the novel, the dilemma that accordingly emerges is one in which the deeper interpersonal bond between family members becomes ideological and fatally mediated – and this applies to all the characters equally. Quentin and his father also articulate the ideological power of the Sutpen paradigm. For them, Sutpen appears in a very similar manner, as a creation "out of thin air" that emerges in the very midst of the community. Although this ideological paradigm has the power to reduplicate itself indefinitely, we see the fractures that emerge in any system where such an abstract epistemology dominates, eventually rupturing not only the ideological surface itself, as we saw with the torn canvas curtain toward the end of the novel, but also the individual relationships that underlie and sustain these surfaces. While this novel is often considered to be the high-water mark of Faulkner's art, it can be more properly understood as the beginning of an extended artistic meditation upon piercing the illusion of permanence and stability that coercive paradigms of social control seem to possess. What we find instead is a view of the South in a constant state of change with competing vertices springing up everywhere. In the novels to come, Faulkner offers a striking reappraisal of human interiority. As we have already seen, systems may become incoherent and collapse, requiring novelty and innovation to reconstitute them into new form. But as the next two chapters show, novelty is not enough. Our social systems cannot be made into something better without immanence and intimate interrelation, which are always the foundations for a coherent social body and human well-being.

CHAPTER 5

Beyond the Tyranny of Textual Space

While many of Faulkner's novels leading up to *Absalom, Absalom!* portray the intractable character of ideology, the creative period afterward was a time in which Faulkner searched more decisively for solutions to the problems set out in his earlier fiction. *The Unvanquished* (1938) continues to depict the Civil War as an entropic event capable of upending the plantation system, but does so with a much greater emphasis upon the role of individual agency. *Go Down, Moses* (1942) presents an even more striking response to the earliest cognitive cartography of the Sartoris plantation house. While ideology continues to be preserved and replicated within the principal nodes of social space, in these works Faulkner turns his attention to the disruptive and resistant activity of a hidden interiority within these systems. He employs a variety of images to evoke this emergent interior dimension – from the creek bottom to the burial mound, to the fiery hearth, to the symbolic motif, most importantly, of a submerged woman in the depths, a motif that begins with Eunice's suicidal act of defiance in *Go Down, Moses*. Around this last image, as we shall see in both this chapter and the next, Faulkner develops the possibility of alterity, of producing an alternative hub of information flow that is capable of resisting, challenging, and even upending the top-down vertical hegemony that defines the cognitive cartographies of the plantation system. In this chapter, I trace this paradigm as an emergent Faulknerian ethics that emphasizes, above all, the possibility of spontaneous and free movement in social space as well as the paramount value of immanence and interpersonal relationships.

Section 5.1 of this chapter explores Faulkner's depiction of novelty in Loosh's destruction of the "living map" that opens *The Unvanquished*. These actions offer a new vision of the human being within complex social systems, and they anticipate the black agency that Faulkner develops in *Go Down Moses*. Section 5.2 explores Faulkner's portrayal of a hidden history whose information flow competes with the cognitive cartography of the

McCaslin plantation complex. While some critics have seen the novel as privileging white agency and, as a result, the white signifying economy, I make the case that Faulkner self-consciously set out to give voice to an emergent interiority capable of unsettling the plantation system from within. Isaac McCaslin's ability to see beyond the dicta of the lien ledgers that govern and regulate the plantation complex is predicated upon unprecedented paradigms of behavior established by the lives of Eunice and her black family. Their protest offers a key ethical paradigm in *Go Down, Moses*, both in its oppositional character to the tyranny of textual space and in its affirmation of the principles of immanence and intersubjectivity. Sections 5.3 and 5.4 explore these principles in three characters of *Go Down, Moses*: (1) Isaac McCaslin with his immersion in the wilderness; (2) Lucas Beauchamp with his eventual affirmation of the interpersonal bonds of family; and (3) Rider, the protagonist of "Pantaloon in Black" who is not a member of the McCaslin line, but serves as perhaps the most striking example of the disruptive novelty that can emerge in systems of high inequality. With these characters, Faulkner gives variable expression to the dynamic relationship between self and social space by examining how the architecture of interior space – as a scaleless dimension in the greater life of the whole – can disrupt and re-route the flow of information through a networked system.

5.1   Disruptions of Vertical Power

Like *Absalom, Absalom!*, Faulkner's next published novel, *The Unvanquished* (1938) explores the Civil War years as an entropic period of time in which the information structures of the antebellum South are upended and remade. The theme of institutional disruption and the spontaneous individual behavior that propels it takes center stage in *The Unvanquished*. Faulkner returns to the Sartoris family and to Bayard Sartoris whom we last saw as an old man in *Flags in the Dust*. Like the patriarch who ritualistically performed the plantation order of the New South, the Bayard that readers find in the opening pages of the later novel is a young boy engaged in mitigating the disruptive reality of war and attempting to reinstate the authority of the Confederacy. With Ringo, his friend and slave, he mimetically recreates the siege of Vicksburg as a "living map" made of woodchips and mud, which the two boys maintain with water from a nearby well:

> Behind the smokehouse that summer, Ringo and I had a living map. Although Vicksburg was just a handful of chips from the woodpile and

the River a trench scraped into the packed earth with the point of a hoe, it (river, city, and terrain) lived, possessing even in miniature that ponderable though passive recalcitrance of topography which outweighs artillery, against which the most brilliant victories and the most tragic of defeats are but the loud noises of a moment. (U 3)

This opening passage establishes the symbolic coda of the novel which entails the dynamic interrelation of culture and consciousness in the midst of the disruptive paradigm of total war. By enacting the siege in miniature, the boys seek to come to terms with the greater social milieu in which they are situated. Their play serves as a "shield" against "doom" (4), a defense against the encroachments of the Union and the potential upending of the planter way of life. The cartographic game they play is "urgent" (7) in that it serves an underlying psychic purpose: Bayard and Ringo are generals engaged in "the most brilliant victories and the most tragic of defeats," but always with the express aim of defending their homeland. Though their game involves taking opposing sides in the conflict, the two boys are not in opposition. Faulkner is explicit that "the two of [them] need[ed] first to join forces and spend [themselves] against a common enemy" (4). To do this, the boys have come to an agreement as to whom will play Generals Pemberton and Grant. Although Bayard has the clear privilege of race, he must nonetheless allow his friend to play Pemberton in every third iteration of the game if Ringo is to continue playing.

Faulkner thereby stages the information flow of the boy's cartographic game upon a far larger geographical and civilizational canvas. Although the boys understand something of the strategic importance of Vicksburg to the Confederacy, they are unlikely to comprehend that the greater trajectory of the war hinges upon it, since the city was a central transportation hub for the South, a vital chokepoint for resources to flow up and down the Mississippi River to and from the great international trade hub of New Orleans. Faulkner accentuates the entropic context threatening this cognitive cartography with a series of individual disruptions, first when Loosh sweeps "the chips flat" (5) and then when Louvinia, Ringo's grandmother, abruptly interrupts the boys' game. Where the "living map" serves as a powerful vertex of social and cognitive space for the boys, a new source of authority intervenes, symbolically possessing a vertical power – that is, a power that acts from above – to flatten the three-dimensional information object the boys have erected and to return it to a dead two-dimensional surface: "Her voice seemed to descend upon us like an enormous hand, flattening the very dust which we had raised, leaving us now visible to one

another, dust-colored ourselves to the eyes and still in the act of throwing"
(7). On one level, Louvinia's intervention in the game is easily explained;
she is merely calling the boys to greet Colonel Sartoris who has returned
home to the plantation. Faulkner's symbolism offers, however, a far
grander vision of individual novelty assuming precedence, for Louvinia's
voice seems to possess the symbolic power of heaven itself: It "descends" to
upend and "flatten" the game.

The dashing of this makeshift information object anticipates the ultimate disruption, the imminent collapse of the slave culture. Here, moreover, Faulkner is constituting a symbolic language for entropy. Quite
unlike the statue, the planter genealogy, the sun-clock, or the many other
mimetic information objects we have analyzed in previous chapters, the
"hurricane" offers a potent image that denotes the other end of the
information spectrum. Instead of storing memory in a lasting way, the
hurricane signifies a vertical, destructive power capable of unsettling a
civilization's information structures. According to Faulkner, the boys have
used the "living map" to become "two supreme undefeated like two moths,
two feathers riding above a hurricane" (7). The demise of the map,
however, leaves the boys "dust-colored," no longer above the hurricane
and, thus, no longer safe from the entropic processes that can unsettle any
information paradigm, no matter how instantiated it may be.

We have seen this type of entropic imagery before. In fact, Faulkner
initially employed this imagery during his trip to France in 1925, writing
that "it looks as if a cyclone had passed over the whole world at about six feet
from the ground" (Selected Letters 28). In the fiction to come, Faulkner
employs this entropic war imagery in describing a variety of characters.
In Light in August, the townspeople envision Hightower's sermons as a
"cyclone" that never touches the ground, and Rosa apprehends Ellen's
propagation of Sutpen's genetics as "a tornado" in which his "face" is
reduplicated "in miniature" and propelled onward by his slaves and the
thunder and fury of his horses (AA 16). The cyclone, the tornado, and the
hurricane all bear one unmistakable insistence: They are vertically elevated
images of entropy acting from above to break apart the memory structures
preserved in social space. To be sure, Hightower, his very name denoting
vertical power, presides over a more gradual failure of institutional space.
In Absalom, Absalom!, Rosa sees Sutpen's disruption of the aristocratic mores
of the South as a harbinger of the Civil War and an end to the antebellum
planter way of life. In The Unvanquished, the stakes are just as high, for
neither individuals nor their institutions can escape the calamity of war for
long, no matter what information object they employ to ensure stability.

In the opening of *The Unvanquished*, the demise of Bayard's cognitive cartography immediately has consequences for how the boy perceives all investitures of power. At the outset of the Yoknapatawpha canon, we saw how Colonel Sartoris transfers himself into an information paradigm which he then places up high in the apex of social space so that it will be preserved and replicated. In striking contrast to this archetypal figuration in Faulkner's fiction, *The Unvanquished* initially emphasizes the demise of the father's power and vitality. Instead of an information object presiding over a thriving planter network, the crumbling of the living map into dust prefigures a whole series of institutional decentralizations and, with them, the institutional investitures of power they entail. The first to fall is the Colonel himself, for his initial appearance is immediately characterized by the dust that has just overwhelmed the map of woodchips and earth:

> We watched them – the big gaunt horse almost the color of smoke, lighter in color than the dust which had gathered and caked on his wet hide … and Father damp too from the ford, his boots dark and dustcaked too, the skirts of his weathered gray coat shades darker than the breast and back and sleeves where the tarnished buttons and the frayed braid of his field officer's rank glinted dully. (U 8–9)

Certainly, Colonel Sartoris has all the accoutrements of authority. Dressed in an officer's uniform, he rides a large stallion, Jupiter, named after the chief deity of the Roman pantheon of gods. Nonetheless, both man and horse have been "caked" and "tarnished" by the dust, leading Bayard in turn to question his father's authority. We can see this with Bayard's perception of size, the fact that, on one hand, he thinks of his father as "big" and, on the other, he is forced to concede that his perception is not at all true:

> He was not big, yet somehow he looked even smaller on the horse than off of him, because Jupiter was big and when you thought of Father you thought of him as being big too and so when you thought of Father being on Jupiter it was as if you said, 'Together they will be too big; you wont believe it.' So you didn't believe it and so it wasn't. (10)

The destruction of the "living map" symbolically initiates a process in which all investitures of authority lose precedence. The discrepancy between Bayard's mental conception of his father and the actual proportions of the man undermines the boy's belief in his father's supremacy and, by extension, in the ideology that underpins the culture of the planter class. Faulkner expresses it most simply: "So you didn't believe it and so it wasn't." Bayard no longer "believes" in the size of his father and, with this loss of belief, the man is no longer big.

Whereas a number of Faulkner's characters perceive the upending of their cognitive cartographies as a dire existential dilemma, such disruption offers the possibility for individual and systemic change in the Yoknapatawpha fictions. The overall narrative arc of the *The Unvanquished* certainly upholds a positive view of such disruption, since the demise of the living map in the opening of the novel corresponds to Bayard's fateful decision at the conclusion to reject the Southern code of honor impelling him to take vengeance for the murder of his father. Since it frames the novel, this narrative coda – the disruption of the living map and Bayard's final act of novelty – certainly assumes prominence, but the theme of spontaneous novelty is established just as fully and perhaps more poignantly in the self-emancipation of members of the black community. Jennie Joiner (2022) insightfully identifies Loosh's act of novelty as the key event that allows for new constitutions of movement, behavior, and thinking for this group. To be sure, Loosh is not incidental to the destruction of the living map. The enslaved individual, Joiner writes, "does not behave as expected" and, as a result, he is "the character who first embodies emancipation and leaves the Sartoris plantation," taking his wife with him and betraying the location of the family silver to the Yankees (40).

Joiner unpacks the symbolic logic of the destruction of the living map, arguing that Loosh at once decenters the symbolic edifice of the plantation South and initiates a far larger and self-organizing pursuit of novelty on the part of the enslaved black population. Here the imagery of "dust" is paramount, for it denotes the failure of institutional power, as we saw above, and is also associated with black individuals and families who liberate themselves from these hierarchies of oppression. Joiner observes that out of the "39 instances of the word 'dust' in the novel, 35 of these occur exclusively between the moment Loosh destroys the living map and the point" (40) at which hierarchal power is reinstated when a thousand black individuals are placed under the authority of Granny Millard by the Union army. Between these two events, Faulkner repeatedly refers to the "former slaves who have emancipated themselves . . . as a 'dustcloud'" (41). Freedom, Joiner concludes, "ceases to be simply an idea; it becomes an action," a vertically oriented movement beyond coercive hierarchy and one that seeks to sustain itself by "returning to life at Jordan, a literal river in the South, but also a symbolic biblical river" (41).

Faulkner's artistic vision of entropy and information, of disruptive novelty and system centralization, is never a simplistic dualism where good triumphs over evil or individualism trumps the collective clustering of the social body. However much readers of *The Unvanquished* might wish otherwise, these self-emancipated individuals do not remain free for long. The plantation system, even within the Civil War, does not entirely lose its power but adapts to curtail the spontaneous behavior that upended its authority in the first place. Thus, the thousand self-emancipated men and women are enfolded back into the plantation system and, as a result, they tragically disappear from the text altogether. Even Ringo who plays a key role in the survival of the Sartorises during the Civil War largely vanishes from view toward the end of the novel. Colonel Sartoris and Bayard himself acknowledge Ringo to be the smarter of the two boys. In the entropic setting of the Civil War, the boy certainly rises to the occasion, becoming a vital source of information-gathering so that Granny's campaign against the Union can succeed. With the reinstatement of plantation power, however, Bayard comes to serve as the sole and final touchstone of individual novelty and agency. Yet we would be amiss not to acknowledge that *The Unvanquished* offers a moral vision of human novelty beyond white identity that becomes increasingly fundamental to the Yoknapatawpha fiction. Faulkner intimates that the individual is the moral measure upon which any coercive system of social control must be weighed. The top-down vertical power of highly centralized systems of social control only appears overwhelming, and whether the individual's attempts to move, behave, and think beyond the dicta of those systems are suppressed, half realized, or successful, each act also possesses its own potential authority to transform the social body.

5.2 The Submerged Woman

The value of individual agency within highly centralized systems becomes much more obvious during the final two decades of Faulkner's writing. In *Go Down, Moses* (1942), where he makes his strongest moral case against the twentieth-century tenant plantation system, Faulkner consciously set out to address the "relationship between white and negro races," as he told his publisher by letter.[1] Here, miscegenation *within* the plantation system becomes the central concern for the first time in his fiction – and he addresses this theme in terms of an escalating incoherence within the system itself. It is not the Civil War that acts as the tipping point toward entropic change. Faulkner examines the McCaslin plantation, the central institution in the novel, as the microcosm of this disruption. At its inception, the plantation was a violent site of miscegenation where the two families lived side by side as one family united through blood, with the black family in perpetual service to the other. As we will see, the striking change in this later fiction consists in Faulkner's insistence upon interiority as a distinct domain that allows for the possibility of change.

Go Down, Moses displays a striking continuity with the older Yoknapatawpha fiction in its representation of how centralized hubs of information and resource flow come to dominate the social space around them. With the McCaslin plantation complex, Faulkner recreates and then answers the violent cartography of consciousness he first identified in the Sartoris manor house and developed with such sophistication. As in these earlier novels, an information object in the form of two lien ledgers presides over the recurrent movement, behavior, and thinking of the social body, subjugating and directing a whole system of labor around it:

> the squared, galleried, wooden building squatting like a portent above the fields whose laborers it still held in thrall '65 or no and placarded over with advertisements for snuff and cures for chills and salves and potions manufactured and sold by white men to bleach the pigment and straighten the hair of Negroes that they might resemble the very race which for two hundred years held them in bondage ... plowlines and plow-collars and hames and trace-chains, and the desk and the shelf above it on which rested the ledgers in which McCaslin recorded the slow outward trickle of food and supplies and equipment which returned each fall as cotton made and ginned and sold (two threads frail as truth and impalpable as equators yet cable-strong to bind for life them who made the cotton to the land their sweat fell on). (GDM 227–8)

The McCaslins are elite planters who have reorganized the conditions of labor in Northeast Mississippi after the Civil War. Instead of the manor house, the commissary serves as a new center of economic and social relations within the plantation complex. By the 1880s, it was common for large landownings to become their own self-contained ecosystems with ginneries and commissaries in which the laborers would purchase the majority of their goods (Charles Aiken 1998: 41–2). As with the Sartoris manor before it, the commissary's architectonics are greater than its overt material structure. The square, wooden building of the plantation commissary exerts an invisible, but "cable-strong" force upon the black laborers in the fields, an energy whose seat of power extends from above in the figure of two lien ledgers that the landlord McCaslin stores high on a shelf within the architectural structure. Faulkner visualizes this new plantation complex by means of an intricate top-down hierarchy that extends upward from the black laborers in the fields to the store "squatting like a portent above" them, and, within this structure, the desk and, above that, the lien ledgers that "bind for life" the tenants to work the land.

At the height of his artistic powers in *Go Down, Moses*, Faulkner explicitly interweaves the symbolism of the Sartoris family bible in *Flags in the Dust* into that of the lien ledgers, so that a mimetic text, once again erected in the apex of social space, the symbolic investiture of power, possesses a quasi-agency that administers the life around it, even while expanding to encompass new selves, surfaces, and resources. Like the Sartoris genealogy, the ledgers remain paradoxical, at once a dead artifact bearing no threat to anyone and a textual surface capable of assuming absolute primacy as the elite planter class continues to write down the names and figures of plantation transactions:

> This time there was no yellowed procession of fading and harmless ledger pages. ... the ledgers, new ones now and filled rapidly, succeeding one another rapidly and containing more names than old Carothers or even his father and Uncle Buddy had ever dreamed of; new names and new faces to go with them, among which the old names and faces that even his father and uncle would have recognized were lost, vanished ... those rapid pages in the bindings new and dustless too since McCaslin lifted them down daily now to write into them the continuation of that record which two hundred years had not been enough to complete and another hundred would not be enough to discharge; that chronicle which was a whole land in miniature, which multiplied and compounded was the entire South, twenty-three years after surrender and twenty-four from emancipation – that slow trickle of molasses and meal and meat, of shoes and straw hats and overalls, of plowlines and collars and heel-bolts and buckheads and clevises, which returned each fall as cotton – the two threads frail as truth and impalpable as equators yet cable-strong to bind for life them who made the cotton to the land their sweat fell on. (277–81)

Here – and necessarily abridged – we have a classic Faulknerian sentence, a virtuoso attempt to compress a vast historical network into the grammatical unit of the sentence. The ledgers run out threads of relation ("threads frail as truth and impalpable as equators yet cable-strong") to all those around them, invisible threads that exert such a powerful social force that they bind and tie individuals to them absolutely, so that the individuals who come and go, year after year, do so as a clustering around, and dispersal from, the information object. Isaac comes to understand the sheer scope and power these mimetic surfaces have assumed across time, as they inscribe and then regulate the flow of information through the nodes of the system – through both animate and inanimate matter. The ledgers are therefore much more than ink and paper, more than mere accounting, discourse, or narrative; they constitute a cognitive cartography that seems to be everywhere, a network that uses abbreviations and "miniatures" of itself as the nodes through which ideology can flow endlessly in a dynamic feedback loop. As a result, this record assumes an uncanny power to link past, present, and future – to connect Old Carothers, the original patriarch of the slave plantation who began the ledgers, to Ike's present perception of them to Cass Edmonds who will continue to add names and figures in these texts once Ike repudiates his inheritance. Although invented, these ledgers are no longer fiction; they are the literal dead center of the plantation complex, the vertical hub in which information and resources centralize and through which they flow out to peripheral nodes or to other network clusters that make up the larger plantation system of the New South.

Faulkner's meditation on written language denotes a tyranny of textual space that assimilates everything it represents and comes to possess that quasi-agency we have so often observed in Faulkner's most coercive information objects. At sixteen years of age, Isaac experiences the quasi-agency of the ledgers, discovering for the first time the incestuous crime of his forefather, Old Carothers, who raped his own daughter Tomasina: "The old frail pages seemed to turn of their own accord even while he thought *His own daughter His own daughter*" (259). Instead of a harmless, dead artifact, the ledgers now appear capable of turning the pages of their own accord and ultimately invading Isaac's being so that they will be "part of his consciousness . . . forever" (259). I contend that this whole sequence is one of Faulkner's most significant as a writer, not only because it represents a culmination of the cartographic symbolism that Faulkner invented at very outset of his Yoknapatawpha fiction, but also because the content of the passage demonstrates a moral maturation on the part of author, a movement beyond the modernist self-reflexive aesthetics of his earlier fiction toward a robust ethical engagement with the other.

Martin Buber's famous essay *I and Thou* (1923) offers a basic tenet with which to distinguish between the cognitive cartographies of *Flags in the Dust* and *Go Down, Moses*. Buber's own distinction between the *I–It* and the *I–Thou* upholds intersubjectivity as an "in between" or "mutual" ontology that overcomes instrumental determinism. For Buber, the "*I–It* relationship, in its most degenerate stage, assumes the fixed form of objects that one can measure and manipulate." By contrast, "human intersubjectivity affirms the polymorphous *I–Thou* encounter. Resting upon the claim that no isolated I exists apart from relationship to an other, dialogue or 'encounter' transforms each figure into an ultimate and mysterious center of value whose presence eludes the concepts of instrumental language."[2] For all its symbolic sophistication, the original plantation prototype in *Flags in the Dust* exemplifies an *I–It* relationship. To be sure, instrumentality dominates the deceptive white simplicity of the Sartoris manor, for at the base of the structure, we find murderous bloodred roses producing a coinage by strangling the wisteria vine and, at the architectural apex of the manor, the Colonel places his own image, a mimetic information object that at once assimilates everything around it and transforms that life into dead lettering. In the context of the Buber paradigm, we may say that in the earlier works the architectonics of interiority are dominated by the fixed form of objects – indeed, the ultimate fixed form of the object: The death's head in the watery page of the family Sartoris bible and, by extension, the monumental statues of the Colonel or the Confederate soldier that are variations of this original paradigm. A similar cognitive cartography occurs in *Go Down, Moses*, with the "yellowed page" of the ledger also becoming a watery surface. Instead of a dead object assuming primacy, however, an intersubjective vision of the other manifests itself through the textual medium. Unlike the skull staring back at the planter in *Flags in the Dust*, Isaac sees a submerged self that does not obey the dicta of the information object that inscribes it. In other words, the depths open to display not a dead object but a beloved being who is expressing a deliberate act of agency.

In experiencing an *I–Thou* relationship, Isaac is able to see beyond the instrumental ideology of calculation and ownership that permeates the textual medium. Most importantly, Isaac's eventual repudiation of his inheritance is based not on himself or the biological web of heredity that props him up in time, but on an original act of repudiation. The precedent for Isaac's act of defiance is set when Eunice, the matriarch of the primary mixed-race family on the plantation, drowns herself in an "icy creek":

> looking down at the yellowed page spread beneath the yellow glow of the lantern smoking and stinking in that rank chill midnight room fifty years later, he seemed to see her actually walking into the icy creek on that Christmas day six months before her daughter's and her lover's (*Her first lover's* he thought. *Her first*) child was born, solitary, inflexible, griefless, ceremonial, in formal and succinct repudiation of grief and despair who had already had to repudiate belief and hope
>
> that was all. He would never need look at the ledgers again nor did he; the yellowed pages in their fading and implacable succession were as much a part of his consciousness and would remain so forever. (GDM 259)

Isaac's repudiation is modelled upon a black matriarch's ultimate sacrifice. At sixteen, Isaac discovers that Old Carothers, the original plantation patriarch, bought Eunice in a New Orleans slave market in 1807, raping and impregnating both her and his own daughter by her, Tomasina, who, in turn, gives birth to Tomey's Turl, the father of Lucas Beauchamp. Eunice, for her part, does not accept this violent dominion over her body willingly. Upon learning of her daughter's pregnancy, she drowns herself on Christmas day in 1832, a tragic event that also becomes the foundational act of agency, novelty, and disruption in the novel, a steadfast refusal to submit to the coercive ideology of the plantation system and enacted at far greater price than the renunciation of property.

Although the ledgers seem omnipotent, Isaac's intersubjective vision elucidates a competing and hidden history that was already present at the ledger's inception and runs right through and beyond its sequence of names, dates, and transactions. Jay Watson (2019) provides a moving and in-depth analysis of Eunice's significance not only within *Go Down, Moses* and the larger Yoknapatawpha corpus, but also in the larger terms of the black Atlantic world. For Watson, Eunice offers a historical "legacy of negation," one which does not monumentalize, but "functions as a *critical memory* . . . where the performances of Eunice and her successors comprise a behavioral repertoire to complement and at times contest the written archive of the McCaslins, whose ledgers already attest to the power of black will and black death to disturb a sensibility handed down from the European Enlightenment to the New World Plantation" (277). Watson provides a key defense of Faulkner's artistic attempt to represent black experience not just as "an oppositional history," although it can be, but as a founding history in his later Yoknapatawpha fiction. Faulkner, Watson concludes, "self-consciously constructs Eunice as a founding figure, positioning her history in a pointed relationship of priority to other such figures and originary scenes" (281).

The ledgers may frame the emotional registry of Eunice's act as a suicide and Ike, for his part, accepts a version of its narrative. However, the black matriarch's tragic but courageous refusal to submit to the tyranny of Old Carothers cannot be circumscribed. Eunice's protest generates the emergence of an interior dimension that gives rise to a host of other disruptive acts of novelty down through the generations which change the plantation system and reconstitute the way in which it functions. Thus, Isaac discovers others capable of renouncing the ideological dictates of the ledgers – Thucydus McCaslin, for example, whom Old Carothers married to Eunice once she became pregnant with his child. Old Carothers left land to

Thucydus, but the enslaved individual refused the inheritance bequeathed to him, choosing instead to work himself out of slavery and open a shop as a blacksmith in Jefferson. Tomey's Turl, the son/grandson of Old Carothers and grandson of Eunice, is another individual in the bloodline who will not stay within the demarcations of the plantation complex. He simply runs away whenever he has a chance so that the plantation masters, his half brothers/uncles Amodeus and Theophilus, repeatedly have to hunt him down and place him back into bondage. His son Lucas Beauchamp is another key example. His own iron will and domineering personality are especially on display in his violent confrontation with Zach Edmonds, the owner of the plantation and Lucas' white cousin, in turn denoting the mounting incoherence of the racial power dynamic that is central to the logic of the ledgers.

5.3 Beyond Ideology, the Immanent and Intersubjective

Although the cognitive cartography of the McCaslin plantation reaches across generations to coerce black and white families with the invisible chains of ideology, Faulkner also articulates another kind of power source within these systems, a different kind of centralized informational hub – associated with individual inwardness and family bonds – that acts from below rather than from above. A primary purpose in Sections 5.3 and 5.4 is to demonstrate that Faulkner's cognitive cartographies cannot be neatly abstracted into a rejection of centralization and hierarchy. Faulkner does not reject hierarchical power systems in themselves, but rather the ways in which they are maintained indefinitely at the price of the individuals who sustain them. Indeed, intractable top-down vertical power suppresses the production of novelty, subordinating the individual who is a source of this novelty and also destabilizing the viability of the system over time.

In these two final sections, I show that Faulkner presents three principal ways to address the supervening ideology of the New South plantation system. One can repudiate it like Isaac, negotiate with it like Lucas, or strike against it as in the case with Rider. This third section explores the answer that Faulkner formulates in the character of Isaac; section 5.4 examines the respective formulations of Lucas and Rider. While each character provides a different response, Faulkner explicitly structures all three with an emphatic affirmation of interior space. We have seen repeatedly how this interior space is subject to invasion; here, however, Faulkner provides a new architectonics that align with his earlier fiction certainly, but offer a powerful reconsideration of how social space can be reconstituted through individual behavior. Isaac and Lucas provide variable instances of emergent individual novelty that actively challenge the "cable-strong" social force that the plantation complex exerts, and Rider demonstrates that, under certain conditions, this novelty can violently deform the vertical paradigms of power that surround him.

We begin by appreciating the greater symbolic contours of the novel's title as both a cry for freedom, as it is typically understood, and an implicit spatial directive towards cognitive depth and interiority. "Go Down Moses" is a well-known phrase that alludes to *Exodus* 5:1 in which Yahweh directs Moses to demand freedom for the Israelites. In the context of the chattel slavery of the United States, the phrase commonly occurred in spirituals signaling a desire for liberty – and gains even more significance for us with its association to Harriet Tubman who used a hymn with the phrase to communicate with self-emancipated individuals on the Underground Railway. Tubman's description offers an evocative spiritual imagery of an "unseen singer" and those who hide in the darkness and "listen eagerly for the words she sings" (Bradford 1869: 26). This context allows us to better comprehend Faulkner's representation of our three aforementioned characters in striking relation to a site in social space which hides from view and is not circumscribed by the institutions and laws of human systems.

As we will see, all three of these characters – Isaac, Lucas, and Rider – negotiate the demands of inwardness or depth in ways that involve, but exceed ideology. In *Go Down, Moses*, the submerged woman, the Indian mound, and the grave of Mannie present an associative symbolic language for these dark architectonics of interiority. On one immediate level, this emphatic emphasis upon the dead body in the depths of cognitive space indicates that Faulkner was using his fiction to work through the death of Caroline Barr to whom he dedicated *Go Down, Moses* with the expression, "To Mammy." There is certainly a homonymic wordplay across the various chapters on the word Mammy with Molly, Mollie, and Mannie as the most obvious examples. Here, moreover, Faulkner affirms interior space in a manner that is only intimated in the earlier fiction, indicating that complex social systems depend upon the smaller self-organizing nodes that constitute them and that may even transform them.

While older scholars tended to affirm Isaac's renunciation of the plantation and his reverence for nature,[3] contemporary critics often view the character as a failure, predicated on a clichéd and deceptive Romanticism. Erik Dussere (2003) makes the most forceful case. "The Bear," he states, is "a parable of the failure of white male selfhood" (23). Christina Thyssen

(2015) provides a more postmodern reading: "Ike's entirely impotent mythologization of the virginal wilderness [entails] his search for a pure origin beyond the doomed plantation" (94). However we are to assess Isaac's success or failure as a character, Faulkner carefully crafted the character to be capable of thinking outside the epistemology of the ledgers. On one level, Isaac's early discovery of the crimes that his white family perpetuated on his black family comes at a personal price, not as absolute as the one Eunice paid certainly, but one that jeopardizes his future ability to remake and nurture the interpersonal bonds of family. Despite the limitations of his character, the ethics of immanence that Faulkner embeds in Isaac is a vital and interlinking facet of this deeper intersubjective repudiation that manifests itself across many individuals, both black and white. The self-reflexive symbolism that Faulkner evokes in Isaac's mental visualization of Eunice's submerging herself in the "icy creek" (259) directly corresponds to his earlier vision of the bear "sink[ing] back into the dark depths of its pool" (201). As we will see in the next section (5.4), this self-reflective symbolism of interior space explicitly maps onto Lucas and Rider as well, indicating that the novel seeks to address the relationship between the ideological and the individual from numerous perspectives.

With Isaac's reverence for the wilderness as his moral compass, Faulkner implicitly comments upon and develops the dilemma that he evoked in Quentin Compson. In the earliest hunting stories that were to become *Go Down, Moses*, Quentin, not Ike McCaslin, is the boy learning to hunt, and Faulkner must have realized that Quentin, the suicide, could not allow him to evoke the moral agency necessary to resist the tyranny of textual space that dominates the plantation complex. Isaac is not only Quentin's narrative successor; he also connects readers to one of Yoknapatawpha's earliest families from *Flags in the Dust*, the MacCallum family. The McCaslin plantation is located on the Yoknapatawpha County map where Faulkner located the MacCallum farm. In the earlier novel, MacCallum Place is a rather modest farm, located deep in the woods and made of "chinked logs" and "hand-trimmed" floor boards (FD 332). While the details of the McCaslin plantation are not uniform across novels, the site itself is among the oldest in the County, a major slave plantation before the Civil War and a bureaucratic center for the sharecropping that comes afterward. In this sense, Isaac is a character in whom two significant strands from the earlier Yoknapatawpha fiction converge. He is a man who confronts the sharecropping plantation system – with its powerful feedback loop of credit compelling its black laborers into a modern form of indentured servitude. Isaac comes to understand that the plantation epis-temology of textual space is predicated upon a wilder principle of being which he identifies at once with a nomadic way of life and with Old Ben, the mythical bear of the Big Bottom in the northwest corner of Yoknapatawpha. From the first, Isaac does not reject all vertical forms of power and, thus, his morality is not based upon a simplistic antagonism to civilization. Indeed, his early relationship with the woods sets up his opposition to the ideology of the plantation with the principle of inviolable immanence.

Throughout "The Bear," Faulkner employs an emphatic vertical imag-ery to portray the big woods and its symbolic representative, the bear, as an underlying and immanent form of power, separate from, but related to the ledgers. In the symbolic language of cognitive cartographies, Isaac perceives a contest between vertical paradigms of power, between the woods, on the one hand, and textuality, on the other. "The Bear" begins with this insistence most of all, for Isaac in boyhood already sees "the wilderness, the big woods, bigger and older than any recorded document" (GDM 183). The wilderness is "bigger" than the ledgers; it "stoops overhead," denoting not simply a fantasy of vertical power in the imagination of Isaac, but a vision of what power can be when it does not seek ideological dominion over others. Faulkner has already preset this spatial vision of the wilderness in "The Old People" as a type of conversation with Isaac holding his breath and, in response, "the wilderness ceas[ing] to breathe also, leaning, stooping overhead with its breath held, tremendous and impartial and waiting" (175). Faulkner's characterization of the breathing wilderness of "The Old People" and "The Bear" is very different from the paradigm we explored in the first two chapters. In *Flags in the Dust*, if we recall, the Colonel appears in the bank breathing above and about his son – and as the narrative unfolds in the attic of the Sartoris house, this uncanny imagery of breath is dramatically multiplied with "a legion of ghosts breath[ing] quietly at [Bayard's] shoulder." In *The Sound and the Fury*, Faulkner heightens the sense of coercion in the way that plantation power disseminates itself as breath in the opening of Quentin's mono-logue. With Isaac's initial engagement of the wilderness above, by contrast, Faulkner offers breath as genuine intersubjectivity. The boy has to enter into a drawn-out dialogue with the wilderness as a dynamic form of mirroring in which the boy holds his breath and, in response, the wilder-ness does the same. The bear eventually emerges as the boy's first under-standing of a vertical power that existed before humans appropriated it with the aim of erecting permanent hierarchies of power.

Go Down, Moses does not dismiss hierarchy, though it emphatically rejects the top-down form of vertical power embodied in the ledgers and, thus, in all the coercive information objects we have seen throughout Faulkner's Yoknapatawpha fiction. From the first, Isaac is capable of thinking in a language that exists outside the ledgers. He already dreams of the bear before he has ever entered into the big woods, and Faulkner continues to employ this immanent symbolism in terms of vertical height, since the creature "looms" and "towers" above: "It ran in his knowledge before he ever saw it. It loomed and towered in his dreams before he even saw the unaxed woods where it left its crooked print" (184). Under the tutelage of Sam Fathers, his half black, half Chickasaw mentor, Isaac learns to see the fuller temporal arc of human social systems that scale from natural processes to become the complex and often coercive assemblages of modernity. Isaac eventually sees beyond the vertically instantiated information objects of human civilization because he understands that they are nestled within an impermanent and wilder domain of existence: "the old wild life which the little puny humans swarmed and hacked at in a fury of abhorrence and fear like pygmies about the ankles of a drowsing elephant" (GDM 185). Isaac visualizes a far larger duration of "wild life" which gradually gives way to the dynamic, but "puny" human hierarchies which "swarm" about and feed off of it.

A major misconception among some scholars is that Isaac's character arc involves stepping out of history and into myth. As a number of critics contend, the boy loses himself in a "timeless" and "mythic past" (Ronald Schleifer 1982: 126; and Paul Harris 1993: 637). On the contrary, the wilderness is not timeless. In the figure of the bear, Faulkner depicts a wilderness that gives way to the swarming human behavior of complex social systems. Yes, the bear possesses a mythic power insofar as it is a grand symbol of the wilderness, but readers should neither dismiss nor minimize Faulkner's portrayal of nature as naive Romanticism or facile mysticism. Isaac's connection to an earlier nomadic way of life makes his later ability to see beyond the dicta of the ledgers conceptually coherent. The deceptive claim of all ideology, as we have seen, is that there is nothing outside of ideology. Whereas the ledgers insist upon this claim, Faulkner does not portray nature in this manner. Like the innermost architecture of the self, it is fragile, subject to invasion and control.

Sam Fathers' tutelage involves recognizing the spiritual dimension in nature as a deeper reality that animates the visible world but does not seek to dominate it eternally. In short, he teaches the boy to see these immanent hierarchies that emerge and dissipate in the natural world. In one of the boy's first hunting experiences which opens "The Old People," Isaac witnesses a "condensed light" or a "source" that both wells up in his prey and is disseminated in its movements:

> Then the buck was there. He did not come into sight; he was just there, looking not like a ghost but as if all light were condensed in him and he were the source of it, not only moving in it but disseminating it, already running, seen first as you always see the deer, in that split second after he has already seen you, already slanting away in that first soaring bound, the antlers even in that dim light looking like a small rocking-chair balanced on his head. (GDM 157)

Faulkner expresses a different kind of cognitive cartography from the ones we have analyzed so far. Whereas coercive information objects force the self to accept their centrality by internalizing and then transmitting their content to others, Isaac perceives the buck as a compression of light and a dissemination of this light in physical space without the threat of violence or force. The intimation that the animal's antlers look like a chair above its head differs markedly from the menacing spectral throne that Bayard imagines superimposed onto his family's genealogy in *Flags in the Dust*; the vertically elevated natural architecture of the antlers does not haunt – "not like a ghost" – but expresses rather an open-ended vista for emergence: some new expression will seat itself upon the head of the buck. Nor is this a fanciful speculation, for it accords with the narrative arc in which Isaac's interaction with the buck prepares for his eventual engagement with the bear.

   In order to renounce his claim to the plantation, therefore, Isaac must first learn to think outside its paradigm, to embrace, in other words, an immersion in the wilderness that will allow him to see that any such claim is impermanent within the fuller scale of historical becoming. Yet his initiation into this way of seeing is no easy task; it is a process of self-emptying and learning to engage nature without the implements of civilization – without the "puny" but "cable-strong" ideological instruments of dominion. Under Sam Fathers' direction, Isaac goes alone into the wilderness with only his "compass and a stick for the snakes" (198), but even these must be given up in order to come face-to-face with the bear. Thus, "leaving the gun was not enough" and therefore compass and watch must be abandoned as well, for the young boy to stand "a child, alien and lost in the green and soaring gloom of the markless wilderness" (199). Stripped of all civilizational implements of measurement and rationality, "he relinquished completely to it. It was the watch and the compass.

He was still tainted. He removed the linked chain of the one and the looped thong of the other from his overalls and hung them on a bush and leaned the stick beside them and entered it" (199). Only in this alien condition, bereft of the implements of ideology, is Ike able to track the bear and confront not merely an animal, but an immanent reality that already permeates the wilderness from within:[4]

> Then he saw the bear. It did not emerge, appear: it was just there, immobile, fixed in the green and windless noon's hot dappling, not as big as he had dreamed it but as big as he expected, bigger, dimensionless against the dappled obscurity, looking at him. Then it moved. It crossed the glade without haste, walking for an instant into the sun's full glare and out of it, and stopped again and looked back at him across one shoulder. Then it was gone. It didn't walk into the woods. It faded, sank back into the wilderness without motion as he had watched a fish, a huge old bass, sink back into the dark depths of its pool and vanish without even any movement of its fins. (200)

Whether readers admire or dismiss this Romantic depiction of the bear, Faulkner's treatment is undeniably positive, an affirmation of a vertically elevated authority whose movements are akin to an entropic "tornado" (201) and impermanent. The bear may leave its "crooked print" on the surface of the earth, but Faulkner repeatedly depicts this surface with the imagery of water, so that all such inscriptions "dissolve away" (199). In the passage above, this insistence is unmistakable, since the bear first appears "immobile" in the midst of physical space. We have seen this immobility before in all the coercive information objects that dominate cognitive and social space, but the bear immediately relinquishes control and sinks back into the "dark depths of its pool."

Faulkner's fascination with depth – "the dark depths" within animate matter – permeates his depiction of the big woods and the bear. The spectral depth we saw in the Sartoris family genealogy, the Colonel's statue, the Sutpen text, or the plantation ledgers involves a violence to, and an invasion of interior space; this is not the case with the portrayal above. Nor are these dark depths easily dismissed as a self-contained essentialism. Contrary to the view that Isaac is seduced by a timeless or mythic past, Isaac's Romanticism is no facile insight about timelessness. Isaac's rejection of the ledgers is an outright rejection of the Keatsian urn image we analyzed in *Light in August*. Like Lena who is able think outside of the static delineations of the urn, Isaac rejects Cass Edmonds' encapsulation of the bear encounter as a poetic truth engraved upon a Grecian urn.

Faulkner reinforces just how vertiginous it is for the modern human being to reject the civilizational claims of permanence. Indeed, just as he discards the urn paradigm offered by "his kinsman, his father almost," Isaac is overwhelmed by a feeling of rootlessness, his very familial bond to Cass irrevocably severed so that the two sit "juxtaposed and alien now to each other against their ravaged patrimony, the dark and ravaged fatherland still prone and panting from its etherless operation" (285). For Isaac, then, truth does not attain centrality, much less immortality, as something instantiated permanently in physical space. Rather, the bear possesses even greater power because it relinquishes its own sovereignty.

The eventual tragedy of an aged Isaac in "Delta Autumn" is that he forgets the moral basis for his renunciation above. As a boy and young man, he is able to see two figures, the bear and Eunice, submerge themselves in the dark depths of being – and this paradigm unfolds as an ethical engagement with other beings. The older Isaac loses this intersubjective ability. On one level, his final stance is a willful evasion of the environmental tragedy unfolding across the arc of his life. This is because Isaac's wilderness has become ideological, his final desire in "Delta Autumn" simply self-centered and solipsistic, since he has decided that there is just enough of the Big Woods left to last out the remainder of his life, as though the wilderness is for him alone. Thus, Isaac no longer engages in the possibility of dialogue between beings, for he sees only how the wilderness is gathering itself into an "inverted-apex" or "one tremendous density of brooding and inscrutable impenetrability" to funnel downward "between hills and River":

> He had watched it, not being conquered, destroyed, so much as retreating since its purpose was served now and its time an outmoded time, retreating southward through this inverted-apex, this ∇-shaped section of earth between hills and River until what was left of it seemed now to be gathered and for the time arrested in one tremendous density of brooding and inscrutable impenetrability at the ultimate funneling tip. (328)

The older Isaac still sees the wilderness as endowed with depth, but it is being directed downward into interior spaces that have no relation to actual living beings. Thus, Isaac's consolation is dramatical different from the intersubjective engagements of his youth, for he imagines that this disappearing "dimension" will become "free of both time and space." Thus, he imagines that whereas "the untreed land [is] warped and wrung to mathematical squares of rank cotton," a deeper interior memory will "find ample room" and preserve both him and the wilderness (339). This visualization is ultimately empty, because it is at once abstract and not tied to real flesh-and-blood beings.

At the close of "Delta Autumn," Faulkner explicitly reveals that interior spaces are still dynamically alive, but only within human beings – and it is Isaac's inability to engage in genuine dialogue with these spaces that reveals the old man's eventual failure. While he was able to recognize the claim of a submerged Eunice in his youth, here, he rejects this method of seeing in later life by effectively instructing Eunice's kin to accept the stipulations of Jim Crow and leave the father of her unborn baby to marry a person of her own race. Thus, a frail Isaac lies beneath his blanket and confronts a mysterious interiority in the unnamed mistress of Roth Edmonds, the granddaughter of Tennie's Jim and thus great-granddaughter of Eunice herself:

> She regarded him, almost peacefully, with that unwinking and heatless fixity – the dark wide bottomless eyes in the face's dead and toneless pallor which to the old man looked anything but dead, but young and incredibly and even ineradicably alive – as though she were not only not looking at anything, she was not even speaking to anyone but herself. (344)

Here, Isaac is still capable of recognizing these dark architectonics when they appear, but this is where we invariably confront the limitations of an individual life that has retreated from contact with other human beings. No matter how fully a self individuates and attempts to work through the greater moral quandary of the social space in which it is embedded, this individual experience inevitably remains a partial engagement and always requires others. Isaac has become ill-equipped to rebuild the interpersonal bonds of family and community – and the great-granddaughter of Eunice is a final reminder of Isaac's inability in this regard. Whereas Isaac's intersubjective engagement with the Big Woods once prepared him to recognize the claims of the submerged Eunice over those of the ledgers, now, he does nothing to help her kin, even though the rejected mixed-race woman who looks down on him similarly represents an immanent dimension within matter. This woman is "ineradicably alive," possessing "dark wide bottomless eyes." But Isaac is no longer present to her or anyone else and is thus incapable of offering the genuine intersubjective engagement of his earlier days. Thus, we conclude with the woman regarding him, but "not looking at anything" and "not even speaking to anyone but herself." This unnamed woman must find a life for herself – away from the white father of her baby and the plantation complex he administrates – and the description above indicates that she is more than equal to the task.

5.4   A Reconciliation and a Warning

In *Go Down, Moses*, Lucas Beauchamp – who is kin to this unnamed mixed-race woman with "dark wide bottomless eyes" – is the character who most fully attempts to work out and negotiate the interpersonal bonds that unite self, family, and community. In Lucas, moreover, we see how the immanent depths of being can be entangled with the ideological snares of the governing social order. Like Isaac, Lucas is ideologically tethered to the plantation complex, but in a subtler and more insidious way. As a young man, Isaac dealt with a very clear ultimatum: either to become the owner of the McCaslin complex, thereby placing himself as the newest successor of old Carothers, or to reject his place in this genealogy. Theresa Towner (2000) illuminates why Lucas cannot indulge in such "a culturally privileged gesture," since "life as a poor man with dark skin has taught him" otherwise (15). Thus, Isaac repudiates the plantation, but he ultimately cannot build a viable life of interpersonal connections outside of it. Lucas' quandary is that he must disentangle himself from an ideology that has secured precedence in the depths of his identity, and he must do so without jeopardizing his marriage to Molly Beauchamp or the wellbeing of his daughter and his son-in-law, all of which are at stake throughout the chapter devoted to him.

Most of "The Fire and the Hearth" takes place in 1940 when Lucas is already "the oldest living person on the Edmonds plantation, the oldest McCaslin descendant even though in the world's eye he descended not from McCaslin but from McCaslin slaves" (GDM 38). The narrative at first appears comedic, depicting Lucas as a stereotypical father who believes that George Ripley, his bootlegging competitor, is not good enough for his daughter, since the younger man is "a fool, innocent of discretion, who sooner or later would be caught" by the law (36). Lucas hatches a plan to thwart the man, and his opening move involves hiding his own moonshine still from Roth Edmonds and the law at the creek bottom. As Lucas descends from his land to the creek bottom, readers begin to see beyond the apparently humorous competition between the men. To be sure, it is here that Faulkner first identifies the nature of Lucas' complicated ideological relationship to the land. Being mixed-race, Lucas could never have inherited the plantation, even though his hereditary claim runs through his paternal side to Old Carothers, whereas the present owner's claim is maternal. At once proud and bitter, Lucas is hyper-aware of his seniority and the fact of his patrimony, nurturing a belief about his dispossession that in his mind gives him a claim over the land that Roth Edmonds, who actually owns all the land, does not have: "But it was his own field, though he neither owned it nor wanted to nor even needed to. He had been cultivating it for forty-five years, since before Carothers Edmonds was born even, plowing and planting and working it when and how he saw fit" (37). Lucas knows the land; he has cultivated it and does not need anyone to confirm his personal relationship with it. In his movement through the night, he demonstrates, moreover, that he is capable of a farsighted perception of this land across time. Like Isaac, he can see far back into the past, beyond his own individual life, tracing the McCaslin relationship with the land all the way back to when Old Carothers "got the land from the Indians in the old time when men black and white were men" (38).

In the opening section of the chapter, Faulkner parallels this temporal visualization with a pattern of spatial descent that will be familiar to the reader. Just as Lucas mentally traces the temporal sequence into the past, he reaches "the creek bottom" (38). Faulkner echoes the coupling of spatial descent and mnemonic interiority he initially employed in *Flags in the Dust* when old Bayard's descent into the somnolent setting of the plantation manor enacts a movement into the depths of the mind. In this later novel, we can see how much Faulkner's craft has developed in the intervening years, for the technique is employed more seamlessly and establishes, moreover, an intersubjective arena of discovery that identifies the dark depths within as paramount. Where Isaac in "The Bear" discovers the black matriarch submerged in an "icy creek," here, in the second line of the earlier chapter, Lucas has to find "some place far enough away and secret enough" to conceal his still. He descends to the creek bottom which is described as a "rank sunless jungle of cypress and willow and brier" (38). While this is a real site within the plantation proper, Faulkner also indicates this sunless and secret place houses a core of hidden power that rises out of the ground "without reason": "Then he saw the place he sought – a squat, flat-topped, almost symmetrical mound rising without reason from the floorlike flatness of the valley. The white people called it an Indian mound" (39). Faulkner skillfully interweaves the mound as a realistic place and a type of non-rational archetypical structure rising out of the depths. White people call this place Indian mound and thereby seek to circumscribe it within their maps. Lucas, for his part, perceives this place to be the "old earth," the very "spirit of darkness and solitude" (40) and, as he shovels out an orifice in the dirt, the mound rises above him with all the power that a vertical paradigm can possess, yet it is also an image of depth, of information that expresses itself from below.

In this way, Faulkner establishes a clear intra-textual symbolic parallel between Isaac and Lucas confronting a paradigm of power in the dark depths of nature. Both men look beyond the mimetic surface – the yellowed ledgers in Isaac's case and the "floorlike flatness of the valley" in Lucas' – to find a site that is older than the McCaslin plantation. Jay Watson (2019) articulates "the creek bottom's history as a zone of black struggle" (275), and I argue that it is an explicit site of cognitive interiority that both underlies and can break through the ideological claims of the plantation regime. Where this older paradigm looms in Isaac's dreams and disappears in the "dark depths of its pool," Lucas' experience of this "spirit of darkness and solitude" possesses very similar spatial architectonics: "It sounded to him louder than an avalanche, as though the whole mound had stooped roaring down at him ... the unchanged shape of the mound which seemed to loom poised above him in a long roaring wave of silence like a burst of jeering and prolonged laughter" (GDM 40). Lucas is by no means a passive recipient in this dynamic. Indeed, as he confronts this power in the creek bottom, he imagines that the looming mound hands him a "single coin" and, in response, "his brain boil[s] with all the images of buried money he had ever listened to or heard of" (40). Here Lucas' ideological identification with the land comes to a head. He may have been unfairly dispossessed of his claim, but the "old earth" has offered him a golden treasure that he will pursue despite the damage it causes to himself and his familial relationships.

Well versed readers of Faulkner know that such a quest for buried gold is always a fool's errand in the Yoknapatawpha fictions, and this scene provides a striking indication of what is really at stake in the chapter. Here, at the bottom of the creek, Lucas is coming face to face not only with his enduring belief in the value of the plantation system, but also with his own buried anger and resentment. Words like "outrage" or "rage" (37, 41, 50, 62, 65, 70, 84, 85, 103, 113, 114, 115) appear so frequently that they locate an emotional register that is paramount throughout the novel, sometimes neglected (as in the case of Isaac), but abiding and ascendant (especially in the cases of Lucas and Rider). Thadious Davis (2003: 111), Christina Thyssen (2015: 95), and Jay Watson (2019: 262), all attend to "an anger so profound" that it has the power to unsettle and destabilize the governing narratives of the plantation system. It is in this spectral exchange between "the old earth" and Lucas where Faulkner links this intergenerational outrage with the imagery of "boiling-over." Later in the chapter, Faulkner gives readers a fuller sense of what precisely is bursting forth in Lucas: "He was raging – an abrupt boiling-over of an accumulation of floutings and outrages covering not only his span but his father's lifetime too, back into the time of his grandfather McCaslin Edmonds" (GDM 102). While this outrage is his own, it exceeds the memory of a single life. Because we have addressed Isaac first, we know that the depths of the creek are imagistically connected to Eunice, Lucas' great-grandmother.

Lucas is not merely projecting his own fantasy about what the land owes him onto the mound; he is confronting an ideology in himself that pivots upon a deeper intersubjective history that arises from below. Throughout the course of the narrative, Faulkner repeatedly takes his readers back in time to show the various experiences that undergird Lucas' beliefs about his place within the plantation. Readers come to find that there are, in fact, two very different versions of Lucas over the sixty-seven years of his life: an earlier Lucas who is the faithful retainer of Zach Edmonds, willing to "risk his life unquestioning at the behest of his employer," and the later man who gains "an enduring awareness of his distinction" from the plantation community (Zender 2003: 121). The older Lucas enjoys, moreover, a financial independence from the plantation. From the first, Faulkner indicates that Lucas has amassed a small fortune for one in his social position: "He already had more money in the bank now than he would ever spend, more than Carothers Edmonds himself" (GDM 35). Unlike his black ancestors, then, he is financially free from the plantation and, therefore, from the ledgers on which his name appears. Yet he is not free from its ideology. He maintains an outrage at this system that, while justified, nonetheless jeopardizes the wellbeing of his person and his family life over time.

The main flashback scene that culminates in Lucas' violent confrontation with Zach Edmonds clarifies the overlapping and contradictory claims upon this black man's historical being: the interpersonal life of family, on the one hand, and his bond to the dicta of the plantation system, on the other. These competing values are developed by means of the chapter's central image – the hearth – whose fire parallels Lucas' fury at the mound: "It was hot, not scorching, searing, but possessing a slow, deep solidity of heat, a condensation of the two years during which the fire had burned constantly above it, a condensation not of fire but of time, as though not the fire's dying and not even the water would cool it but only time would" (52). This passage describes the heat of a hearth that Lucas Beauchamp has kept constant during his wife's two-year absence. Molly, Lucas' wife, lives with his white cousin Zach Edmonds and cares for the plantation owner's new-born son whose own mother died in childbirth. Lucas, for his part, has been given no say in this state of affairs. Lucas' heritage certainly informs his anger and suspicion, since his own great-grandfather raped his slaves, Lucas' great-grandmother and grandmother, and sired two lines of descendants, his white heirs and his mixed-race children, legally bound to the McCaslins as private property and then remaining in the service of the white family long after emancipation.

The heat of the hearth is no simple image, therefore, for it contains a compound symbolism of overlapping claims upon the self. On one obvious level, the hearth is the literal center of the domestic sphere, a centralized hub around which the family clusters across time. Yet it has come to reflect the boiling resentment that Lucas first expresses at the mound and spills over in this flashback in violent confrontation. Still, the hearth is substantially more than this, underscoring a strategy central to Faulkner's cognitive cartographies. The passage displays Faulkner's paradigmatic effort to compress time in imagistic representation. The author is explicit that the heat of the heath is a temporal "condensation." More than temperature alone, the heat of the hearth serves as an informational source for the intergenerational movement and behavior that props Lucas up in time and propels him onward to new action. To parse the significance of the hearth, the reader must acknowledge it as a principal hub of social space, while also attempting to discover what trajectories of historical occurrence presently converge upon this particular condensation of time in space. This is no simple task, since it entails discovering no less than the life of the entire community as it moves, behaves, and thinks in social space. Lucas may command our attention at this point in the text, yet the hearth's heat articulates an intergenerational outrage that can be located in countless moments in time, including the specific demands of the plantation on Lucas and the ways it invades and usurps his family life. When Lucas eventually acts, it is not some flight of fancy on his part or perceived injustice. Holding a razor and standing above the sleeping body of his white cousin, Lucas acts alone while simultaneously acting as a compression of all these previous moments in time as they manifest themselves in present action.

Though Isaac's dilemma takes a very different form, both he and Lucas confront the self-same phenomenon. In Lucas' perception, both of these centralized nodes – the dark mound and the scorching hearth – are in danger of being appropriated by the ideology of the plantation. In the first instance, the ideology of inheritance exerts itself even in "the old earth," within the very orifice of the mound – and, in the second iteration, the hearth as the communal center of the family has been disrupted by the external demands of Zach Edmonds upon Lucas' wife. Faulkner frames

Lucas' individual experience to reflect and intersect in striking ways with the experience of all those around him. Faulkner establishes these parallels between selves by emphasizing both the variability of each personal experience and the fact that these separate subjective experiences tend to cluster around certain weighted nodes of social space. Faulkner's representation of Roth Edmonds' emotional makeup and spatial movements also reflects those of his cousin Lucas, though the two men's social, racial, and economic circumstances are so different. As the plantation owner reaches the "Old Injun's mound" in pursuit of Lucas, the man also feels a rage rising within him – and Faulkner directly repeats the imagery previously used to describe Lucas at the hearth: "The rage was not cold now. It was hot, and there was an eagerness upon him, a kind of vindictive exultation as he plunged on" (84). Within the larger context of the novel, selves converge and diverge across time, pulled in different ways by the mysterious gravity of certain places of precedence and privilege.

Like Isaac in renouncing the plantation, Lucas will ultimately repudiate his ideological claim over the land when he gives up his search for buried treasure. A different set of external pressures, however, makes Lucas' repudiation an act of novelty in its own right, for he affirms the interpersonal bonds of family over the claims of the plantation. Lucas chooses the hearth, but must withdraw the burning outrage that he has projected onto this hub of cognitive and social space. In short, Lucas attempts to preserve the hearth as its own independent vertical principle. Though it may still lie within a broader centralized system of racial inequality, Faulkner indicates that the power of the overarching system is never absolute, but perilously negotiated within each individual life.

By giving up the ideology of the plantation and engaging in a legal negotiation that involves rather than excludes Roth Edmonds, Lucas symbolically purifies the dark depths of the mound that lie at the creek bottom. This site is the place at which Lucas' rage is first fully articulated and, in the fuller context of the novel, it is connected to his great-grandmother Eunice's original act of agency. Eunice's creek bottom connects us with one of the earliest symbolic paradigms in the Yoknapatawpha fiction that offers an alternative authority to the ideological power of the plantation. The creek bottom of *The Sound and the Fury* was the place where the Compson children played, and Caddy muddied her bottom. Faulkner recognized it as part of the matrix of imagery from which the novel initially emerged. To be sure, the creek is the site at which Benjy remembers his sister, Caddy, as "that fierce, panting, paused, and stopped wet figure which smelled of trees" (6).[5] Benjy's tragedy is that, with the loss of his sister, he can "never grow beyond this moment," but, imperiled as the memory may be, the creek bottom provides a vision of intersubjectivity that cannot be extinguished.

In *Go Down, Moses*, Faulkner returns to the symbolism of the creek bottom as a space of interiority and sensuous immanence, a site capable of disturbing the power of the ledgers in Isaac's narrative and one at which Lucas begins to confront the plantation's claims upon his own personhood. Lucas' narrative ultimately affirms that human beings can move, behave, and think beyond the system in which they are nestled. The interior architecture of the self, moreover, is not some fantastical illusion to which we stubbornly cling, a mere artifact of ancestral superstition; rather, it is the site within the individual self through which the information of the larger system flows; as a consequence, it is the site in which we can reorganize the system of which we are a part, whether in subtle or profoundly disruptive ways. "Pantaloon in Black" poignantly registers the latter, and the chapter serves as our final example of how a black individual life can pierce through the overarching social system and potentially change the behavior it expresses across time.

The double narrative structure of "Pantaloon in Black" establishes the two principal paradigms of the greater novel – (1) the intersubjective architecture within the self; and (2) the plantation ideology that governs the social body – as separate, albeit overlapping realities. In the second narrative, Faulkner explicitly presents the institutional thinking of the social body, a form of cognitive capture that distorts the meaning of Rider's mourning. Without doubt, the sheriff and his wife dismiss Rider's actions and actively misread every incident leading up to his ultimate lynching, but the very point of structuring Rider's narrative in this juxtaposed and overlapping manner is that it forces readers to engage in Rider's experience beyond the bounds of the white signifying economy.[6] The opening paragraph establishes a cognitive cartography that emphasizes interiority at the gravesite of Rider's dead wife Mannie. Here, a network of agents is involved in ritualistic burial, and their work implicitly structures an interior dimension within both the external landscape and the protagonist himself, an interior dimension that arises from below and does not obey the governing dicta of the plantation economy. There is a peculiar, but obvious parallel between this site and the other sites of burial or submergence we have seen in the novel. Like the Indian Mound that rises out of the creek bottom, the gravesite of Mannie serves as a centralized node of power, in this case a vertex rising out of the actions of the social body, but possessing a mysterious and underlying power that cannot be reduced to its constituent parts.

Individuals may be producing this mound, yet Faulkner insists upon a complex agency of things, both inanimate and animate, that contributes to its generation. The "shovels" seem to have a life of their own and, as Rider takes one up, he participates in a momentum already well underway:

> [Rider] restored the hand to the moving shovel, flinging the dirt with that effortless fury so that the mound seemed to be rising of its own volition, not built up from above but thrusting visibly upward out of the earth itself, until at last the grave, save for its rawness, resembled any other marked off without order about the barren plot by shards of pottery and broken bottles and old brick and other objects insignificant to sight but actually of a profound meaning and fatal to touch, which no white man could have read. (131)

There is no initiation to the action, since a momentum already flows through agents – both animate and inanimate – producing, moreover, a vertex that possesses a quasi-agency of its own. The shovel seems to be moving of its own accord, and even the mound itself appears to be "rising of its own volition," indicating that this site operates beyond the intentionality and control of any one self. Although the mound arises as a hub of information, it is not like the ledgers for it is expressly nonideological. We are now very familiar with the way that coercive information objects operate: They supervene from above upon their constituent parts using an epistemology of textual space to reinforce their dicta. Faulkner is adamant that this is not the case here. The grave is "not built up from above but thrusting visibly upward out of the earth itself." Thus, we have an emergent intersubjective phenomenon arising from below and dynamically self-organizing through the activity of a network of agents. The mound, moreover, does not relate to vision, at least not a vision predicated upon the demarcations of the white plantation system. The burial is surrounded by other broken objects that are similarly "insignificant to sight," and Faulkner even concludes with a provocation that "no white man" can read the language of the site.

Like Eunice's submerged body, the dark depths into which the bear sinks, and the "old earth" which Lucas confronts at the Indian mound, this site possesses "a profound meaning" that is not just oppositional to the ledgers that administer from above; this site has an interior significance of its own, arising as it does from below. Whereas some critics have fruitfully argued that black outrage in the novel "has to do with a failure of representation" or a "nonidentification" (Thyssen 2015: 98), we must clarify that Mannie's burial plot is a site of novelty generating its own alternative language. We should be wary, I suggest, of circumscribing blackness within a paradigm that is solely characterized by disruption and a rejection of the dominant order. Faulkner provides a symbolic language that registers precisely through its own architecture of immanence, even while establishing just how much power such interior sites can possess. Where Lucas negotiated a settlement at the conclusion of "The Fire and the Hearth" in order to preserve his family life, Faulkner presents a decisive variation that will produce a different outcome. In Rider's life, the interpersonal bonds of family – those vital networks that exist within, but are not absolutely beholden to, larger systems of social control – are broken. This site thereby functions "without order," at least not the order governing from without, and there is a powerful indication that any system that loses or negates the interpersonal bonds within it will become unstable. This was the dilemma that Lucas faced and ultimately sought to resolve both with his wife and through a legal settlement. In the case of Rider, the interpersonal dimension within has been tragically effaced. In place of Mannie the actual woman, there is a "barren plot" that is marked by brokenness and is "fatal to touch," a clear foreshadowing of the murder that concludes the first narrative of the chapter.

The immanent power of Mannie's grave exhibits itself, first, in Rider's inability to re-incorporate himself into the social order. The sign economy of the plantation pales in comparison to the gravity that her grave exerts upon the bereaved husband. Perhaps for the first time in his life, Rider begins to see the systemic racial inequality that governs his life and that is assuaged by the interpersonal bonds of family. Having buried Mannie, he immediately returns home, despite the protests of family who want to care for him. As he arrives at his cabin, he realizes that the cabin is "not his" at all, "but rented from Carothers Edmonds, the local white landowner" (133). The work that the couple have put into the cabin over the first six months of their marriage suddenly appears in a radically different light, as belonging not to the newlyweds, but to the landowner who ultimately benefits when his tenants "refloor the porch and rebuil[d] and roof the kitchen" (133). Faulkner also parallels Rider building a "fire on the hearth on their wedding night" to Lucas Beauchamp's building of a fire "forty-five years ago and which had burned ever since" (134). Here, different selves are paralleled across time, with an emphasis on the variability of these information patterns. Indeed, Rider – who has felt compelled to return home, back to the cabin that he and his beloved rebuilt together and to the hearth that was kindled upon the consummation of their marriage – realizes that without the immanent and the interpersonal, the plantation economy of signs has no meaning at all for him: "But when he put his hand on the gate it seemed to him suddenly that there was nothing beyond it. The house had never been his anyway, but now even the new planks and sills and shingles, the hearth and stove and bed, were all a part of the memory of somebody else" (134).

Faulkner's representation of Rider brings to a crisis an ontological view of the self within networked systems. Faulkner's initial presentation of Rider provokes an open question, a dilemma that is reinforced by the character's very name: as a rider, does he direct the flow of information through the network of which he is a part or is he simply subject to the chain of cause and effect that flows from external system through the individual life? At first, Rider may seem to possess no agency at all. In the first paragraph that I quoted above, the moving shovel seems to have precedence over him: "He restores the hand to the moving shovel" (131). This imagistic insistence that objects about the self already have momentum only grows throughout the narrative. When Rider eats, the lifeless stew is doing the moving. When he goes to the logging mill the next day, he does not merely pick up the massive log; instead, Faulkner depicts Rider as part of a complex chain of cause and effect that flows from objects to the individual self: "It was as if the unrational and inanimate wood had invested, mesmerized the man with some of its own primal inertia" so that "the log seemed to leap suddenly backward over his head of its own volition" (141–2). All these objects seem to act out of their own agency, and Faulkner repeatedly characterizes Rider in the mimetic terms of a shadow (eight instances that appear on pages 137, 138, 143, 144, 146, and 147). Like Quentin Compson or Joe Christmas before him, Rider stands "in the middle now of the unimpeded shadow" (146), a mimetic pattern that seems to have a life of its own and to flow "unimpeded" through the self in order to gain expression.

Yet Rider is present, as a self, as an agent, in a way that these earlier characters are not. From the first paragraph, Faulkner encodes Rider's agency as an express validation of the depths of the burial site. Yes, the momentum of the ritual flows through and into Rider, but he responds by manifestly substantiating the burial site as a paradigm of vertical power: "Then he straightened up and with one hand flung the shovel quivering upright in the mound like a javelin and turned and began to walk away" (131). Here, in actively sustaining the burial site, Rider presents the first part of a symbolic coda that culminates when Rider kills the "boss-man."

Faulkner captures a powerful intentionality, hidden though it may at first appear, in this act of violence and self-defense. Indeed, the "boss-man," as the black loggers call him, has been cheating these workers in a crooked dice game for years, his white authority allowing him to swindle part of their weekly pay.

What we have is a small, centralized hub of power within the larger plantation complex, one that grows symbiotically with the sharecropping economy. We may place this iteration of the plantation alongside all the various temporalities that this site possesses in Faulkner's Yoknapatawpha fiction to visualize a modernizing arc, from the modest farms of the MacCallums and the McCallums, located deep in the woods, to the McCaslin plantation as a large-scale business engaged in clearing the wilderness to make way for the sharecropping economy. Indeed, the plantation is run by labor-lords who lease tracts of uncleared land to lumber companies not just to extract its raw resources, but also to clear the land so that it can be prepped into sharecrops that, in turn, will be contracted out to individual black farmers at steep interest rates, thereby "binding for life" (228) these men and women to the ledgers that record the transactions that sustain the institution. In "Pantaloon in Black," it is this complex network of labor and environmental destruction that Rider finally refuses. Faulkner's description is a frightening and marvelous one, capturing the complex agency of things around the man, while also ultimately affirming Rider's own emergent agency in his act of self-defense:

> The razor hung between his shoulder-blades from a loop of cotton string round his neck inside his shirt. The same motion of the hand which brought the razor forward over his shoulder flipped the blade open and freed it from the cord, the blade opening on until the back edge of it lay across the knuckles of his fist, his thumb pressing the handle into his closing fingers, so that in the second before the half-drawn pistol exploded he actually struck at the white man's throat not with the blade but with a sweeping blow of his fist, following through in the same motion so that not even the first jet of blood touched his hand or arm. (148–9)

While the sheriff and his wife later interpret this act as senseless, readers bear witness to an act that follows and gradually overcomes the mimetic and metonymic momentum with which Faulkner has characterized Rider so far. Indeed, we begin with the "razor" hanging and then "the motion of the hand" bringing it forward and freeing it. Again, Rider at first seems to be absent as an agent here; he obeys a momentum that flows through a complex network of objects – both animate and inanimate – most immediately, the boss-man's draw as well as the blade's motion and opening. But gradually through the meticulously constructed sentence, Rider appears to us, at first his "thumb pressing the handle into his closing fingers," another metonym that gives way to a sudden agency as "he," Rider, preempts the bullet, to strike so swiftly at the boss-man that the blade itself is secondary, following in the wake of the man's own hand, that "sweeping blow of his fist." Rider's coda of agency, therefore, begins when he "fl[ings] the shovel quivering upright in the mound" and ends when "he actually struck at the white man's throat." In both cases, the individual does more than obey the momentum of the network about him; he funnels, channels, and directs an underlying "fatal" energy that finally upends a long-standing and seemingly intractable node of institutional power. Thus, Rider actively and self-consciously destroys a vertical hub of white power within the McCaslin complex, and the impetus for his capacity to do so signifies through an associative symbolism of interior space that is central to the narratives of Isaac and Lucas.

Rider's action can be seen in the context of an emergent and hard-won vision on Faulkner's part. As stable as the plantation economy may appear with its ostensibly intractable vertices of ideology and culture, the individuals within this system are constantly in movement, many of them caught within the lien-centered feedback loop of sharecropping and industry, but others offering paradigms of alterity and novel variation. Eunice is, of course, the foundational example of this immanent alterity, innovating movement, tragic though it may be, outside the bounds of the plantation. Many of her kin follow in this diaspora away from the ideological dicta of the slave system and Jim Crow. As we have seen, Thucydus McCaslin, Eunice's husband, works himself out of slavery. Tomey's Turl continually escapes his bonds, despite the concerted effort of his masters to contain him. Others after the Civil War engage in similar paradigms of movement, moreover. James Beauchamp ("Tennie's Jim") leaves the plantation and seems to wind up in Indiana, Samuel Worsham Beauchamp relocates to the urban north where he presumably ends up in a Chicago-era prison, and James' daughter with the "dark wide bottomless eyes" returns to find that the plantation of her father offers her nothing. The lives of these individuals are difficult, beset with challenges and tragedy, but they offer an ethical dimension to the novel, instantiating a mercurial unknown that can never be fully quantified within the calculating rubric of the plantation ledgers.

Rider's act of self-defense must, I submit, be considered alongside theirs. Like Eunice, he aligns with an underlying paradigm of immanence, intersubjectivity, and alterity. In Rider, moreover, Faulkner offers a stark warning of what happens when the immanent and interpersonal delineations of a human life are effaced within a system of inequality and injustice. It is no hyperbole to insist upon Faulkner's prescience in the fuller context of the twentieth and twenty-first-century United States. The drug war and the prison industrial complex that symbiotically scaled alongside it were key elements in devastating the black family and thus destabilizing the agency and self-expression of the black man. While Richard Nixon may have officially launched the war on drugs in 1971, its institutional origins can be traced back to Faulkner's own time, most infamously to the 1930 appointment of Harry Anslinger as the founding commissioner of the Treasury's Federal Bureau of Narcotics. Anslinger was a lifelong propagandist for a war on drugs, and his zealotry hinged upon vilifying minority groups, black Americans especially. It would take generations for the effects on black communities throughout the country to become apparent, as the changing industrial conditions of the 1940s and 1950s created a diaspora of black individuals and families leaving the rural life they had known to move into cities. We continue to grapple with the ongoing consequences of jeopardizing black individual and familial autonomy, and we still debate the ways to reform these structures. Rider's violence is a warning, for the man can be understood as an escalating inevitability within a complex social system that fails to affirm the immanent and interpersonal or to build an infrastructure that would allow these elements to flourish.

CHAPTER 6

Architecture of Interiority

I have proceeded chronologically through the Yoknapatawpha fiction so far, but I make an exception in this final chapter with *The Hamlet* so as to treat the Snopes trilogy as a whole – and, more specifically, to read the trilogy as a clear-sighted study of immanence and interiority that responds in a self-contained way to the whole of Faulkner's study of complex systems as outlined in this book. In *The Hamlet*, as we saw last chapter in *Go Down, Moses*, the symbolism of the submerged woman offers Faulkner's clearest portrayal of an immanent underlayer to our networked social systems that gives value and dignity to the individual life. Individual behavior, no matter how seemingly insignificant, can remake social space and, with it, the cognitive cartographies that are embedded in its structure. Though there may be a chaotic quality to the expression of such individual forms of novelty, this does not mean that the larger networked process is blind. For Faulkner, individual experience serves as both a moral anchorage for the larger expression of the social body and an ever present wellspring for social change. Indeed, these later novels emphasize not the permanence of vertical paradigms of power; rather, as we saw in *Go Down, Moses*, the various iterations of the plantation economy are in a perpetual state of transformation – and the Snopes trilogy similarly emphasizes how the novelty of spontaneous individual interaction can decenter and reform these networks of power. Again, we see how immanent configurations are springing up from below, from the individual and intersubjective interactions that bestow a mercurial quality to the New South, making it open to the possibilities of change.

In Sections 6.1 and 6.2, I concentrate on *The Hamlet* (1940) in order to show how Faulkner develops a pattern of clustering and dispersal in social space as he builds to the narrative of the horse auction. Faulkner was personally invested in the horse auction, having drawn "upon [his own] childhood experience" to create "the precipitating event of the Snopes saga" (Carl Rollyson 2020: 164). I examine three textual sequences that provide an interpretative context for the auction: (1) the behavior of Eula's suitors; (2) Lump Snopes' financial exploitation of his cousin's obsession with Jack Houston's cow; and (3) Mink Snopes' botched concealment of Houston's body. In Sections 6.3 and 6.4, I consider *The Town* (1957) and *The Mansion* (1959) in terms of Faulkner's explicit effort to reinstate an immanent underlayer to his characters' participation in complex social systems. I conclude with his final articulation of the mimetic crisis in the relationship of Flem and Mink Snopes. These two men reanimate the conflict between textual space and immanence, now with a poignant emphasis upon the latent power of the disenfranchised. Faulkner's trilogy allows us to recapitulate the argument of this book in tracing the simultaneous emergence and decentering of hierarchical paradigms of power, which for all their complexity depend upon the immanent life of the subject.

6.1   Swarming about the Vertex

Faulkner opens *The Hamlet* by establishing an overarching chronology for the community of Frenchman's Bend, emphasizing distributed processes that are not wholly dependent on any particular site of social space, no matter how centralized.[1] In the first two paragraphs, more than a century is compressed to portray the changing social structure of this north Mississippi community. Frenchman's Bend, we read, "was a section of rich river-bottom country" that became the "site of a tremendous pre-Civil War plantation ... parceled out now into small shiftless mortgaged farms" (H 3–4). In a similar manner as in *Go Down, Moses*, *The Hamlet* presents the transition from the wilderness to the various organizations of the plantation economy – first slave, then tenant – as the land of Frenchman's Bend, once dominated by an elite planter class, becomes subject to the crop-lien system of the New South. Faulkner thus presents the resilience of this plantation economy even when the Frenchman's original plantation dream, most visibly figured in the decaying Frenchman's Place, is replaced by a new centralized node of social space. Whereas the Frenchman's manor once constituted the central hub of social space during slavery, under the crop-lien system the furnish store – running on credit and often charging high interest to the sharecropper – came to replace it. Under the new system, it was through these furnish stores that information and resources flowed to the community and back again in a feedback loop that primarily enriched the landowner or, as the historian Gavin Wright (1986) termed these New South landowners, "laborlord" (18). *The Hamlet* portrays the clustering of the social body around the furnish store in a dynamic manner. Under certain conditions, the individuals of *The Hamlet* group around one spatial node of exchange, while in other circumstances, they select new centers – and these patterns of movement over long periods of time lead to the emergence of new social and cultural behavior, even while constituting the overarching hierarchal dimensions of Frenchman's Bend with the furnish store at its center.

What becomes clear throughout the novel is that Frenchman's Bend is composed of many interacting and overlapping networks, some of which emerge only to die out, but all of which are dynamically linked to, affect, and are affected by the aggregate behavior of the whole. Where Faulkner opens the narrative with a compression of histories of movement in physical space, he soon slows the narrative pace in order to present the individual interactions that constitute this evolving social body. The most obvious interaction network that emerges early on is Eula Varner and the suitors who besiege her once she reaches puberty. Faulkner indicates that this pattern of social behavior arises without the express intentionality on the part of any one agent; he emphasizes an instinctual clustering around the young girl who does nothing actively to provoke the activity: "She would take no part in them, yet she would dominate them. Sitting beside the stove exactly as she had sat during the hours of school, inattentive and serene amid the uproar of squeals and trampling feet, she would be assaulted simultaneously beneath a dozen simultaneous gingham or calico dresses in a dozen simultaneous shadowy nooks and corners" (H 127). Even when Faulkner limits the narrative purview to focus on a single interaction network, we find that he represents not merely one event, not one "assault," but a cluster of events that expresses itself in a "dozen" similar "nooks and corners" and thus becomes a predictable network played out across time and extended over physical space.

In the passage above, Eula sits "amid the uproar of squeals and trampling feet" of the children and youths, and this description of relatively free movement serves as fitting prelude to a more intricate consideration of how beings – both human and nonhuman – cluster in social space and produce spontaneous order. While appearing chaotic, the uproarious movement of the children self-organizes into a more stable pattern, overlapping with the varying assaults of the suitors who come from neighboring counties to join the aggregate pattern in question. In anticipation of his later representation of nonhuman beings in the novel, Faulkner tropes the young suitors as a swarm of insects whose movement and behavior self-organizes concentrically around Eula:

> It would have but one point, like a swarm of bees, and she would be that
> point, that center, swarmed over and importuned yet serene and intact
> apparently even oblivious, tranquilly abrogating the whole long sum of
> human thinking and suffering which is called knowledge, education, wisdom,
> at once supremely unchaste and inviolable: the queen, the matrix. (127)

The imagery of bees and their queen at the center articulates an arrangement of social space predicated on the aggregate movement of the social
body. Eula does not direct the individuals around her; no one individual
directs them. The "sum" of the individual interactions spontaneously self-
organizes without direction or guidance from any one governing will or
agency, and Eula, as the vertex around which the swarm of young men
cluster, continues to be profoundly unaware of the suitors as well as of "the
sum of human thinking and suffering" to which their movements
are related.

Faulkner describes Eula as a "matrix," moreover, employing a term that
already anticipates a systems vocabulary. According to the Cambridge
Online Dictionary, a matrix is "the set of conditions that provides a system
in which something grows or develops." In this respect, Faulkner visualizes
the swarming pattern of the suitors about Eula as a network configuration
with her as hub, producing an emergent phenomenon. He does not simply
describe suitors attacking Eula; he establishes the collective behavior of all
the children as a chaotic uproar out of which an assault organizes, emerging in different locations and over an extended period of time. Faulkner
also continues to trope this swarming or clustering activity as insect
behavior. "Through that spring and through the long succeeding summer
of her fourteenth year, the youths of fifteen and sixteen and seventeen who
had been in school with her and others who had not, swarmed like wasps
about the ripe peach which her full damp mouth resembled" (141).
No longer bees, but now wasps, this imagery provides a variable articulation of the cluster pattern as it seeks a source of sustenance that Faulkner
interweaves with the imagery of Eula's mouth – the part of the body that,
as we have seen in *Sanctuary* and *Light in August*, gives access to the
immanent domain. Yet again, Faulkner emphasizes no one individual,
but the "dozen" suitors who "form a group, close, homogeneous, and
loud, of which she was the serene and usually steadily and constantly
eating axis, center" (141). In these depictions, we find a hierarchal group-
ing in which value and weight are given to one node of social space – Eula,
the "constantly eating axis" – but without any top-down governance.
Eula's profound disinterest is equally matched with the persistent lack of

planning on the part of her suitors: "One night they charged the moving buggy from the roadside shadows and were driven off by the whip because they had no concerted plan but were moved by a spontaneous combustion of rage and grief" (152).

Faulkner depicts the network clustering around Eula as one that produces predictable results across time, while remaining non-linear and highly variable. The suitors swarm in different locations – and Eula is similarly mobile. There is an express lack of individuality in this behavior: The young men may as well be iterations of the same person. The schoolteacher Labove seems the exception. Despite his misanthropic nature, he is also a suitor, moved by the faceless instinct that pervades the group of young men. And while his behavior may differ from the others, his movements similarly cluster about Eula through that year and into the next. Labove may be a "militant fanatic" ready to turn his "uncompromising back upon the world" (117), but he only differs in degree, not in kind, from the group of which he is a member. Labove's inclusion helps define the interaction network not simply as a faceless and mindless swarm, but as a spontaneous and varied pattern produced by individuals of differing personalities and motivations.

Faulkner's ingenious characterization of Labove suggests that variables cannot escape the overarching social pattern, even while they continue to create new clusters of behavior. Labove is part of the interaction network that groups around Eula, but his own behavior inadvertently serves as a catalyst for new configurations of spontaneous order. Thus, Faulkner describes in detail how Labove moves into an "unheated lean-to room in Frenchman's Bend" (122), and how the community adapts to the strange young man in its midst. The description is worth quoting in full, since it indicates how thoroughly Faulkner interweaves the idea of interaction networks – the dynamic relations between a smaller number of nodes – into his narrative technique and content:

> It was in the house of a widow who lived near the school. He owned a razor, the unmatching coat and trousers he stood in, two shirts, the coach's overcoat, a Coke, a Blackstone, a volume of Mississippi Reports, an original Horace and a Thucydides which the classics professor, in whose home he had built the morning fires, had given him at Christmas, and the brightest lamp the village had ever seen. It was nickel, with valves and pistons and gauges; as it sat on his plank table it obviously cost more than everything else he owned lumped together and people would come in from miles away at night to see the fierce still glare it made. (122)

For his night studying, Labove possesses "the brightest lamp" the community has ever seen. Although he does not care about the community, the "fierce glare" of his lamp assumes a quasi-religious value among the members of the community who repeatedly come mothlike "from miles away" to see it. We can therefore observe a new concentric clustering in social space, one that is unintended but ritualistically manifest in people's movements around the lamp.

This description of Labove indicates that one's position in the community – indeed the very way that a person comes to live amongst others – depends upon multiple interacting nodes of agency that give rise to unexpected, self-organizing outcomes. Another striking example of this clustering pattern within Frenchman's Bend is Lump Snopes' financial manipulation of Ike, his cousin, which mirrors Flem Snopes' ability to manipulate any financial transaction to his own advantage. While the mentally disabled Ike knows little beyond his instinctual desire for the cow, Lump builds a business model involving the recurrent movement of the community's men that establishes, however briefly, a new center of social space. Faulkner's description of V. K. Ratliff's discovery of the business echoes the earlier clustering behavior of Eula's suitors. Instead of any moralizing condemnation of either Ike's bestiality or Lump's exploitation of his cousin's obsession, Faulkner emphasizes emergent pathways of movement:

> That lot was beyond the house from the road; the rear wall of the stable was not in sight from either. It was not directly in view from anywhere in the village proper, and on this September forenoon Ratliff realized that it did not need to be. Because he was walking a path, a path which he had not seen before, which had not been there in May. Then that rear wall came into his view, the planks nailed horizontally upon it, that plank at head-height prized off and leaning, the projecting nails faced carefully inward, against the wall and no more motionless than the row of backs, the row of heads which filled the gap. (216–17)

The stable in which Ike copulates with the cow "was not directly in view from anywhere in the village proper," but has become visibly linked to the village by a newly emergent "path." As Ratliff follows it, he comes to join "the row of heads" that habitually groups around the spectacle. Just as the suitors concentrically crowded around Eula's mouth, here, the townsfolk cluster about another "orifice" (217). Ratliff's humanity becomes apparent in this case, but not because he deviates from the movements of the community. He too walks the freshly formed path and, unlike his friend Bookwright, he beholds the spectacle, projecting himself into the consciousness of Ike: Ratliff "did look, leaning his face in between two other heads; and it was though it were himself inside the stall with the cow, himself looking out of the blasted tongueless face at the row of faces watching him" (217). Lump's business effectively ends in this moment – and readers learn that although some nodes of social space may take prominence, the centrality of one location cannot be sustained indefinitely. Indeed, a cluster pattern can be disrupted by even one small change in group behavior. In this case, Ratliff's ability to see through the eyes of another is enough to disturb the centrality of the stable. This underscores Ratliff as a humanizing force in the community, even while demonstrating the power that individuals possess to reorganize social space.

Where *The Hamlet* unquestionably emphasizes network centrality, it just as powerfully values individual behavior as a wellspring of novelty and change. Indeed, network centrality and novelty form an interlocking pattern: Individual expressions of novelty, moral or otherwise, may evoke change for the better, but like any other behavior, these expressions are subject to unexpected pattern formations within complex systems. A telling example of this blend of novelty and unpredictability is Mink Snopes' tragic bungling of Houston's murder. Again, the sequence of cause and effect is separated over space and time, another feature, we may recall, of complex systems. To be sure, through an intricate web of events, Mink commits the violent act and, in his attempt to conceal Houston's body, he finds himself a victim of the clustering behavior of social groups. As in earlier passages, the new pattern that unveils itself involves the clustering of animals – bees and buzzards. Mink chooses a hollow tree in which to conceal Houston's body, not fully appreciating that this node once served as a center around which other beings clustered and could very well do so again:

> He seemed to know exactly where he was, he did not even look over his shoulder until he released the body at last and stood erect and laid his hand upon what he sought – the shell of a once-tremendous pin oak, topless and bout ten feet tall, standing in the clearing which the lightning bolt or age or decay or whatever it had been, had created. Two years ago he had lined a wild bee into it; the sapling which he had cut and propped against the shell to reach the honey was still in place. (249–50)

The activity of the wild bees once produced a vertex around which beings – both human and nonhuman – grouped. With this architecture "still in place," the oak serves again as a center of activity. Three days after Mink disposes of the corpse, he wakes to see a new assemblage of movement. Much like the suitors who swarmed about Eula or the townsfolk who nightly gravitate toward Labove's bright lamp, the buzzards circle Houston's dead body in the dead hollow of the oak, thwarting Mink's laborious efforts to conceal his crime: "He just watched the black concentric spiraling as if [the buzzards] followed an invisible funnel, disappearing one by one below the trees" (257). Despite his intentions, then, Mink's actions have created yet another coordinated social ritual in nature. The "limitless freedom of the sunny sky" is filled with "black concentric spiraling," a visualization that underscores how unintended patterns of behavior can self-organize and concentrically cluster anywhere.

6.2   Hives, Horses, and Human Hierarchies

Faulkner's horse auction achieves a scale of complexity that dwarfs all of the clustering interaction behavior we have seen thus far. While Faulkner composed much of the novel's final section two years before returning to his work on *The Hamlet*, the horse auction is among the oldest of Faulkner's Yoknapatawpha fiction, since it "forms the bulk of the uncompleted 'Father Abraham' manuscript, written in late 1926 or early 1927" (Greiner 1968: 1133). Faulkner continued to rewrite the auction "several times, from several different narrative points of view and submitted it to magazines under several titles." He eventually published it as "Spotted Horses" in *Scriber's Magazine* in 1931.[2] In the 1940 novel, the previous story is transformed again. With virtually the whole of Frenchman's Bend engaged in the buying and selling of spotted ponies, the fourth section portrays something far more ambitious than individual exchange or concentric social clustering: It narrates how many interacting nodes, each with different motivations and interests, can produce a widespread aggregate pattern of nonlinear behavior that temporarily groups in social space – while also emphasizing the underlying immanence that is emergent in this pattern.

   The crowd behavior of this narrative sequence may suggest uniformity, but Faulkner concentrates on the intricate interdependencies among the many parts of the crowd, depicting the simultaneous and independent operation of its variables. In his most intricate portrait of systems complexity, Faulkner emphasizes the roiling chaos within the social body that continually threatens to break free, the way in which a chaotic system is sensitive to each of the variables that compose it. This context also helps to explain why Faulkner blurs any firm distinction between so-called natural and human systems. *The Hamlet* involves the bustling activity of beehives, the menacing concentration of wasps, the circling movement of buzzards and, in section four, the frenetic behavior of wild horses – all of which mirror the behavior of their human counterparts and thereby serve as expressions of how the social body moves, behaves, and thinks in space.

On one level of analysis, there is a clear dialectical tension between humans and horses. From the opening of the section, coercion and restraint are decisive parts of this process of assemblage, a human/nonhuman tension that mirrors the social and economic inequality of the sharecropping system in which the community of Frenchman's Bend is nestled. Flem Snopes and Buck Hipps arrive at the store with the ponies "shackled to one another and to the wagon itself with sections of barbed wire" (H 300). Despite the normalizing imposition of their shackles, Faulkner emphasizes the behavioral diversity of the animals. As their "mismatched eyes rolled wild and subdued, they huddled, gaudy motionless and alert, wild as deer, deadly as rattlesnakes, quiet as doves" (300). With its amalgamation of varying, even contradictory characteristics (wild, deadly, peaceful), the herd's quivering energy expresses itself fluidly as surges or waves of movement: "the movement of its surge against the wire which held it travelling backward among the rest of the band in a wave of thuds and lunges" (300). Here, Faulkner captures the *modus operandi* of an interaction network; the horses' undulating motion, their surging and wavelike tactile interaction, transmits an energy throughout the group: "The Texan grasped the wire and began to draw the first horse up to the wagon, the animal plunging and surging back against the wire as though trying to hang itself, the contagion passing back through the herd from animal to animal until they were rearing and plunging again against the wire" (303). A "contagion" moves "from animal to animal," inciting the beings assembled to act in ways they would not otherwise have done individually. If we recall Hofstadter's theory of the self-mirroring that occurs in brains and ant colonies, the interaction pattern Faulkner depicts constitutes a form of communication that travels through an extensive network to produce self-organization. Importantly, it is not the surging of the horses alone that evokes this behavior, but also the coercive actions of Buck that again come to be mirrored by the community of Frenchman's Bend.

Here, in the self-mirroring activity of horses and humans, we can discern yet another feature of system complexity in which the tense dynamic between humans and horses gives way to larger, more all-encompassing behavior. Like the one-on-one interaction of the horses, the men of Frenchman's Bend begin to imitate the activity of Buck Hipps whose pattern of behavior therefore corrals not simply the horses, but also the men. It takes just a few participating nodes to spark such a surge through the social body. Flem may have introduced the Texan by arriving with him, but it is another man of influence, Jody Varner, who gives Buck his first participant (302). With Jody's acquiescence, Eck Snopes "grasped the wire also" (303) and, within a twenty-four-hour period, virtually the whole community of men has adopted his movements by employing "wire," "stakes" (310) and "plow-line" (331) to subdue the wild ponies and cluster them into a hub of social space.

One must note that this emergent aggregate pattern is not without opposing variables. Ratliff, who as we saw exercised great social influence before, warns the men assembled at Varner's store of Flem's hidden hand in the swindle afoot. Even as he countered Lump's ability to manipulate a centralized node of social space, this last section narrates the failure of Ratliff's influence. Not heeding his warning, the men succumb to the advantages of paying less for a team of horses, and the emerging pattern of self-mirroring propels them toward a fateful decision. As the horses communicate with each other by rubbing bodily against each other and producing a collective wave of motion, so the men converse and their verbal exchange produces "something stubborn, convinced, and passive" (306) in them. Gradually increasing in size from "six men" in Mrs. Littlejohn's lane (308) to "more than fifty men standing along the fence" (314), the crowd comes from miles around to see the Texas horses up for auction. Some of these men speak, although, like many of the men at Varner's store, they are largely described as "one of the others" (309, 311, 313, 332) or "a second," "third," or "newcomer" (309, 320, 322) without individual characteristics. As the men speak, moreover, they are no longer visualized as agents, but as "silhouettes" in darkness, whose language is immediately echoed by a "bird, a shadow, fleet and dark and swift, [which] curved across the moonlight, upward into the pear tree and began to sing" (306). This symbolic logic may initially be difficult to tease out, but we have repeatedly seen how Faulkner employs birds to portray a mimetic, imitative or self-mirroring pattern that is transposed from the shadowy men to the "shadow" of a "mockingbird."

The pear tree in which the mockingbird sings operates, moreover, as an imagistic touchstone throughout the depiction of the event. While the men imitate Buck Hipps in roping and constraining the horses, the pear tree constitutes an alternative hub of information: "The pear tree across the road opposite was now in full and frosty bloom, the twigs and branches springing not outward from the limbs but standing motionless and perpendicular above the horizontal boughs like the separate and upstreaming hair of a drowned woman sleeping upon the uttermost floor of the windless and tideless sea" (306). Here, Faulkner introduces the paradigmatic symbolism of the drowned woman that operates so powerfully in the figure of Eunice in *Go Down, Moses*, a novel that was published two years after *The Hamlet*, but whose composition nonetheless overlaps with the earlier novel. Like the figure of Eunice, the tree offers a model of resistance, one which prefigures the wild horses bursting free from their barbed-wire confinement in the lot. Like Eunice in *Go Down, Moses*, the tree is initially imagined as a "drowned woman" (306) or "drowned silver" (331), and the wild horses are similarly submerged as "phantom fish" (304, 331). The pear tree, moreover, is associated with the action of bursting forth: "Then the pear tree came in sight. It rose in mazed and silver immobility like exploding snow" (339).

Though there is clearly a variety of ways to interpret such a condensed symbolism, one key to the pattern in question is Faulkner's insistence that the tree is composed by an alignment of the vertical "twigs and branches" that "stand" above the "horizontal boughs." In this configuration of the vertical and the horizontal, the above and the below, we have an imagistic parallel for the alignment of the clustering of the social body around a vertex and the simultaneous urge for flight, to break free from the wire bonds, as the horses ceaselessly attempt to do. With this imagistic alignment of opposites, all beings – horses, mockingbirds, and men – come to resemble each other: the horses as phantoms, the mockingbirds as shadows, and the men as silhouettes (305, 311, 312, 331, 333). My analysis in Chapter 5 helps to clarify the pattern in question, for here, with the image of the pear tree, we do not have a coercive information object but something more fundamental, an object that possesses both vertical height and immanent power. In the context of Isaac's experience with the bear who manifests from, and then returns to, the dark depths of the earth, the rising of the drowned tree can be interpreted as the emergence and expression of an immanent principle in being – an *élan vital*, to use Henri Bergson's term.

The "rising" and "exploding" pear tree provides a node of information that informs the conclusion of the horse auction for the men and women of Frenchman's Bend. After all, the auction is built upon containing a wild and irrepressible energy and is highly sensitive to small changes that can disrupt its aggregate behavior. Buck Hipps' departure may be one of these factors, although Lon Quick's forgetting to close the lot gate (333, 364) clearly operates as the decisive and unintended action that decenters the behavioral cluster. Whatever the case, the freedom of the horses is, on one level at least, a victory against confinement that any reader is likely to appreciate – and it reverberates further as an underlying paradigm of alterity within the logic of the sharecropping economy that Flem has come to administrate. At first, the escape of the horses is subtly established by a reversal or *chiasmus* of the earlier models of swarm behavior that we have seen so far: the suitors clustering about Eula's mouth (141); the men looking through a hole at Ike and the cow (217); and Mink thrusting Houston's body "into the growing orifice" of an oak (281). In these later scenes both before and after the auction, Faulkner intimates that this center of confinement cannot hold; indeed, the wild energy of the horses will push back against confinement. The horses are thus repeatedly associated with metaphors of interiority, both mouth and orifices that are by no means placid. In the barn, for instance, the "entire interior exploded into mad tossing shapes like a down-rush of flames" (312), and the horses become a "towering parti-colored wave full of feet and glaring eyes and wild teeth, which overtopping, burst into scattered units, revealing at last the gaping orifice and the little boy still standing in it, unscathed, his eye still leaning to the vanished knothole" (312). Here the horses rise, jumping through the doorway back into the lot and eviscerating the knothole or "orifice" through which Wallstreet Snopes peers. This pattern comes to a finale when the horses are once again pinned into the shadow of the barn, forced as it were into mimetic confinement, only to explode outward like "a gaudy vomit of long wild faces and splotched chests" (333) that "crash through the gate" and pour outward toward freedom.

We can identify an insistent Romanticism in Faulkner's narrative that resonates powerfully with our own present inclinations and values in humanistic discourse. The narrative fulfills the audience's own predilections for flight and novelty, reflecting undoubtedly a hunger for interior authenticity – an underlying modernist disenchantment with bureaucratic or industrial mechanization. Indeed, Faulkner persistently questions the mechanisms of control that operate in the sharecropping economy and affirms the lived, material worlds of those – both animal and human – that populate his fiction. In the words of Christina Colvin (2014), "Faulkner's effort to represent animals . . . as members of lived, material worlds invites an interrogation of the ways Faulkner's animals resist human systems of discourse" (95). Yet this perspective is by no means univocal, since Faulkner also provides his readers with a means of eschewing such distinctions between human and nonhuman. In *The Hamlet*, all beings concentrically cluster and produce privileged vertices of social space – and while Faulkner invites us to question the structures they make or, more appropriately, that we make, there is nonetheless an open-endedness that persistently relies on the reader's response to the patterns in question.

Part of grappling with this open-endedness is the realization that nothing is final in Yoknapatawpha. Faulkner's later vision presents centralization within the greater context of a system on the *edge of chaos*, a system, if we recall, that continuously adapts and self-organizes from the bottom up. While Flem ceaselessly manipulates the clustering of the social body to his advantage, he is invariably part of the system's dynamical expression. Thus, just as Flem secures his victories in Frenchman's Bend, he joins the wagon trains that take him and his family to Jefferson. Flem's departure implicitly signals a new dispersal and clustering pattern that occurred *en masse* in the South, the flight from rural to urban life. As Carl Rollyson (2020) argues, the "spotted-horse auction marks a momentous change in the economy of Frenchman's Bend, disrupting traditional, normative practices and launching Flem's takeover not only of business but of the way to do business" (166).

Within the concentric clustering and dispersal of the social body, we confront, above all, the suffering and endurance of individuals like Mrs. Armstid who is the person most disadvantaged by Flem's auction scheme. Carolyn Porter (2007) addresses the "distinctively dark side" of *The Hamlet*'s final section by noting the "inevitable rise of the cash nexus as the central locus of power in the novel's world" and, more viscerally, in "Mrs. Armstid's plight" that "remain[s] to haunt us" (178). Porter does not identify, however, why Armstid's plight serves as the measure for Flem's unjust "cash nexus." Readers may well feel the smart of the blows that her husband rains down upon the woman or lament the loss of the money over which she has labored. Faulkner also forces his readers to see through Mrs. Armstid's eyes, to perceive an invocation of complex order that, though beautiful in its vastness and interconnection of parts, is still the system that binds and holds this woman in place:

> After a time Mrs. Armstid raised her head and looked up the road where it went on, mild with spring dust, past Mrs. Littlejohn's, beginning to rise, on past the not-yet-bloomed (that would be in June) locust grove across the way, on past the schoolhouse, the weathered roof of which, rising beyond an orchard of peach and pear trees, resembled a hive swarmed about by a cloud of pink-and-white bees, ascending, mounting toward the crest of the hill where the church stood among its sparse gleam of marble headstones in the somber cedar grove where during the long afternoons of summer the constant mourning doves called back and forth. (H 349)

Mrs. Armstid has just asked Flem Snopes for the return of her money as she was promised by Buck Hipps. Flem's refusal is taken as a victory: "By God," Lump laughs, "you cant beat him" (351). Mrs. Armstid herself does not argue, not in this node of social space that Flem has so clearly secured for himself. But, on the threshold of Varner's store, she sees the greater pattern of which she is a part "rising" with one level stacked upon another and the trees resembling a hive of bees that ascend further toward the highest promontory of the community. Like so many of Faulkner's characters before her, she is mastered by this aggregate pattern, but this fact does not render her suffering absurd or meaningless. Indeed, her anguish is implicitly manifest in the circulation of information through the larger social body, operating not just in her position below, but also in the "back and forth" communication of "the mourning doves" above. Here again, we see the self-mirroring that can spread through an aggregate pattern of behavior. Like the mockingbirds that repeat the language of the men, the doves residing above the community echo the pattern of suffering below, suggesting that no part is too small to affect the life of the whole.

As all beings cluster and disperse in social space, the rub, Faulkner insists, is individual in nature. Thus, Flem, moving to Jefferson, may repeat in stages what he has achieved in Frenchman's Bend, beginning with a side-street restaurant and gradually appropriating the central hubs through which resources flow into the wider community, first the power plant and then his final victory, the Sartoris bank. But there is an immanent volatility to the complex design of the social body suggesting that, while nothing is final, the life of the whole rests at last upon the individual self. T. S. Eliot (2002) captures this poetically in "Preludes" when he confesses that even though our individual experiences are replicated in "a thousand furnished rooms," his mind still curls round and clings to the "notion of some infinitely gentle/ Infinitely suffering thing" (24–5). In *The Hamlet*, this idea is poignantly realized in Faulkner's affirmation of Mrs. Armstid, for after Flem's refusal, the woman "descends the steps" of Varner's store, and it becomes clear that she herself is the "drowned woman" that we saw figured initially and powerfully in the pear tree: "The gray folds of the garment once more lost all inference and intimation of locomotion, so that she seemed to progress without motion like a figure on a retreating and diminishing float; a gray and blasted tree-trunk moving, somehow intact and upright, upon an unhurried flood" (H 351).[3] The whole pattern rising from the depths is reenacted as Mrs. Armstid appears "a gray and blasted tree-trunk" moving above the water, just as "the upstreaming hair of the drowned woman" rose above to become "exploding snow."

The horses are one facet of this emergence, and their escape is some small victory against constraint, but Mrs. Armstid is that member of the system who is most damaged by their flight. In stark contrast to, and as a result of, their explosive flight, she is left as a "blasted tree-trunk moving ... without motion" (351), thereby fulfilling the initial imagistic insistence that this tree appears locked in place, as "motionless" above as she was below at the bottom of a "windless and tideless sea" (306).[4] The imagery is certainly intricate, but this is the point of humanistic inquiry. Visualizing structure alone is not enough. Faulkner's process invariably involves our participation – not simply to see through the eyes of the other, but to affirm that other as a measure of ourselves. Mrs. Armstid's plight so poignantly haunts us because it ripples right through the system itself, not just at the lower rungs of the social hierarchy, but up above as well in the circulation of information through the entire structure. Conquered, beaten, and dispossessed, Mrs. Armstid is nonetheless the means through which we come to understand the complex system in which we are nestled. And though, in this instance, her suffering cannot disrupt Flem's power, some future iteration most certainly will.

6.3   Vertical Control and Immanent Perception

The horse auction presents a conflictual and interlocking relationship between top-down vertical control and disruptive novelty that composes the changing face of Frenchman's Bend. Faulkner upholds these two principles throughout the Snopes trilogy, visualizing, on the one hand, the greater concentric clustering of Yoknapatawpha's social body in very similar terms to the horse auction and, on the other hand, the immanent principle bound up, but always capable of breaking free to open up the possibility of new forms of order. These final two sections conclude my analysis of Faulkner's cognitive cartographies by showing how *The Town* and *The Mansion*, respectively published seventeen and nineteen years after *The Hamlet*, employ these two principles to portray the complex social order of Yoknapatawpha. In *The Mansion* particularly, the two characters of Flem and Mink Snopes strikingly embody the interlocking trajectory of these two principles of top-down vertical control and immanent novelty. As in the earlier fiction, the human being can still be mastered and overwhelmed by the contours of the greater social order, but Faulkner explicitly reconstitutes the immanent domain as a site of both tragedy and vigorous resistance.

The larger Snopes trilogy indicates that, on some basic level, any system of complexity requires both the clustering and dispersal of the social body. The immanent principle that underlies these two seemingly opposing forces is not an empty or abstract spiritual placeholder. Rather, the Snopes trilogy repeatedly gives this immanence value and character and sets it in stark contrast to the figure of Flem Snopes whom I take up first as a representation of the perils of system centralization and the financialization of the New South that we saw expressed in Jason Compson. Throughout the trilogy, Faulkner carefully crafts a composite imagery that aligns Flem with all the Yoknapatawpha proxies of top-down vertical control we have analyzed so far: from Colonel Sartoris to Jason Compson to Popeye to Sutpen. Some critics routinely interpret Flem as an embodiment of capitalism itself, rather than an ever present moral hazard within the capitalist system. Michael Wainwright (2005) makes the case most forcefully, arguing that the "capitalist system" is "personified by Flem Snopes" (75). Richard Godden (2007) calls for a more nuanced appraisal of Flem, stating that the character "may be misread if he is too readily allegorized as the agent of something as generic as 'capital'" (18). Indeed, Flem is not a condemnation of capitalization writ large, but a nuanced illustration of the dangers of centralization, monopoly, and financialization. In one respect, he is the polar opposite of Ratliff, the travelling salesman whose business is built through interpersonal exchange. Flem, by contrast, cares nothing for others; rather, he relentlessly goes about usurping the principal hubs of exchange in Yoknapatawpha – Varner's store, the Jefferson power plant, and the Sartoris bank – manipulating the flows of capital and resources to build his empire.

From the first, Flem is an express antagonist of interior space, a man associated with opaque, mimetic surfaces. In his first appearances in *The Hamlet*, he possesses eyes "the color of stagnant water" (H 24, 57) – and this watery surface is soon imagined with the machinic imagery of the white-and-black page itself. When Flem takes over the running of Varner's store, he attempts to look the part. Faulkner embeds a well-established textual symbolism in the description of Flem's dress, for his white shirt serves as a surface upon which a "machine-made," black "symbol" is impressed: "He wore not only a clean white shirt but a necktie – a tiny machine-made black bow which snapped together at the back with a metal fastener ... a tiny viciously depthless cryptically balanced splash like an enigmatic punctuation symbol against the expanse of white shirt" (63–4).

Flem's vicious lack of depth echoes one of the first depictions of Popeye we discussed in Chapter 3. Where Popeye operated as industrial proxy for the hyper-mimetic proliferation of surfaces, Flem's rapaciousness in manipulating these surfaces is more carefully developed. Indeed, Flem does not operate exclusively within the sharecropping economy or industry; like Jason Compson, he utilizes finance in a bid to control the various flows of capital and resources within the New South.

Faulkner also grafts a statue symbolism into his depiction of Flem, giving a predatory quality to Flem once attributed to Colonel Sartoris. In *The Hamlet*, for instance, Faulkner depicts the clerk as a bizarrely crafted aesthetic object whose original nose the craftsman has swapped with "a tiny predatory nose like the beak of a small hawk" (57). This symbolism is developed to suggest the invasion of interior space by a voracious mimetic paradigm. With his white shirt and minute bowtie, the clerk lurks spiderlike among the "ultimate shadows" of the Varner store's "interior" space in order to trap his prey: "that squat reticent figure in the steadily-soiling white shirts and the minute invulnerable bow, which in those abeyant days lurked among the ultimate shadows of the deserted and rich-odored interior with a good deal of the quality of a spider of that bulbous blond omnivorous though non-poisonous species" (64). With Flem now in control of the central hub of economic exchange in Frenchman's Bend, the store has effectively become a lair whose interior space is overtaken by mimetic shadows and the stink of a cunning predator.

Flem emerges as an antagonist of interior space, a man who seeks to dominate the principal hubs of social space with no regard for others and driven by an instinct for absolute control. Nowhere is this better articulated than in *The Mansion* in which Flem finally ascends the social hierarchy, usurping at once the bank presidency and the house of his competitor, De Spain. Although his new mansion has all the aesthetic qualities to signal success, Faulkner emphasizes two features of Flem's behavior above all. Within the massive house, Flem simply sits alone in a swivel chair with his feet propped up against the side of a fireplace, chewing mechanically upon the empty air. Readers learn how the man once chewed tobacco and then gum, but gives up the first because he cannot bear the unnecessary expense and the second because he hears that folk believe that a bank president is rich enough not to chew anything (173). Still, Flem does not give up the activity of chewing, and he steadily chews a "little mouth-sized chunk of air" (174) or a "nothing," an appropriate metaphor for a man propelled by a momentum without meaning.

Flem's posture here, which is simultaneously his final posture since Mink shoots him while in this attitude, serves as the overarching symbol of top-down vertical control for the final novel. Flem has been the predatory hawk or spider in previous iterations, but in the final novel, he is a man who holds to only one private ritual – that is, to sit with his "feet propped on the white paint [of the fireplace mantle], scratching it a little deeper ever day with the pegs in his heels" (173). Flem solves the deface-ment of the mantle by having "a little wood ledge, not even painted, nailed to the … mantelpiece at the exact height for [him] to prop his feet on it" (173). Faulkner visualizes this wood ledge in terms of vertical height and parallels Flem's use of the ledge with an "alpine climber" who clings to a ledge "panting, gathering his-self for that last do-or-die upsurge to deface the ultimate crowning pinnacle and peak with his own victorious initials" (176). Flem's ledge is no longer aspirational, if it ever was. It is, however, the only spiritual remnant that remains in his otherwise empty existence:

> But not this [ledge]; and here was that humility again: not in public where it would be a insult to any and all that held Merchants and Farmers Bank alpine climbing in veneration, but in private like a secret chapel or a shrine: not to cling panting to it, desperate and indomitable, but to prop his feet on it while setting at his ease. (177)

With his feet propped up on, and violently etching into, this apex of social space, Flem has achieved mastery over the world around him. He is no longer the spider of *The Hamlet* trapping and consuming his prey through attending to the bureaucratic paperwork of the store. Instead, he has become an empty symbol of centralized finance, an empire of signs and figures amassed not to serve an "economy" of living beings, but "belong-ing," as we are told during Flem's funeral, "simply to Money" (461).

Throughout the trilogy, this centralizing paradigm of vertical control is repeatedly juxtaposed with an ethics of interiority. In *The Town*, for instance, Gavin Stevens explicitly articulates this tension when he observes that Flem's inability to see the true humanity of the other stems from his own interior pollution, that stagnant depth within that originally charac-terized the petty tyrant: "You couldn't see behind Mr Snopes' eyes because they were not really looking at you at all, like a pond of stagnant water is not looking at you. Uncle Gavin said that was why it took him a minute or two to realise that he and Mr Snopes were looking at exactly the same thing: it just wasn't with the same eye" (T 175). The three narrators of *The Town* – Gavin Stevens, Charles Mallison, and V. J. Ratliff – attempt to elicit this inner domain through attentive acts of reading so as to resist

Flem Snopes' takeover of Jefferson.[5] Though the Faulkner of the late
1950s is still fascinated with the power of textual space, he now places
this within a framework of learning to read both within and beyond
bureaucratic processes.[6] It is essential to add that these three narrators
are capable of such readings precisely because they can attest to the
immanent and interpersonal dynamics that exist within individuals and
underlie the formation of the greater social body with its proliferation of
texts, culture, and ideology.

In the most iconic scene of *The Town* and perhaps of his whole fiction,
Faulkner crafts a cartography of interiority that exemplifies the importance
of the immanent gaze of the later fiction. From the vantage point of
Seminary Ridge, Gavin Stevens sees the whole county laid out before
him – and through his eyes, Faulkner directly addresses the reader: "And
now, looking back and down, you see all Yoknapatawpha in the dying last
of day beneath you" (330). Here, Faulkner depicts a luminescence gathering and pooling just above the surface of the earth. Textual space still
functions as one level of emergent order, but it is situated within a grand
articulation of three-dimensional space. Faulkner begins this cognitive
cartography with Stevens ascending upward, driving "a mild unhurried
farm road presently mounting to cross the ridge" (330). As he climbs
toward a God's-eye view of Yoknapatawpha, the stars appear above, and a
"soundless murmur" similarly rises across the landscape: "There are stars
now, just pricking out as you watch them among the others already coldly
and softly burning; the end of day is one vast green soundless murmur up
the northwest toward the zenith" (330).

The vision that initially emerges is one that powerfully echoes the horse
auction from nearly two decades earlier. Like the barbed wire or plow lines
that harness the horses, the diverging roads "tie" the diffuse rural land to the
center, binding a "living water" into "concentric rings" (331). From Stevens'
point of view, moreover, Frenchman's Bend, an "ant-heap" (332), is similarly
secured to road-spokes that arc at once to the center and outward "to the
world" (330). Yet, as every careful reader of Faulkner knows, this God's-eye
view is neither the sole nor even most important measure of hierarchies in his
fiction. Indeed, this heightened perception is made possible by the immanent
murmur that rises upward to animate and compose the various levels of
order, first through fireflies and then through voices, cries, and words that
comprise the "whole sum" of our individual experiences:

> Then, as though at signal, the fireflies – lightning bugs of the Mississippi
> child's vernacular – myriad and frenetic, random and frantic, pulsing; not

questing, not quiring, but choiring as though they were tiny incessant
appeaseless voices, cries, words. And you stand suzerain and solitary above
the whole sum of your life beneath that incessant ephemeral spangling. First
is Jefferson, the center, radiating weakly its puny glow into space; beyond it,
enclosing it, spreads the County, tied by the diverging roads to that center
as is the rim to the hub by its spokes, yourself detached as God himself for
this moment above the cradle of your nativity and of the men and women
who made you, the record and annal of your native land proffered for your
perusal in ring by concentric ring like the ripples on living water above the
dreamless slumber of your past; you to preside unanguished and immune
above this miniature of man's passions and hopes and disasters – ambition
and fear and lust and courage and abnegation and pity and honor and sin
and pride – all bound, precarious and ramshackle held together, by the web,
the iron-thin warp and woof of his rapacity but withal yet dedicated to
his dreams. (331)

Scholars have emphasized the tension in this passage between literal and
figurative space. Leonard Lutwack (1984), for instance, sees this depiction
as both "a geographical area and a metaphor for the literary creation of an
author" (43). Elizabeth Kerr (1983) extends this tension to the body
politic itself, so that the map beneath the reader's gaze serves as "a
microcosm peripheral to the navel of America" (18). And Joseph Urgo
(2004) insightfully interprets the passage by invoking a "sense of dual lives,
one material, one deeper, more profoundly inaccessible, [that] animates
Yoknapatawpha" (648). Yet the "deeper" life that Urgo identifies in the
passage is not entirely inaccessible. Such an assessment more accurately
describes the "inverted-apex, this ∇-shaped section of earth" (GDM 328)
that an aged Isaac perceives retreating from the world, as we saw in our
analysis of "Delta Autumn." In *The Town*, Faulkner is adamant that the
"light [is] not being subtracted from the earth" (T 330).

   While the two respective visions begin in a nearly identical way, Gavin's
experience is precisely the opposite to that of the McCaslin man. The older
Isaac saw the disappearing wilderness "gathered and for a time arrested in
one tremendous density of brooding and inscrutable impenetrability at the
ultimate funneling tip" (GDM 328). Gavin similarly sees the light as "one
vast green soundless murmur ... gathered, pooling for an unmoving
moment yet, among low places of the ground" (T 328). Unlike the
retreating wilderness in the earlier novel, the light of Gavin's epiphany
pools along the earth and then rises upward to self-organize on different
levels of signification and to infuse Steven's vision so thoroughly that
readers have a new sense of information flow in Yoknapatawpha. To be
sure, there is neither a tyrannical information object supervening on the

structure below, nor a network whose nodes circulate an ideology that seeks to invade the fragile domain within. Instead, Gavin witnesses a deeply infused and interconnected social body, which is composed out of the random, chaotic, and self-organizing behavior of the individual beings below – a system truly pushed to the *edge of chaos*, at once producing hierarchal order, yet capable of adaptation and genuine change.

The imagery and spatial delineations of Faulkner's passage portray, therefore, a complex system in which the immanent domain constitutes itself from below and self-organizes through multiple levels of emergent expression. At the lowest level, there is only reflected light, one that makes the earth "luminous," but is "unmoving" with the trees "standing darkly and immobile out of it" (330). But this express mimetic predicament is answered by the fireflies immediately above that in turn giving rise to a living language that the onlooker perceives, even while above him the stars are becoming visible. Certainly, this whole order is already established to some extent; twilight has begun to assume dominance, indicating some form of closure in which the county appears in "miniature" like the textual surface itself, invariably static and immovable. Yet this cartography of consciousness remains dynamically open. As the passage begins to elicit semantic height through a complex expression of individual agencies, the words on the page cease to be stationary. Indeed, what was dissonant and chaotic on one level of significance achieves a new coherent social form of communication, for the fireflies are "not questing, not quiring, but choiring as though they were tiny incessant appeaseless voices, cries, words."

Like the cloud of pink-and-white bees swarming upward after the horse auction in *The Hamlet*, these fireflies arise "myriad and frenetic, random and frantic," their behavior communicating "words" that circulate the information of all the parts through the whole of the structure. In Mrs. Armstid's vision in *The Hamlet*, there is a quality decidedly melancholic about "the somber cedar grove" above Frenchman's Bend where the bees swarm, a grove "where during the long afternoons of summer the constant mourning doves called back and forth" (349). As I observed, Mrs. Armstid's personal calamity is not hers alone, but is transmitted intact through the whole social body. In *The Town*, Gavin similarly recognizes the suffering implicit in being part of the whole: "Because the tragedy of life is, it must be premature, inconclusive and inconcludable, in order to be life; it must be before itself, in advance of itself, to have been at all" (333). For Faulkner, then, the answer to the mimetic dilemma – to the textual surface being already written – is not some ultimate metaphysical consolation; rather, the mimetic cartography stirs itself to life and language, and this self-constitution involves a "truth" which is always "one last chance to choose, decide" (333). Certainly, our agency is constrained by circumstance, constrained by the cartography of which we are a part. Like Judith's vision of the loom in *Absalom, Absalom!*, we are woven into a pattern with others around us, each trying to establish his or her own individual expression. Yet for Faulkner, such a struggle for dominance represents only one facet of our shared experience; in each moment, the world offers itself as a complex network of relations and requires our participation, which may yet change the constitution of the whole. Gavin's lyrical vision out on Seminary Hill may seem entirely positive and hopeful, but it just as surely corresponds with tragedy. Indeed, the vision of the whole contains all the various individual members that compose it, including Eula who is making "one last choice" of her own – namely, suicide.

The iconic passage here entails the most striking example of a way to read and pierce through the bureaucratic texts of Flem's cash empire so as to perceive a multifaceted and immanent social order in which our agency is both constrained by the cartography about us and yet a vital avenue of transformation and change. Textual space is still present as one layer of signification, but it does not form a self-enclosed system of signs. Rather, there always emerges "one last choice" to submit to, or change, the greater flow of information. In *The Town*, readers can see several such examples of illuminated reading. For instance, through Gavin, readers are able to see a dramatically different Eula from the earlier Snopes novel. Whereas Eula was never fully present as a self in the earlier novel, now she becomes a woman of stunning, even frightening depth, which makes her eventual suicide all the more poignant.

In Gavin's closest and most sexually dangerous encounter with Eula, we have a sense both of his desire for the ever suffering wife of Flem and of her very being as a virtually unlimited depth of field: Eula "never had looked at me but that once as she entered. She simply confronted me across her shoulder with that blue envelopment like the sea, not questioning nor waiting, as the sea itself doesn't need to question or wait but simply to be the sea" (97). Eula's eyes are an "unbearable and unfathomable blue, speculative and serene" (99) – and Faulkner insists upon this spatial and natural depth inside the woman throughout the entire encounter and subsequently remaps Gavin's perception of Eula's interiority onto Linda, Eula's daughter, with an additional mythic element: Linda's eyes "were not gray at all. They were darkest hyacinth, what I have always imagined that Homer's hyacinthine sea must have had to look like" (203). In these instances, we better understand Gavin's motivations. He may pine after

Eula like so many other men before him, but his dedication to these two women aligns with his larger recognition of immanent being, a domain that Flem, as the exponent of depthless surfaces, seeks to appropriate, even while being incapable of understanding its significance.

The Mansion is even more emphatic in its recognition of immanence, and Faulkner's portrayal of his characters accordingly assumes a greater empathetic resonance. Eula serves again as a powerful example. Even while living within Flem's bureaucratic empire of textual space, she is forced to develop a fragile immunity to her environment, which is, once again, constituted in terms of depth: "that-ere bubble-glass thing somewhere inside her like one of them shimmer-colored balls balanced on the seal's nose, fragile yet immune too jest that one constant fragile inch above the smutch and dirt of Snopes as long as the seal dont trip or stumble or let her attention wander" (M 152). Here, Faulkner imagines Eula's preservation of immanence as a game of amusement with extremely high stakes. In this case, the immanent domain is figured as a ball of shimmering color that Eula, as a creature of the sea and, thus, of the deep, must balance upon her nose, lest it fall into the dirt of Snopes' empty ambitions. That Eula eventually chooses suicide indicates, moreover, that this delicate balancing act to preserve an immanent domain succumbs, in this instance, to an environment profoundly hostile to it.

Faulkner emphasizes this notion of immanent personhood by mapping it onto unlikely characters, showing that immanence is not always negated in such hostile environments. Miss Reba Rivers, whom we last analyzed in Chapter 3 as an exponent of Popeye's mimetic transgression of Temple, appears in *The Mansion* as a woman who preserves "something in or behind" the "eyes" that "shouldn't have been there" (88). We recall that, in *Sanctuary*, Reba and her dogs represent an already polluted internal space. The "wheezy, flatulent sounds" of the dogs correspond to the "rich pneumasis of [Reba's] breast," which in turn gives rise to asthmatic coughing and a thousand conflicting sounds (S 143), all of which convince Temple that she has no authentic nature and thus must internalize Popeye's mimetic transgression of her body. Despite Reba's hard life, the former prostitute and madam of the Memphis brothel retains an immanent and interpersonal dimension that cannot be taken from her. Her continuing grief over the loss of her beloved partner, Mr. Binford, elicits this underlying fragile dimension in a way that thoroughly humanizes her and evokes our compassion:

> It shouldn't have been there: the rat raddled face and body that had worn themselves out with the simple hard physical work of being a whore and making a living at it like an old prize fighter or football player or maybe an

old horse until they didn't look like a man's or a woman's either in spite of the cheap rouge and too much of it and the big diamonds that were real enough even if you just did not believe that color, and *the eyes with something in or behind them that shouldn't have been there*; that, as they say, shouldn't happen to a dog. Minnie passed the door going back down the hall. The tray was empty now. (88; emphasis added)

Although the internal space "in or behind" the eyes should not be there, it is, even in someone "worn out" from the "hard physical work" of prostitution. Faulkner, however, subtly embeds a caveat to the expression of this inner life. Immanence may be a necessary underlayer to our interpersonal being, but under certain conditions and external pressures, it also disappears from all view, from all representation. Faulkner undercuts Reba's immanent dimension by turning the narrative's attention to Minnie who continues the action outside the room. This is no casual detail, for it reinscribes the dilemma of *Sanctuary* in a new, but interrelated way. Although Reba signals that her inner domain survives in the memory of her beloved Binford, there is nonetheless no external referent for it in the social space of the brothel. Minnie passes by and her tray is "empty now," in turn indicating that the immanent underlayer to our being can be constrained and jeopardized by our environment.

6.4   "A Single Tree Somewhere Deep in Memory"

Among the many characters of the Snopes trilogy who offer a view of the fragile depths of the self, Mink Snopes functions as the primary touchstone for immanence and disruptive novelty in *The Mansion*. To be sure, Mink's character arc exemplifies the survival of the immanent depths within the self even in environments profoundly unfavorable and hostile to them. In the pairing of Flem and Mink, Faulkner readdresses the conflict between vertical control and immanent being that has been a central preoccupation of his entire Yoknapatawpha fiction. It is important to consider that this pairing does not unfold entirely in oppositional terms. While both men are set against each other, Mink does not hate Flem. From the first, he has a "grudging admiration, almost pride" (109) for his cousin. In short, his belief in Flem – or what Flem represents – is a core constituent of his worldview. Thus, with Mink eventually shooting Flem and bringing a halt to the man's ceaseless chewing of the empty air, Faulkner indicates that the pairing of these two men unfolds dialectically, each representing two aspects of the social body's behavior as it clusters and disperses across time.

The Mansion therefore depicts Mink and Flem's relationship in complex and enigmatic terms – at once oppositional and complementary. Mink's faith in Flem initially contradicts his own better sense. Although Mink almost certainly knows that Flem cannot come to Mississippi to aid him, he kills Zach Houston anyway. The Snopes man continues to call for Flem from his cell and pays little attention to his own trial or sentencing, looking away from the judge and jury and back toward the courtroom door for the approach of his cousin. Even after serving some thirty-six years, Mink still articulates his admiration for Flem: "he would think, say aloud, without envy even: 'That Flem Snopes. You cant beat him. There aint a man in Missippi nor the U.S. and A. both put together that can beat Flem Snopes'" (M 109). Faulkner establishes the quasi-religious dimension of Mink's faith in his cousin early on with an insistence that, in Mink's mind, the benevolent Christian God has been superseded by the power of the social body. For Mink, Flem is the only one capable of navigating a social order administered by an all-powerful and all-knowing "Them."

From the first pages of the novel, then, Faulkner grafts the "Them" of *The Town* onto Mink's abstract idea of a social body that possesses an omniscience once assigned to the metaphysical deity of the Christian faith. Where in *Matthew* 10:29, it is promised that not one sparrow will fall without the Father knowing of it, in the opening pages that narrate Mink's trial, this "Them" possesses a similar omniscience:

> He had not forgotten that his cousin would not be there. He simply couldn't wait any longer. He had simply had to trust *them* – the *Them* of whom it was promised that not even a sparrow should fall unmarked. By *them* he didn't mean that whatever-it-was that folks referred to as Old Moster. He didn't believe in any Old Moster. He had seen too much in his time that, if any Old Moster existed, with eyes as sharp and power as strong as was claimed He had, He would have done something about. (5)

Mink's belief in the power of "*Them*" is matched by a view that all spiritual notions are simply a form of trickery, a way in which those in power manipulate the powerless in order to fill up a lack in themselves:

> Besides, he, Mink, wasn't religious. He hadn't been to a church since he was fifteen years old and never aimed to go again – places which a man with a hole in his gut and a rut in his britches that he couldn't satisfy at home, used, by calling himself a preacher of God, to get conveniently together the biggest possible number of women that he could tempt with the reward of the one in return for the job of the other – the job of filling his hole in payment for getting theirs plugged. (6)

Mink imagines the spiritual nature of the human being in terms of a depth that needs to be filled up, but his interpretation of this paradigm is initially seen as the "hole" in the "gut," intimating that this desire or yearning is only carnal in nature and needs to be alleviated through the "rut in a man's britches." As a result, Mink's contempt for the minister lies in his perception that the man of God fraudulently "plugs" this interior yearning by trickery and thereby satisfies his desires under the guise of religion.

This lack of a belief in an interior domain has tragic consequences for Mink. Faulkner repeatedly describes the man as someone irresistibly compelled by external forces. Take, for instance, the portrait of Mink sitting in the Warden's office once he has been sentenced for life: He "was completely still, just blinking a little, his hands hanging empty but even now shaped inside the palms like the handles of a plow and even his neck braced a little as though still braced against the loop of plowlines" (94). Fashioned by a life of sharecropping, Mink resembles a beast of burden. His hands are empty, but shaped by the plow, his neck similarly "braced ... against the loop of plowlines" even when they are not harnessing him. And now he is incarcerated in a penitentiary, the name of which Faulkner took from a real prison in Mississippi and that also connects with the ultimate constraining surface in Faulkner's fiction, a textual surface. Indeed, Parchman as a surname comes from the French "parcheminier," meaning parchment. Mink, therefore, has never been free, trading one life of confinement for another; more tragically, he has never yearned for freedom, until now. The man begins to yearn for the world outside his cage. Unfortunately for the sharecropper, even this nascent desire is turned against him when his cousin Montgomery convinces Mink to escape in accordance with Flem's directive to add more time to Mink's sentence:

> "Just five years more, then you'll be out where the free sun and air can shine on you without any man with a shotgun's shadow to cut it off. Because you'll be free."
>   "Free," [Mink] said, not loud: just like that: "Free." That was all. It was that easy. (94)

The dynamic here is simple, but it goes to the heart of the conflict we have seen throughout the greater Yoknapatawpha fiction: the mimetic power of an institution to confine the self and the immanent desire to escape such confinement. The "shadow of the shotgun" cuts the prisoner off from the "free sun and air," and Montgomery uses Mink's desire for the world beyond to extend the poor man's incarceration.

When Mink is finally released, his new-found freedom awakens an immanent architecture within him that has been either dormant or non-existent. Faulkner's previous depiction of the mysterious "something that shouldn't have been there" in Miss Reba intimates the type of interiority that is awakening in Mink, for it entails an inner landscape that cannot be fully sustained outside of memory, as with Reba. Nonetheless, Faulkner offers a moving portrait of a man learning to move, behave, and think outside of the *Them* that has always tyrannized his existence. When Mink is finally released from Parchman Penitentiary, his interior world stirs within him, perhaps for the first time, and he becomes capable of combatting the withered and dying landscape of the Delta swamp with a golden memory of his "home in the hills":

> It was fall, almost October, and he discovered that here was something else he had forgotten about during the thirty-eight years: seasons. They came and went in the penitentiary too but for thirty-eight years the only right he had to them was the privilege of suffering because of them: from the heat and sun of summer whether he wanted to work in heat of the day or not, and the rain and icelike mud of winter whether he wanted to be out in it or not. But now they belonged to him again: October next week, not much to see in this flat Delta country which he had misdoubted the first time he laid eyes on it from the train window that day thirty-eight years ago: just cotton stalks and cypress needles. But back home in the hills, all the land would be gold and crimson with hickory and gum and oak and maple, and the old fields warm with sage and splattered with scarlet sumac; in thirty-eight years he had forgotten that. (116)

After thirty-eight years of institutional confinement, Mink is beginning to claim ownership over his own experiences. The seasons under which he struggled as a convict "belong to him again" and, as the process unfolds, he is able to access memories that have lain dormant for too long. The withered "cotton stalks" and "cypress needles" that characterize Mink's external environment can no longer overpower him, for he has remembered something long forgotten, his home awash in the golden and crimson beauty of the fall. Mink has thereby become capable of an interior reflection that was impossible for him before, when his vision of the world was solely characterized by power or the lack thereof.

As we have seen in previous Yoknapatawpha novels, the natural world so often functions as an immanent source within the self – whether this is displaced with Benjy associating the smell of trees with his absent sister Caddy or realized in a life-sustaining way with Jewel and his horse. As these examples suggest, nature in Faulkner is not some abstract, self-contained ideal landscape; in order to be nourishing, it must afford access to others. This dynamic underscores precisely the interior transformation taking place in Mink. His freedom from confinement is more than a realignment with nature – with a "home" of "gold and crimson with hickory and gum and oak and maple, and the old fields warm with sage and splattered with scarlet sumac." Mink's reclamation of this interior, mnemonic landscape is ultimately an attempt to access the interpersonal foundations of his being. This place "deep" in his memory is a site of correspondences, "a single tree" that, as we saw in *The Hamlet*, exerts a disruptive power on the constrictive external network. Here, Mink's memory of home ultimately involves an experience of maternal love that now exists "somewhere deep" within:

> When suddenly, somewhere deep in memory, there was a tree, a single tree. His mother was dead; he couldn't remember her nor even how old he was when his father married again. So the woman wasn't even kin to him and she never let him forget it: that she was raising him not from any tie or claim and not because he was weak and helpless and a human being, but because she was a Christian. Yet there was more than that behind it. He knew that at once – a gaunt harried slattern of a woman whom he remembered always either with a black eye or holding a dirty rag to her bleeding where her husband had struck her. Because he could always depend on her, not to do anything for him because she always failed there, but for constancy, to be always there and always aware of him, surrounding him always with that shield which actually protected, defended him from nothing but on the contrary seemed actually to invite more pain and grief. But simply to be there, lachrymose, harassed, yet constant. (117)

In this passage, Faulkner upholds the paradigmatic image of the submerged mother that was originally prefigured in Dilsey who "ris[es] like a ruin or a landmark" out of watery depths and then developed powerfully in Eunice of *Go Down, Moses* and Mrs. Armstid of *The Hamlet*. These women may have been damaged by external circumstance, raped as Eunice is by old Carothers, or swindled out of her hard-earned money as Mrs. Armstid is by Flem. But they offer access to the immanent depths within being, Eunice as the source of an alternative symbolic order to that of the plantation ledgers, and Mrs. Armstid as the moral measure of Flem's nascent empire. Mink's stepmother is also the mother "deep within memory," a woman who in life was "harassed" and battered by her husband, but whose "constancy" has outlasted her mortal body as she emerges in Mink's memory as an underlying source of meaning and solace. Faulkner indicates, moreover, that this immanent and interpersonal experience is also beyond ideological institutions. On the face of it, Mink's stepmother assumes responsibility for a child who is not hers "because she was a Christian." Faulkner indicates, moreover, that "there was more than that behind it." The mother's constancy is thus imagined in immanent and spiritual terms, for she at once resides "deep within memory" and is "always there and always aware of him, surrounding him always with that shield." Faulkner creates a consoling ambiguity about the memory within. Although the woman is gone, she nonetheless remains steadfast and constant, the key repetition of "always" subtly asserting that her constancy signifies across time.

While Faulkner continues to answer the crisis of interiority that so permeated his earlier fiction, he does not sentimentalize these characters. Mink's creative interiorization of his experience cannot be fully sustained in a landscape to which he is unaccustomed and in which the human identification with the land has been jeopardized. As he travels from the Mississippi state prison to Tennessee, Mink's search for inner significance aligns him with others who similarly attempt to find meaning in a landscape that has become alienating and disaffecting. His labor both at Sister Holcomb and Brother Goodyhay's houses involves a collective attempt to rebuild some kind of coherent order out of a chaotic and haphazard external environment. Goodyhay's house particularly under-scores this severe confusion between inner and outer, private and public:

> In fact, this house had no shades nor curtains whatever to be spied from behind. Indeed, as he really looked about it for the first time, the whole place had an air of violent transience similar to the indiscriminate jumble of walls and windows and doors among which he and the other man worked: merely still nailed together and so standing upright; from time to time, as the stack reclaimed planks and the pile of fire-lengths to which his saw was reducing the spoiled fragments slowly rose. (297)

After thirty-eight years, Mink's experience of life beyond the prison indus-trial complex is deeply unsettling, and Faulkner makes clear that he is not alone. What was his interior revelation after coming out of prison is now specifically played out as he attempts to reclaim order from the piles of diffused chaotic buildings. In this sense, the attempt to rebuild, renew, and repurpose the past into new order is what symbolically connects Mink's mnemonic epiphany with the work of Goodyhay's congregation to build a new chapel. A landscape characterized by "violent transience," "spoiled fragments," and "the indiscriminate jumble of walls and windows and doors" comprises a far larger collective crisis in the life of the New South.

We learn, moreover, that, similar to Mink, Goodyhay recounts his wartime experience that led to a revelation deep within, at the "bottom of the Pacific" which brought him to the "edge of Memphis, Tennessee" to build a church (295). While Goodyhay's account of his revelation is absurd with Jesus cast as a commanding officer, Faulkner indicates that Mink shares a deeper interior architecture with Goodyhay and his ragtag congregation. In these passages, Faulkner is at his best, at once refusing to sentimentalize the congregation's plight and intimating that their yearning for meaning can be both absurd and consequential at the same time. Goodyhay and his congregation are socialized by custom, yet capable of greater, if temporary, reconciliation through shared suffering. During Goodyhay's Sunday service in a "Negro Schoolhouse," the congregation assembles with a bereaved white "woman" in a "yellow hat" in the front row and segregated behind her, "a big Negress alone on the back one" (307). On one hand, Faulkner indicates that the husband's war-time sacrifice remains "unreconciled by [a widow's] meagre and arid tears which were less of tears than blisters." On the other hand, these irreconcilable aspects of human experience can be overcome, if only temporarily:

> The solitary Negro woman got up from her back bench and walked down the aisle to where the young woman's soiled yellow hat was crushed into the crook of her elbow like a child in a child's misery and desolation, the white people on the bench making way for the Negress to sit down beside the young white woman and put her arm around her. (310)

The congregation is capable of crossing lines of separation and communing; in this instance, the black woman offers compassion and solace when no one else can. Similarly, Mink's isolation from this group is not overcome; to be sure, he watches them, "himself alien, not only unreconciled but irreconcilable" (310), but it is this community nonetheless that responds to his monetary need, propelling him on to Memphis to experience the city in a state unfettered and unencumbered by custom or habit.

With Mink's approach to the city, Faulkner reinstates that evocation of complex social order that he has so developed through the Snopes trilogy. Similar to Mrs. Armstid's vision of the bees rising up above Frenchman's Bend or Gavin's God's-eye view of the luminescence of Yoknapatawpha, Faulkner's depiction of Mink seeing Memphis again as a lambent landscape emphasizes the sheer vertical power of the city. On the edge of his seat in the truck, Mink sees a city fully electrified for the first time in his life, "the low glare on the sky as into some monstrous, frightening, unimaginable joy or pleasure":

> That was how he saw Memphis again under the best, the matchless condition for one who hadn't seen it . . . at night, the dark earth on either hand and ahead already random and spangled with the neon he had never seen before, and in the distance the low portentous glare of the city itself, he sitting on the edge of the seat as a child sits, almost as small as a child, peering ahead as the car rushed, merging into one mutual spangled race bearing toward, as though by the acceleration of gravity or suction, the distant city; suddenly off to the right a train fled dragging a long string of lighted windows as rapid and ephemeral as dream; he became aware of a convergence like the spokes of a gigantic dark wheel lying on its hub, along which sped dense and undeviable as ants, automobiles and what they told him were called buses as if all the earth was hurrying, plunging, being sucked decked with diamond and ruby lights, into the low glare on the sky as into some monstrous, frightening, unimaginable joy or pleasure. (312)

Mink may have given birth to an incipient immanent architecture, but he, like us, moves antlike along the newly paved highways and is completely subject to the irresistible and concentric gravity of the city. In fact, the city possesses a godlike vertical power too big to be grasped by the intellect and overwhelming through sheer scale and scope:

> Now he was in what he knew was the city. For a moment it merely stood glittering and serried and taller than stars. Then it engulfed him; it stooped soaring down, bearing down upon him like breathing the vast concrete mass and weight until he himself was breathless, having to pant for air. (313)

The city is initially "taller than stars" and descends upon Mink with a power akin to that of Yahweh to breathe life into him. The man is so mystified and overwhelmed that he has to pant for air. Here, we see the old metaphysical verities reimagined ominously in modern terms. Mink is that self shaped by a transcendent force that descends from above and compels those ant-like humans to participate in this historical sublation into modern totalization – with cart replaced by automobile, dirt road by asphalt, and candle by electricity. Indeed, the advent of the wheel – and thus the quintessential innovation of early civilization – is so all-encompassing that we are always a part of that "gigantic dark wheel lying on its hub."

Yet, Mink – a man at the bottom of the social hierarchy, a man who cannot even bear to look at the electric city without terror – is the one who ultimately unseats Flem from his perch of power toward the conclusion of the novel. As we saw last section (6.3), Flem's final posture explicitly stages a vertical paradigm of authority, for the banker sits perpetually in his swivel chair at the center of his mansion, "chewing steady on nothing" with "his feet propped on that little wooden additional ledge nailed in unpainted paradox to that hand-carved and -painted mantel" (174). When Mink finds his cousin positioned in this way, there is no need for conversation or protestation. Flem's jaw simply "cease[s] chewing in mid-motion," and the banker "lowers his feet from the ledge" before he resumes "chewing faintingly again" (455–6). Mink may have spent his entire life shaped and constrained by external social forces, first the sharecrop and then the prison industrial complex, but he is not powerless to resist. Indeed, Flem's mechanical chewing pauses momentarily before Mink brings his cousin's machinations to an end forever.

Like Rider who kills the "boss-man" in "Pantaloon in Black," Mink brings down Flem's empire, indicating that as overpowering as this vertical organization of power may seem, no variable is too small or inconsequential that it cannot upend it. This is the rub of any proliferating, totalizing vertex of social space: It is measured at last not by sheer size or by prevailing power, but in terms of the ever suffering individual whose very being is shaped to its service, yet carries within them a mysterious element that cannot be wholly subsumed. We have seen this ethical dimension of Faulkner's systems view in a number of characters thus far: Caddy who falls into dishonor and shame, but whose memory continues to reverberate through *The Sound and the Fury*; and Eunice in *Go Down, Moses* whose despair and defiance in suicide survive on as an alternative site of alterity within the plantation regime. This is no less true of Mink's role in bringing down Flem's seemingly intractable vertex of power. Although Flem's vertex of power appears omnipotent and ubiquitous, the larger system itself is poised at the *edge of chaos* and is thereby highly responsive to subtle changes in behavior and capable of adapting from within.

As he does with Rider's killing of the boss-man, Faulkner offers a subtle, yet stark warning in his description of the murder itself. Faulkner ultimately minimizes the weapon's part in the process, for the "report of the pistol" is "nothing." Rather, the chair upon which Flem sits serves as catalyst, since it is the seat of power itself that appears to act of its own accord, producing a sound so loud that it can wake the entire social body from its slumber: "When the chair finished falling and crashed to the floor, the sound would wake all Jefferson" (457). As we saw in Rider's narrative, all elements – both animate and inanimate – are part of a complex agency of things capable of destroying any paradigm of power. Strikingly symbolized by the empty air that Flem chews and the cruel biting of the banker's boots upon the ledge, this particular centralized hub of social space has become increasingly incoherent and can no longer sustain itself. Mink is that reminder to us that no element is incidental; that, at a certain level of analysis, there isn't even any conflict, just the sound of a vertex of power suddenly foundationless and, as a result, buckling under its own mammoth weight and producing an opportunity for new forms of social order.

Conclusion
Between Image and Ideology

> The past is never dead. It's not even past. All of us labor in webs spun
> long before we were born, webs of heredity and environment, of
> desire and consequence, of history and eternity. Haunted by wrong
> turns and roads not taken, we pursue images perceived as new but
> whose providence dates to the dim dramas of childhood, which are
> themselves but ripples of consequence echoing down the generations.
> The quotidian demands of life distract from this resonance of images
> and events, but some of us feel it always.
>
> (Greg Iles, *The Quiet Game,* 1999)

When I first read the words above, I was attending a lecture in which the
speaker attributed the passage to Faulkner. Sitting in the audience,
I googled the final sentence and found it similarly credited on dozens of
webpages. I certainly recognized the first two sentences from *Requiem for a
Nun* (1951). They have become iconic Faulkner, quoted and misquoted
by many and famously cited by President Obama to articulate an
American history that is ongoing and challenges its participants to create
a more perfect union. Still, the rest of the quotation was unfamiliar to me.
It sounded Faulknerian, although too perfect of an encapsulation, possessing an advantage of distance to address a complete and finished artistic
vision. By contrast, Faulkner's long sentences often bear an undeniable
tension, attempting, as we have seen, to compress entire histories of
movement, behavior, and thinking into a grammatical structure that can
barely withstand the pressure.

Yet, if there is anything like a credo in Faulkner's Yoknapatawpha
fiction, Greg Iles, a Mississippian himself, conveys the dilemma of the self
in history: As the individual moves in the apparent novelty of the present
moment, the impression of autonomy wavers and the deeper temporal
flow in which this self is nestled can be intuited. I have called Faulkner's
constitution of this spatiotemporal form a cognitive cartography and
explicated the author's idiosyncratic and farsighted visualization of the

ways in which the individual is nestled within vast intergenerational networks of social relationships. On one level, Faulkner's spatial practice is a direct inheritance of the Romantic desire to locate the individual within the vast progressive arc of history itself. What sets Faulkner's spatial practice apart is his painstaking study of the social body as a collective entity that invents culture and embeds self-directing and self-replicating information within the objects and nodes of its networks.

From *Flags in the Dust* onward, there is virtually no difference beyond that of scale between the individual artwork and the institution-building in which the social body engages. Yet there is simultaneously a problem with this symbiotic relationship between culture and signification which Faulkner repeatedly recognizes. Our cultural artifacts can be individuated, but they cannot stand individually, separate, or alone. As a result, art does not merely offer a mirror of the individual's interior world; rather, the complex systems of which we are a part are enabled by a mimetic mechanism within us that allows us both to generate culture and to replicate it endlessly. In Faulkner's Yoknapatawpha, the individual artwork thereby gives way to cultural production and reproduction. Faulkner was especially cognizant of the ways in which textuality is employed in this arc toward complex and centralized social order. In his first description of the plantation complex, he visualizes the manner in which a text or aesthetic object is placed in a central vertex of social space so that its ideology can be reproduced in the movement, behavior, and thinking of the social body as it reinforces the maxims of the cultural order. With this, the author developed a symbolic shorthand that he employed frequently throughout his Yoknapatawpha fiction and one that allowed him to understand the ways in which all manner of texts – aesthetic, architectural, and economic – are fundamental to the development and maintenance of a highly administered society. Throughout Faulkner's fiction, this text erected at the center of social space takes many forms: most prominently, a planter genealogy written on the flyleaves of a family bible, the monumental statue of the planter patriarch and the Confederate soldier, and the lien ledgers that organize the sharecropping plantation system. All these are not simply artifacts of power, but information objects that have acquired a quasi-agency; they are not conscious, but they mediate centralized nodes of social space in which intergenerational memory is stored and through which capital, resources, and information flow.

With this portrayal of storing and instantiating information in the structures around us, Faulkner vividly explores how the self is intimately involved in, and composed of, such activities at a level below volition or choice. As a result, the division between artistic creation and societal production necessarily blurs and, with it, the capacity of art to represent that interior domain in the self wavers and threatens to disappear altogether. Yet there remains a spiritual vision in Faulkner nonetheless, one that cannot be wholly subsumed within these webs of biology and culture, a vision that we perilously term immanence, soul, spirit, *élan vital* – while wary that such a placeholder might send us down the path toward ideology and institution-building. The twenty-first-century critic is bolstered and encumbered by post-structural legacies of interpretation in assessing this vexed tension between culture and immanence in Faulkner's work. Beginning in the late 1970s, Faulkner scholars increasingly began to abandon the Faulkner of spiritual interiority. Often with a twinge of nostalgia, these scholars rebelled against notions of immanence and the various architectures through which, they believed, it was historically represented. They tended to see the Romantic concept of immanence as the assertion of an essentialism employed to prop up and naturalize social hierarchy or cultural hegemony.

This book has argued for a different conception of the Faulknerian self without denying that Faulkner was intently absorbed in exploring the wide-ranging implications of the self's social construction. The Romantic belief of immanence – that unsettled territory within the human self – is still very much alive in Faulkner's earlier work, repeatedly serving as a battleground rather than simply as a poeticized domain of inspiration. With this, Faulkner presents a view remarkably contemporary in its emphasis upon social conditioning, a view of the self not fully autonomous, but shaping and being shaped in dynamic interrelation with its environment. We should also acknowledge, I have argued, that Faulkner assumes immanence as a very real ontological facet of our collective and individual experience, and his novels repeatedly lament the ways in which complex social systems circumscribe and seek to control this domain. Quentin Compson, as we saw, is the most acutely tragic representation of this dilemma, but he is not the only model for this interplay between immanence and cultural construction. Indeed, I have analyzed a number of characters who transcend, however partially, the cultural circumscription of interior space – all of whom are able to express novelty to some degree or other. As Faulkner's artistic vision matured, so did his insistence upon the importance of this interior domain. *Go Down, Moses* and the Snopes trilogy attest, more than any of his other novels, to a dynamic view of immanence as a source of human novelty and social change. While one could say that such novelty remains inevitably contained within highly adaptive social systems, Faulkner's view is not that there is a definitive outside to the social networks of which we are a part, but that these social networks remain viable and arc toward justice precisely because the immanent domain within the self generates variability within the greater system itself.

That Faulkner wrote in an age increasingly circumspect of articulations of immanence makes his defense all the more compelling, especially in our own time where the concept is sometimes met with outright hostility among humanists. In our time, Faulkner's warning acquires a renewed relevance when it is the lonely, embattled interior domain of the individual that struggles to survive amid the immeasurably complex proliferations of digital networks. It is important to recognize that Faulkner saw his defense of the individual as patently nonideological and for good reason. Noel Polk provides an illuminating portrait of Faulkner's intense wariness of ideologies during the Cold War period.[1] Like the French existentialists, Faulkner saw individual freedom not as some assured Enlightenment ideal, but as a necessary process of freeing oneself from ideological manipulation. The author rejected the view of two competing ideological systems during this period on precisely this ground. "Only one of the opposed forces is an ideology," he wrote. "The other is that simple fact of Man" (ESPL 102). This is not because Faulkner believed that the United States was free of all ideology; his entire fiction attests to the fact that he perceived otherwise; rather, he believed that his country still upheld the basic proposition that the individual life was sacrosanct, even if it was everywhere under assault.

I argue that this vision invests his whole Yoknapatawpha canon – and that we, removed from the tenor of the time, often confuse this value and, even worse, conflate it with a straw figure of humanist belief or Western essentialism. Wary of ideological structures, Faulkner imagined the individual life beyond or, more appropriately, before institutions; in his own words, the individual could be a "sanctuary" able to resist the "the old established closed-corporation hierarchies of arbitrary power which had oppressed him as a mass" (ESPL 62). These "hierarchies of church and state had compressed and held him individually thrilled and individually impotent." Thus, when we speak about immanence in Faulkner, we are not speaking about the spiritual assurances that institutions and their ideologies uphold. Nor are we speaking about individualism, at least not the "stubborn, uncompromising individualism" that some have claimed to be foundational in Faulkner (Bleikasten [1983: 36]). As we have seen repeatedly, the individual is always nestled within social relation.

In short, the social body is the foundation upon which an architecture of the self can become coherent at all.

Faulkner's belief that the immanent domain is at the heart not just of the individual, but also of the social informs his 1950 Stockholm Nobel address. From the first sentence, he upholds the "agony and sweat of the human spirit" (ESPL 119) as the foundation upon which he can refuse to accept the "end of man" (120). While he is clearly responding to the prevalent postwar fears over nuclear war, Faulkner's statement arises out of his entire body of work. If we are to understand the writer's vision at all, we must at least attempt to make sense of these words, whether or not we agree: "I believe that man will not merely endure: he will prevail. He is immortal, not because he alone among creatures has an inexhaustible voice, but because he has a soul, a spirit capable of compassion and sacrifice and endurance. The poet's, the writer's, duty is to write about these things" (120). Some critics have expressed dismay, even outright disappointment at these words. Ellen Douglas (1981) calls this passage "overblown, sentimental language," an exercise in "self-indulgence and confusion" (300). It "succeeds only in confusing me," Douglas confesses. "Man is not immortal because he has an inexhaustible voice? Why should he be, any more than birds are immortal because they sing? Man is immortal because he has a soul? It this not a tautology? Man is immortal because he is immortal?" (300). But if we attend to Faulkner's prose, especially the works that immediately follow *Absalom, Absalom!* in which he attempted to address the dilemmas of ideology articulated in his early fiction, the answer becomes much clearer. The Mississippian is not proposing some circular metaphysics of presence, coercive or confused. It is rather a modern affirmation of the Romantic turn that sprang up historically when our social systems became all-encompassing, when hamlets, towns, cities, and nations were linked together in a dizzying array of systematizing infrastructure. The thought of an Emerson, Thoreau, or an Ellison was not to disavow this emergent material reality, but to remember a self not wholly subsumed by its intricacies, a self that had a deeper, sustaining language of story, myth, and symbol that "can be one of the props, the pillars to help [the human being] endure and prevail" (120), as Faulkner concludes in his Nobel speech. Is this really confusion? Or is it an act of self-care, an attending to the older rhythms and co-evolved symbolic tools that we as humans have carried with and within us from before we clustered into permanent settlements and created gods and laws to enforce their nascent order?

Faulkner's belief, then, is in humanity not as a metaphysical abstraction but as an activity in time. "We pursue images" – this is the activity that is at the heart of the passage I quoted at the outset of the conclusion. We should not pass over this declaration without consideration, for Iles' articulation of pursuing the image down through time, through the webs of biology and culture, goes to the heart of Faulkner's mission as a writer. Indeed, the Yoknapatawpha fiction implicitly urges us to consider the primal image as a different kind of inheritance altogether from that of ideology. "The dark pool," "the icy creek," the spring that wells up among the beech trees, the pear tree, the single tree in memory, the drowned woman – these images are not so much vehicles of signification or meaning-bearing devices as they are personal memories, remnants of a threatened interior landscape, sources of sanctuary in the Yoknapatawpha fiction. Unlike the omnipresent aesthetic artifacts that impose specific ideological directives upon their observers – the Confederate statues, sun-clocks, lien ledgers, biblical genealogies – Faulkner's primal images are places of uncharted depth, elements that elude rational systemization and, therefore, resources for resisting the top-down ideological directives of centralized social institutions. That this primal place can be appropriated and invaded – this is the explicit fear that runs through the Yoknapatawpha fiction. But Faulkner also insists on the power of these primal images to yield transformation. This is what Isaac grapples with when he turns the pages of the plantation ledger and sees the text give way to a watery surface into which Eunice, the black matriarch, disappeared generations ago. Or what Lucas confronts at the Indigenous burial mound, coming eventually to give up his own personal claim to the land his family toiled over for generations. Or again what Mink enacts as he gives rise to an interior landscape within his being. The conviction that consciousness – soul, spirit, depth, immanence, interiority, all the names that we traditionally ascribe to it – does better than exceed our cartographies of movement, behavior, and thinking; it can transform them. In Faulkner's fiction, this can be as significant as the repudiation of the social system around us or as simple as escaping the manipulations of an uncle, climbing to freedom through an open window and descending a blooming pear tree in spring.

Notes

Introduction

1 See also Charles S. Aiken (2009: 2).
2 Mark Newman (2010: 2).
3 See Sedgewick (2011: 566).
4 See Klimovskaia et al. (2020).
5 My definition is adapted from Christof Teuscher (2022). See also Mark Taylor's description of architectural pace that "approaches the edge of chaos" (2001: 46).
6 Various literary scholars have provided network terminology for narrative structure. Two seminal examples are Alex Woloch (2003), and Franco Moretti (2011). For Faulkner studies, see Charles Hannon (2015: 91–9), and John F. Padgett (2018: 406–78).

Chapter 1

1 See Faulkner, *William Faulkner Manuscripts 5, Volume 1* (1987), 8–15, for the attic encounter, and 1–37 for the primary description of the house.
2 See Ruth Anne Voth (1958); Guy Cardwell (1969); Cleanth Brooks (1978); Elizabeth Kerr (1979); Noel Polk (1996); Susan Donaldson (1997, 2007); and Itoh Shoko (2001).
3 Clukey (2013: 506–9). See also Clukey and Jeremy Wells (2016: 1–10). Jennifer Greeson (2011) likewise traces a "wider view of the pervasiveness of the South in the broader history of the US novel" so that the South "becomes foremost a site of connection . . . to the larger world, to Western history, to a guilty colonial past and an imperial future both desired and feared" (236–7). In Faulkner Studies, John T. Matthews (2012) links "New World colonial history" and "an emerging new form of global domination: a transnational complex of financial and military powers" (226). Peter Schmidt (2015) follows this line of inquiry (179).
4 See also Wright (1986: 84–90).
5 See Sven Beckert (2016: 55–9) and Aiken (1998: 35–7).

6 See also Elizabeth Kerr (1979: 85).
7 For Faulkner's early emphasis upon vision, see Arthur F. Kinney (1978: 123).
8 *William Faulkner Manuscripts 5, Volume 1* (1987), 2.12.
9 Quoted in Jay Watson (2011: 20).
10 For a commentary on the "continuous circulation" of information through "a discontinuous series of heterogeneous elements," see Bruno Latour (2013: 33).
11 For a comparison of the Sartoris and Falkner families, see Franklin E. Moak (1985: 264–6) and Bleikasten (2017b: 23–5).
12 See also Charles Aiken (1998: 39) and Jeffrey Hummel (2002: 314).

Chapter 2

1 See Gail Morrison (2008: 5). For the debate about the short and long versions of the introduction, see James Meriwether (1973); and Philip Cohen and Doreen Fowler (1990: 263–4).
2 Faulkner, *Selected Letters* (1977: 235).
3 I am quoting from the William Faulkner Papers, 1925–50, Box 1.
4 On the novel's spatial self-reflexivity, see Carolyn Wynne (1964: 59–68); Paul Hedeen (1985: 624); William Sowder (1988: 67–8); Arthur Brown (1995: 409–15); Doreen Fowler (2000: 34); and Marjorie Pryse (2009: 17–35).
5 William Faulkner Papers, 1925–50, Box 1.
6 For the externalization of the psyche, see Bleikasten (2017a: 64).
7 For Quentin's dilemma of authorship, see Jackson Benson (1971: 143); and Jeffrey Folks (2002: 36–43). For the destabilization of Quentin's identity in related contexts (psychological, biographical, and gendered respectively), Gail Mortimer (1983: 34); Nathaniel Miller (2005: 39–40); and John Duvall (2002: 46).
8 For Jason's ascent, see James Berger (2014: 83–4).

Chapter 3

1 For female characters as spaces of disruption, see Minrose Gwin (1990: 8–16).
2 William Faulkner Papers, 1925–50, Box 1.
3 Quoted from Erin Penner and Stephen Railton's "Faulkner's 'Appendix Compson: 1699–1945.'" "Digital Yoknapatawpha," http://faulkner.iath .virginia.edu.
4 See Irving Howe (1952: 137–8).
5 See John K. Simon (1963); Stephen Ross (1979); Arthur Kinney (1989); and Elizabeth Hayes (1992).
6 Michel Deville (1994) gives a Lacanian variation that emphasizes instability and decentering (66–8), and James E. Caron (2015) interprets this dynamic as an inversion of Emersonian metaphysics 82–4.

7 In a similar vein, Michael Zeitlin (2001) provides a powerful reading of "a living soul's depth of field."

8 See John T. Matthews (1992: 85).

9 Eric Sundquist (1985) faults the novel for failing to establish a compelling social criticism (55), and Greg Forter (2015) contends that "*Sanctuary* mystifies the historical forces whose grip on the present it seeks to understand" (98).

10 For the pervasive cultural effects of industrialization on the New South, see Ted Atkinson (2005). Notably, Jolene Hubbs (2008) has termed "Faulkner's focus on rural life" a form of "rural modernity" (461).

11 See Terry Heller (1989: 247–8); John T. Irwin (1992: 543–66); and Nicole J. Camastra (2011: 323–40).

12 See Richard Godden (2007) for an interpretation of counterviolence (105).

Chapter 4

1 See Paul Douglass (1986: 126–43).

2 For the urn figure as containment, see Caroline Levine (2015: 30–1).

3 On the perils of abstraction, see Panthea Reid Broughton (1974: 117–201).

4 For the comparison of Colonel Sartoris and Thomas Sutpen, see Bleikasten (1981) who emphasizes the men not as real individuals, but symbolic paradigms; and Carolyn Porter (1994) who analyzed the marked difference between these two men: "If Sartoris ends as a statue, Sutpen remains a ghost." For Porter, the most important consideration is that "Sutpen is not just dead, he is absent. Between *Sartoris* and *Absalom, Absalom!*, something has happened" (84).

Chapter 5

1 Quoted from Theresa Towner et al. "Faulkner's *Go Down, Moses.*" *Digital Yoknapatawpha*. University of Virginia, 2016.

2 Michael Zank and Zachary Braiterman, "Martin Buber," 2020.

3 See R. W. B. Lewis (1951: 641–2); and Otis B. Wheeler (1959: 134).

4 See also Sarah Gleeson-White (2009: 398–9).

5 Faulkner Papers, Box 1.

6 See also Erin Penner's analysis of the way in which Rider's elegiac self-expression genuinely exists outside the bounds of the plantation structure (2019: 167).

Chapter 6

1 On Faulkner's narrative as a distributed network, see Charles Hannon (2015: 94–5).

2 See Dye, Dotty, and Stephen Railton. "Faulkner's 'Spotted Horses.'" *Digital Yoknapatawpha*, 2014.

3 See Hodge (2015) who addresses how the wood metaphor functions in Faulkner's *As I Lay Dying* and how it is related, particularly to gender (13–24).
4 See Lorie Watkins (2011) on female mobility (164–70).
5 Carl Rollyson (2020) lays out the biographical dimension for this tension (480–1).
6 See Merve Emre (2017) on Snopes' bureaucratic textuality (187–8).

Conclusion

1 For an account of Faulkner's convictions against ideological institutions, see Noel Polk (1995: 297–328).

Bibliography

Abel, Darrel. "Frozen Movement in *Light in August*." *Boston University Studies in English*, vol. 3, 1957, pp. 32–44.

Aiken, Charles S. *The Cotton Plantation South since the Civil War*. Johns Hopkins University Press, 1998.

William Faulkner and the Southern Landscape. University of Georgia Press, 2009.

Atkinson, Ted. *Faulkner and the Great Depression: Aesthetics, Ideology, and Cultural Politics*. University of Georgia Press, 2005.

Bailey, Devan. "Allegory, Culture Industry, and William Faulkner's Sanctuary." *Studies in American Fiction*, vol. 47, no. 1, 2020, pp. 71–96.

Baldwin, Marc D. "Faulkner's Cartographic Method: Producing the Land through Cognitive Mapping." *Faulkner Journal*, vol. 7, nos. 1–2, 1991–2, pp. 193–214.

Bassan, Maurice. "Benjy at the Monument." *English Language Notes*, vol. 2, no. 1, 1964, pp. 46–50.

Beckert, Sven. "Cotton and the US South: A Short History." In *Plantation Kingdom: The American South and Its Global Commodities*, edited by Richard Follett et al. Johns Hopkins University Press, 2016, pp. 39–60.

Benson, Jackson J. "Quentin Compson: Self-Portrait of a Young Artist's Emotions." *Twentieth Century Literature*, vol. 17, no. 3, 1971, pp. 143–59.

Berger, James. *The Disarticulate: Language, Disability, and the Narratives of Modernity*. New York University Press, 2014.

Bleikasten, André. "Fathers in Faulkner." In *The Fictional Father: Lacanian Readings of the Text*, edited by Robert Con Davis. University of Massachusetts Press, 1981, pp. 115–46.

"For/Against an Ideological Reading of Faulkner's Novels." In *Faulkner and Idealism: Perspectives from Paris*, edited by Michel Gresset and Patrick Samway, S. J. University of Mississippi Press, 1983, pp. 27–50.

The Ink of Melancholy: Faulkner's Novels from The Sound and the Fury to Light in August. Indiana University Press, [1990] 2017a.

William Faulkner: A Life through Novels. Indiana University Press, 2017b.

Bradford, Sarah H. *Scenes in the Life of Harriet Tubman*. W. J. Moses, 1869. https://docsouth.unc.edu/neh/bradford/bradford.html.

Brooks, Cleanth. "The Community and the Pariah." In *Twentieth Century Interpretation of Light in August*, edited by David L. Minter. Prentice-Hall, 1969, pp. 55–70.

  William Faulkner: Toward Yoknapatawpha and Beyond. Louisiana State University Press, 1978.

Broughton, Panthea Reid. *William Faulkner: The Abstract and the Actual*. Louisiana State University Press, 1974.

Brown, Arthur A. "Benjy, the Reader, and Death: At the Fence in *The Sound and the Fury*." *Mississippi Quarterly*, vol. 48, no. 3, 1995, pp. 407–20.

Brown, Calvin. *A Glossary of Faulkner's South*. Yale University Press, 1976.

Camastra, Nicole J. "'Waters of the Fountain Salmacis': Metamorphosis and the Ovidian Subtext in William Faulkner's *Sanctuary*." *Mississippi Quarterly*, vol. 64, no. 3/4, 2011, pp. 323–40.

Cardwell, Guy. "The Plantation House: An Analogical Image." *Southern Literary Journal*, vol. 2, 1969, 3–21.

Caron, James E. "Emerson's Sublime Pastoralism, Parody, and Second Sight in Faulkner's *As I Lay Dying*." *Faulkner Journal*, vol. 29, no. 1, 2015, pp. 71–99.

Clark, Thomas. *Dionysius. The Greening of the South: The Recovery of Land and Forest*. University Press of Kentucky, 1984.

Clukey, Amy. "Plantation Modernity: *Gone with the Wind* and Irish-Southern Culture." *American Literature*, vol. 85, no. 3, 2013, pp. 505–30.

Clukey, Amy, and Jeremy Wells. "Introduction: Plantation Modernity." *Global South*, vol. 10, no. 2, 2016, pp. 1–10.

Cobb, James C. *Industrialization and Southern Society*. University Press of Kentucky, [1984] 2004.

Cohen, Philip, and Doreen Fowler. "Faulkner's Introduction to *The Sound and the Fury*." *American Literature*, vol. 62, no. 2, 1990, pp. 262–83.

Colvin, Christina M. "'His Guts Are All out of Him': Faulkner's Eruptive Animals." *Journal of Modern Literature*, vol. 38, no. 1, 2014, pp. 94–106.

Cox, Karen L. *Dixie's Daughters: The United Daughters of the Confederacy and the Preservation of Confederate Culture*. University Press of Florida, 2003.

Davis, Thadious M. *Games of Property: Law, Race, Gender, and Faulkner's Go Down, Moses*. Duke University Press, 2003.

DeLanda, Manuel. *A New Philosophy of Society: Assemblage Theory and Social Complexity*. Continuum, 2006.

  Assemblage Theory. Edinburg University Press, 2016.

Deville, Michel. "Alienating Language and Darl's Narrative Consciousness in Faulkner's *As I Lay Dying*." *Southern Literary Journal*, vol. 27, no. 1, 1994, pp. 61–72.

Domby, Adam H. *The False Cause: Fraud, Fabrication, and White Supremacy in Confederate Memory*. University of Virginia Press, 2020.

Donaldson, Susan. "Making a Spectacle: Faulkner and Southern Gothic." *Mississippi Quarterly*, vol. 50, no. 4, 1997, pp. 567–84.

"Faulkner's Versions of Pastoral, Gothic, and the Sublime." In *A Companion to William Faulkner*, edited by Richard C. Moreland. Blackwell, 2007, pp. 359–72.

Douglas, Ellen. "Faulkner in Time." In *"A Cosmos of My Own": Faulkner and Yoknapatawpha, 1980*, edited by Doreen Fowler and Ann J. Abadie. University Press of Mississippi, 1981, pp. 284–302.

Douglass, Paul. *Bergson, Eliot, and American Literature*. University Press of Kentucky, 1986.

Doyle, Don Harrison. *Faulkner's County: The Historical Roots of Yoknapatawpha*. University of North Carolina Press, 2001.

Dussere, Erik. *Balancing the Books: Faulkner, Morrison, and the Economies of Slavery*. Routledge, 2003.

Duvall, John N. "Postmodern Yoknapatawpha: William Faulkner as Usable Past." In *Faulkner and Postmodernism: Faulkner and Yoknapatawpha, 1999*, edited by John N. Duvall and Ann J. Abadie. University Press of Mississippi, 2002, pp. 39–56.

Eliot, T. S. *Collected Poems: 1909–1962*. Faber and Faber, 2002.

Emre, Merve. *Paraliterary: The Making of Bad Readers in Postwar America*. University of Chicago Press, 2017.

Faulkner, William. "An Introduction to *The Sound and the Fury*," William Faulkner Papers, 1925–50, Accession #9817, Special Collections, University of Virginia Library, Charlottesville, Va., Box 1.

Selected Letters of William Faulkner, edited by Joseph Blotner. Random House, 1977.

Sanctuary: The Original Text. Random House, 1981.

William Faulkner Manuscripts 5, Volume 1: Flags in the Dust, Holograph Manuscript, edited by Joseph Blotner. Garland, 1987.

Absalom, Absalom! Vintage International, 1990.

As I Lay Dying. Vintage International, 1990.

Go Down, Moses. Vintage International, 1990.

The Sound and the Fury. Vintage International, 1990.

The Hamlet. Vintage International, 1991.

Sanctuary. Vintage International, 1993.

Light in August. Modern Library, 2002.

Essays, Speeches and Public Letters, edited by James B. Meriwether. Modern Library, 2004.

The Mansion. Vintage International, 2011.

Requiem for a Nun. Vintage International, 2011.

The Town. Vintage International, 2011.

Flags in the Dust. Vintage International, 2012.

Ferguson, Niall. *The Square and the Tower: Networks and Power, from the Freemasons to Facebook*. Penguin Books, 2018.

Folks, Jeffrey J. "Crowd and Self: William Faulkner's Sources of Agency in *The Sound and the Fury*." *Southern Literary Journal*, vol. 34, no. 2, 2002, pp. 30–44.

Foner, Eric. *A Short History of Reconstruction, 1863–1877*. Harper, 1990.

Forter, Greg. "Faulkner and Trauma: On *Sanctuary*'s Originality." In *The New Cambridge Companion to William Faulkner*, edited by John T. Matthews. Cambridge University Press, 2015.

Fowler, Doreen. *Faulkner: The Return of the Repressed*. University Press of Virginia, 2000.

Fujie, Kristin. "'Through a Piece of Colored Glass': Faulkner, Race, and Mediation." *MFS Modern Fiction Studies*, vol. 65, no. 3, 2019, pp. 411–38.

Gillespie, Stanley. "Light in Faulkner's in *Light in August*." *Interpretations*, vol. 14, no. 2, 1983, pp. 39–47.

Girard, René. *Violence and the Sacred*, translated by Patrick Gregory. Johns Hopkins University Press, 1979.

Gleeson-White, Sarah. "William Faulkner's *Go Down, Moses*: An American Frontier Narrative." *Journal of American Studies*, vol. 43, no. 3, 2009, pp. 389–405.

Godden, Richard. *William Faulkner: An Economy of Complex Words*. Princeton University Press, 2007.

Gordon, Deborah M. *Ant Encounters: Interaction Networks and Colony Behavior*. Princeton University Press, 2010.

Greeson, Jennifer Rae. "Imagining the South." In *The Cambridge History of the American Novel*. Cambridge University Press, 2011, pp. 236–51.

Greiner, Donald J. "Universal Snopesism: The Significance of 'Spotted Horses.'" *English Journal*, vol. 57, no. 8, 1968, pp. 1133–7.

Gwin, Minrose C. *The Feminine and Faulkner: Reading (beyond) Sexual Difference*. University of Tennessee Press, 1990.

Handy, William J. "*As I Lay Dying*: Faulkner's Inner Reporter." *Kenyon Review*, vol. 21, 1959, pp. 437–51.

Hannon, Charles. "Topologies of Discourse in Faulkner." In *Faulkner in Context*, edited by John T. Matthews. Cambridge University Press, 2015, pp. 91–9.

Harris, Paul A. "Fractal Faulkner: Scaling Time in *Go Down, Moses*." *Poetics Today*, vol. 14, no. 4, 1993, pp. 625–51.

Hartley, Roger C. *Monumental Harm: Reckoning with Jim Crow Era Confederate Monuments*. University of South Carolina Press, 2021.

Hayes, Elizabeth. "Tension between Darl and Jewel." *Southern Literary Journal*, vol. 24, no. 2, 1992, pp. 49–61.

Hedeen, Paul M. "A Symbolic Center in a Conceptual Country: A Gassian Rubric for *The Sound and the Fury*." *Modern Fiction Studies*, vol. 31, no. 4, 1985, pp. 623–43.

Heller, Terry. "Mirrored Worlds and the Gothic in Faulkner's Sanctuary." *Mississippi Quarterly*, vol. 42, no. 3, 1989, pp. 247–59.

Hinrichsen, Lisa. "Open Spaces, Open Secrets: *Sanctuary*'s Mysterious 'Something.'" In *Faulkner and Mystery*, edited by Annette Trafzer and Ann Abadie. University Press of Mississippi, 2014, pp. 162–77.

Hodge, Amber. "The Casket in the Corpse: The Wooden (Wo)man and Corporeal Impermanence in *As I Lay Dying*." *Southern Quarterly*, vol. 53, no. 1, 2015, pp. 13–24.

Hofstadter, Douglas R. *Gödel, Escher, Bach: An Eternal Golden Braid.* Penguin Books, [1979] 1994.

Howe, Irving. *William Faulkner: A Critical Study.* Vintage Books, 1952.

Hubbs, Jolene. "William Faulkner's Rural Modernism." *Mississippi Quarterly* vol. 61, no. 3, 2008, pp. 461–75.

Huffard Jr., R. Scott. *Engines of Redemption: Railroads and the Reconstruction of Capitalism in the New South.* The University of North Carolina Press, 2019.

Hummel, Jeffrey. *Emancipating Slaves, Enslaving Free Men.* Open Court, 2002.

Hussey, James. "'A Sort of Madman with Poetic Gifts': Darl Bundren and Henri Bergson." *Explorations: A Journal of Language and Literature*, vol. 3, 2015, pp. 56–69.

Huyssen, Andreas. *After the Great Divide: Modernism, Mass Culture, and Postmodernism.* University of Indiana Press, 1986.

Irwin, John T. "Horace Benbow and the Myth of Narcissa." *American Literature*, vol. 64, no. 3, 1992, pp. 543–66.

Joiner, Jennie. "Locations, Ownership, and Information Flow." In *Digitizing Faulkner: Yoknapatawpha in the Twenty-First Century,* edited by Theresa Towner. University of Virginia Press, 2022, pp. 34–50.

Kartiganer, Donald. "The Meaning of Form in *Light in August.*" In *Modern Critical Interpretations: William Faulkner's Light in August*, edited by Harold Bloom. Chelsea House Publishers, 1988.

  "'So I, Who Had Never had a War...': William Faulkner, War, and the Modern Imagination." *Modern Fiction Studies*, vol. 44, no. 3, 1998, pp. 619–45.

Kelso, J. A. Scott. *Dynamic Patterns: The Self-Organization of Brain and Behavior.* MIT Press, 1995.

Kerr, Elizabeth M. *William Faulkner's Gothic Domain.* Kennikat Press, 1979.

  William Faulkner's Yoknapatawpha: "A Kind of Keystone in the Universe." Fordham University Press, 1983.

Kinney, Arthur F. "The Family-Centered Nature of Faulkner's World." *College Literature*, vol. 16, no. 1, 1989, pp. 83–102.

  Faulkner's Narrative Style as Vision. University of Massachusetts Press, 1978.

Klimovskaia, Anna, et al. "Poincaré Maps for Analyzing Complex Hierarchies in Single-Cell Data." *Nature Communications*, vol. 11, no. 2966, 2020, https://doi.org/10.1038/s41467-020-16822-4.

Lanier, Jaron. *You Are Not a Gadget: A Manifesto.* Alfred A. Knopf, 2010.

Latour, Bruno. *An Inquiry into Modes of Existence: An Anthropology of the Moderns*, translated by Catherine Porter. Harvard University Press, 2013.

Lester, Cheryl. "As They Lay Dying: Rural Depopulation and Social Dislocation as a Structure of Feeling." *Faulkner Journal*, vol. 21, no. 1–2, 2005/2006, pp. 28–50.

Levine, Caroline. *Forms: Whole, Rhythm, Hierarchy, Network.* Princeton University Press, 2015.

Lewis, R. W. B. "The Hero in the New World: William Faulkner's 'The Bear.'" *Kenyon Review*, vol. 13, no. 4, 1951, pp. 641–60.

Liddell, Henry George, and Robert Scott. *A Greek-English Lexicon*. Clarendon, 1972.

Lutwack, Leonard. *The Role of Place in Literature*. Syracuse University Press, 1984.

Lurie, Peter. *Vision's Immanence: Faulkner, Film, and the Popular Imagination*. Johns Hopkins University Press, 2004.

Matthews, John T. *The Play of Faulkner's Language*. Cornell University Press, 1982.

"The Elliptical Nature of Sanctuary." *Novel: A Forum on Fiction*, vol. 17, no. 3, 1984, pp. 246–65.

"*As I Lay Dying* in the Machine Age." *Boundary 2*, vol. 19, no. 1, 1992, pp. 69–94.

Seeing through the South. Wiley-Blackwell, 2012.

Meriwether, James B. "Introduction for *The Sound and the Fury*." *Mississippi Quarterly*, vol. 26, 1973, 410–15.

Miller, J. Hillis. *Topographies*. Stanford University Press, 1995.

Miller, Nathaniel. "'Felt, Not Seen Not Heard': Quentin Compson, Modernist Suicide and Southern History." *Studies in the Novel*, vol. 37, no. 1, 2005, pp. 37–49.

Moak, Franklin E. "On the Roots of the Sartoris Family." In *Critical Essays on William Faulkner: The Sartoris Family*, edited by Arthur F. Kinney. G. K. Hall and Company, 1985, pp. 264–6.

Moretti, Franco. "Network Theory, Plot Analysis." *New Left Review*, vol. 68, 2011, pp. 80–102.

Morrison, Gail M. "The Composition of The Sound and the Fury." *In Bloom's Modern Critical Interpretations: William Faulkner's The Sound and the Fury*, edited by Harold Bloom. Infobase Publishing, 2008, pp. 3–30.

Mortimer, Gail L. *Faulkner's Rhetoric of Loss: A Study in Perception and Meaning*. Texas University Press, 1983.

Mumford, Lewis. *Technics and Civilization*. 1934. University of Chicago Press, 2010.

Newman, Mark. *Networks: An Introduction*. Oxford University Press, 2010.

Orvell, Miles. "Order and Rebellion: Faulkner's Small Town and the Place of Memory." In *Faulkner and Material Culture: Faulkner and Yoknapatawpha*, edited by Joseph R. Urgo and Ann J. Abadie. University Press of Mississippi, [2004] 2007, pp. 104–20.

Padgett, John F. "Faulkner's Assembly of Memories into History: Narrative Networks in Multiple Times." *American Journal of Sociology*, vol. 124, no. 2, 2018, pp. 406–78.

Page, Scott E. *Diversity and Complexity*. Princeton University Press, 2011.

Penner, Erin. *Character and Mourning: Woolf, Faulkner, and the Novel Elegy of the First World War*. University of Virginia Press, 2019.

Pettey, Homer B. "Perception and the Destruction of Being in As I Lay Dying." *The Faulkner Journal*, vol. 19, no. 1, 2003, 27–46.

Pikoulis, John. *The Art of William Faulkner*. Macmillan Press, 1982.

Polk, Noel. *Children of the Dark House: Text and Context in Faulkner.* University Press of Mississippi, 1996.

"'Polysyllabic and Verbless Patriotic Nonsense': Faulkner at Midcentury – His and Ours." In *Faulkner and Ideology*, edited by Donald Kartiganer and Ann Abadie. University Press of Mississippi, 1995.

Porter, Carolyn. "The Problem of Time in *Light in August.*" *Rice University Studies*, vol. 61, no. 1, 1975, pp. 107–25.

"Symbolic Fathers and Dead Mothers: A Feminist Approach to Faulkner." In *Faulkner and Psychology: Faulkner and Yoknapatawpha,* edited by Donald Kartiganer and Ann Abadie. University Press of Mississippi, [1991] 1994, pp. 78–122.

William Faulkner: Lives and Legacies. Oxford University Press, 2007.

Pryse, Marjorie. "Textual Duration Against Chronological Time: Graphing Memory in Faulkner's Benjy Section." *Faulkner Journal*, vol. 25, no. 1, 2009, pp. 15–46.

Rapaport, Herman. "Fantasies of Settlement: Heidegger, Tocqueville, Fichte, Faulkner." *Modern Fiction Studies,* vol. 63, no. 1, 2017, pp. 9–28.

Reidy, Joseph P. "Economic Consequences of the Civil War and Reconstruction." In *A Companion to the American South*, edited by John B. Boles. Blackwell Publishers, 2002.

Robinson, Owen. *Creating Yoknapatawpha: Readers and Writers in Faulkner's Fiction.* Routledge, 2006.

Rollyson, Carl. *The Life of William Faulkner, Vol. 2.* University of Virginia Press, 2020.

Romine, Scott. "Designing Spaces: Sutpen, Snopes, and the Promise of the Plantation." In *Faulkner's Geographies*, edited by Jay Watson and Ann J. Abadie. University Press of Mississippi, 2015, pp. 17–34.

Ross, Stephen M. "'Voice' in Narrative Texts: The Example of *As I Lay Dying.*" *PMLA*, vol. 94, no. 2, 1979, pp. 300–10.

Schliefer, Ronald. "Faulkner's Storied Novels: *Go Down, Moses* and the Translation of Time." *Modern Fiction Studies*, vol. 28, 1982, pp. 109–27.

Schmidt, Peter. "'Truth So Mazed': Faulkner and US Plantation Fiction." *William Faulkner in Context*, edited by John T. Matthews. Cambridge University Press, 2015, pp. 169–84.

Sedgewich, Robert and Kevin Wayne. *Algorithms*, 4th Edition. Pearson Education, 2011.

Shoko, Itoh. "Poe, Faulkner, and Gothic America." *Faulkner Journal of Japan*, vol. 3, 2001, pp. 17–32.

Simon, John K. "What Are You Laughing At, Darl?: Madness and Humor in *As I Lay Dying.*" *College English,* vol. 25, 1963, pp. 104–10.

Singal, Daniel J. *William Faulkner: The Making of a Modernist.* University of North Carolina Press, 1997.

Sitte, Renate. "About the Predictability and Complexity of Complex Systems." In *From System Complexity to Emergent Properties*, edited by Moulay Aziz-Alaoui and Cyrille Bertelle. Springer, 2009, pp. 23–48.

Smith, Mark. *Mastered by the Clock: Time, Slavery, and Freedom in the American South*. University of North Carolina Press, 1997.

Southern Poverty Law Center. "Whose Heritage? Public Symbols of the Confederacy." February 1, 2019: https://www.splcenter.org/sites/default/files/com_whose_heritage.pdf.

Sowder, William. "William Faulkner's Benjy Compson and the Field of Consciousness." *Journal of Phenomenological Psychology*, vol. 19, no. 1, 1988, 59–74.

Spillers, Hortense J. "Topographical Topics: Faulknerian Space." *Mississippi Quarterly*, vol. 57, no. 4, 2004, pp. 535–68.

Stonum, Gary Lee. *Faulkner's Career: An Internal Literary History*. Cornell University Press, 1979.

Sundquist, Eric. *Faulkner: The House Divided*. Johns Hopkins University Press, 1985.

Taylor, Mark C. *The Moment of Complexity: Emerging Network Culture*. University of Chicago Press, 2001.

Teuscher, Christof. "Revisiting the Edge of Chaos: Again?" *BioSystems*, vol. 218, 2022, https://doi.org/10.1016/j.biosystems.2022.104693.

Thyssen, Christina. "'Aj Kin Pas Wid Anything': Blackness as Figural Excess in Faulkner's *Go Down, Moses*." *Faulkner Journal*, vol. 29, no. 2, 2015, pp. 89–108.

Towner, Theresa. *Faulkner on the Color Line: The Later Novels*. University Press of Mississippi, 2000.

Urgo, Joseph R. "Where Was That Bird: Thinking America Through Faulkner." *Faulkner in America*, edited by Joseph R. Urgo and Ann J. Abadie. University Press of Mississippi, 2001.

"The Yoknapatawpha Project: The Map of a Deeper Existence." *Mississippi Quarterly*, vol. 57, no. 4, 2004, pp. 639–55.

Voth, Ruth Anne. *William Faulkner and the Gothic Tradition*. University of Maryland Press, 1958.

Wainwright, Michael. "The Enemy Within: Faulkner's Snopes Trilogy." In *Faulkner and the Ecology of the South*, edited by Joseph R. Urgo and Ann J. Abadie. University Press of Mississippi, 2005, pp. 61–80.

Darwin and Faulkner's Novels: Evolution and Southern Fiction. Palgrave Macmillan, 2008.

Watkins, Lorie. "Women in Motion: Escaping Yoknapatawpha." *Faulkner's Geographies*, edited by Jay Watson and Ann J. Abadie. University Press of Mississippi, 2011, pp. 163–74.

Watson, James G. *William Faulkner: Self-Presentation and Performance*. University of Texas Press, 2000.

Watson, Jay. *Faulkner and Whiteness*. University Press of Mississippi, 2011.

William Faulkner and the Faces of Modernity. Oxford University Press, 2019.

Weinstein, Philip M. *Faulkner's Subject: A Cosmos No One Owns*. Cambridge University Press, 1992.

Wheeler, Otis B. "Faulkner's Wilderness." *American Literature*, vol. 31, no. 2, 1959, pp. 127–36.

Wilhelm, Randall. "Framing Joe Christmas: Vision and Detection in Light in August." *Mississippi Quarterly*, vol. 64, no. 3–4, 2011, pp. 393–408.

Woloch, Alex. *The One Vs. The Many: Minor Characters and the Space of the Protagonist in the Novel*. Princeton University Press, 2003.

Woodman, Harold. "The Political Economy of the New South: Retrospects and Prospects." In *Origins of the New South, Fifty Years Later: The Continuing Influence of a Historical Classic*, edited by John B. Boles and Bethany L. Johnson. Louisiana State University Press, 2003, pp. 238–60.

Wright, Gavin. *Old South, New South: Revolutions in the Southern Economy since the Civil War*. Basic Books, 1986.

Wynne, Carolyn. "Aspects of Space: John Marin and William Faulkner." *American Quarterly*, vol. 16, no. 1, 1964, pp. 59–71.

Zank, Michael and Zachary Braiterman. "Martin Buber." *Stanford Encyclopedia of Philosophy*, edited by Edward N. Zalta, 2020, https://plato.stanford.edu/archives/win2020/entries/buber.

Zeitlin, Michael. "Interiority and Depth of Field in *As I Lay Dying*." *The Faulkner Journal of Japan*, vol. 3, 2001, http://www.faulknerjapan.com/journal/No3/EJNo3.htm.

"The Uncanny and the Opaque in Yoknapatawpha and Beyond." *Mississippi Quarterly*, vol. 57, no. 4, 2004, 619–37.

Zender, Karl. "Lucas Beauchamp's Choices." *Faulkner in the Twenty-First Century*, edited by Robert W. Hamblin and Ann Abadie. University Press of Mississippi, 2003, pp. 119–36.

Index

Abel, Darrel, 111
Adorno, Theodor, 94
Aiken, Charles, 2, 152, 218, 219
alterity, 14, 16, 111, 145, 177, 189, 190, 210
Anslinger, Harry, 178
antiracism, 7
anti-Semitism, 61

Bailey, Devan, 94, 96
Baldwin, Marc, 4
Barr, Caroline, 75, 158
Bassan, Maurice, 66
Beckert, Sven, 218
Berger, James, 47, 77, 219
Bergson, Henri, 110–11, 189
Bible, 18, 36–8, 39, 41, 59, 68, 116, 213
    fall of a sparrow, 203
    Yahweh's creation of Adam, 54, 209
    Yahweh's creation of the world, 85, 132
Bleikasten, André, 22, 47, 66, 219, 220
Brooks, Cleanth, 110, 218
Brown, Calvin, 2
Buber, Martin, 154
Buckley, G. T., 2

capitalism, 194
Cardwell, Guy, 218
Christian civilization, 113
Civil War, 29, 37, 126, 138, 145, 146–51
Clukey, Amy, 19
Cold War, 215
Colvin, Christina, 190
commodification, 94, 95
Confederate monuments, 7, 44, 52, 69, 93, 124, 142, 213, 217
    Confederate statues in Oxford, 69–70
    related imagery of, 127, 195
    statue of Colonel Sartoris, 15, 19, 40–2, 51, 58, 68, 119
    statue of Confederate soldier, 16, 45, 59, 65–72, 74

consciousness
    cognitive interiority, 4–5, 7, 25, 27–39, 42, 48, 50, 55, 57, 73, 80, 99–102, 110, 111, 123, 130, 168
    cognitive mapping, 3–5, 7
    collective memory, 28, 31
    comparison to ant colony, 11, 187
    human and nonhuman, 30, 39, 173
    immanence, 1, 3, 11, 17, 45, 48, 53, 56, 62, 76, 78, 86, 90, 93, 95, 97, 117, 118, 124, 144, 145, 156, 157, 172, 177, 189, 193–4, 196–202, 215–17
    and nature, 78, 113, 158–65, 205
    interpersonal, 82, 90, 93, 107, 112, 144, 145, 171, 206
    mystification, 4, 34, 60, 65, 90, 101, 102, 141
    and social space, 31, 39, 44, 51
    systems view of, 11, 74
    theory of mind, 85, 91, 111
coronavirus pandemic, 7
cotton, 9, 19, 24–5, 41, 44
    financialization of, 60
    production of, 21, 80, 135, 152
Cox, Karen L., 69

Davis, Thadious, 168
Deleuze, Gilles, 11
Deville, Michel, 91, 219
disability, 47
Domby, Adam H., 68
Donaldson, Susan, 218
Douglas, Ellen, 216
Doyle, Don Harrison, 8
Dussere, Erik, 158

ecological crisis, 115, 176
economic precarity, 80, 111, 114, 115
Eliot, T. S., 192
Ellison, Ralph, 216
Emerson, Ralph Waldo, 216
Euclidean geometry, 10

Printed in the United States
by Baker & Taylor Publisher Services